THE ʿABBĀSID REVOLUTION

THE 'ABBĀSID REVOLUTION

M. A. ṢHABAN

Lecturer in Arabic,
School of Oriental and African Studies,
University of London

CAMBRIDGE
AT THE UNIVERSITY PRESS
1970

Published by the Syndics of the Cambridge University Press
Bentley House, 200 Euston Road, London N.W.1
American Branch: 32 East 57th Street, New York, N.Y.10022

Library of Congress Catalogue Card Number: 75-112474

ISBN 0 521 07849 0

Printed in Great Britain
at the University Printing House, Cambridge
(Brooke Crutchley, University Printer)

To my teacher
Professor Sir Hamilton Gibb

CONTENTS

PREFACE

The genesis of this book was a doctoral thesis, *The social and political background of the Abbasid Revolution in Khurasan*, submitted to Harvard University in 1960. I am very grateful to Professor Sir Hamilton Gibb who taught me the art of using source material, an art of which he is the undisputed master. I am equally grateful to Professor Richard Frye for his unfailing help, guidance and much needed encouragement over a period of several years. Professor Charles Beckingham was kind enough to read the typescript of this book with his usual thoroughness and made many invaluable suggestions for which I must acknowledge my deep gratitude. I am similarly indebted to Professor John A. Boyle and Professor Bernard Lewis for their encouragement and help. I am also grateful to Mr Hugh Kennedy for compiling the index of this book. My special thanks go to Miss Carolyn Cross of Cambridge, Mass. and Mrs Dawn Hubbard of Cambridge, England for their skilful typing of a fairly difficult manuscript. Mr Kenneth Hubbard, also of Cambridge, England, was kind enough to help in the preparation of the typescript. My thanks are due to the Cambridge University Press for the publication of the book. I am particularly indebted to the editorial staff and to the printers for the great care they have taken and the patience they have shown in the production of the book.

Cambridge 1970 M.A.S.

INTRODUCTION

Over thirty years ago, Daniel C. Dennett decided that the time had come to challenge the general conclusions of J. Wellhausen about Umayyad history. He explained that although subsequent researches had added an immense amount of detail to our information, they had done so without a critical examination of the principal theses advanced in *Das Arabische Reich*. Furthermore, it had become necessary to revise these conclusions in the light of new material which Wellhausen did not have at his disposal.[1] Dennett made a good start in this direction, but his untimely death deprived us of the full benefit of his efforts.

Almost ten years ago, I made a similar attempt to draw attention to the dangers of following Wellhausen's outdated conclusions.[2] In recent years, a number of studies have been published concerned with various aspects of Umayyad history. One striking feature in all these studies is their unquestioning acceptance of Wellhausen's conclusions. It is indeed surprising to find Professor W. Montgomery Watt, with his continuously enquiring mind, and Professor Claude Cahen, with his keen historical sense, accepting many of these conclusions without any argument.[3] Starting from the same premises, Professor Bernard Lewis referred us to the "well-known" conclusions of Wellhausen, but again without questioning them.[4] Professor C. E. Bosworth realized that "a reinterpretation of events in Khurāsān during the decades preceding the 'Abbāsid Revolution is given by M. A. Shaban, correcting many of the views of Van Vloten, Wellhausen, etc.".[5] Nevertheless he continued to rely on these erroneous conclusions.

1 D. C. Dennett, "Marwān ibn Muḥammad; The passing of the Umayyad Caliphate", unpublished Ph.D. thesis, Harvard University, 1939, p. 3; J. Wellhausen, *Das Arabische Reich und sein Sturz*, Berlin, 1902, tr. *The Arab Kingdom and its Fall*, G. Weir, Calcutta, 1927.

2 M. A. Shaban, "The Social and Political Background of the 'Abbāsid Revolution in Khurāsān", unpublished Ph.D. thesis, Harvard University, 1960.

3 W. M. Watt, "Shī'ism under the Umayyads", *Journal of the Royal Asiatic Society* (1960), pp. 158–72; *idem*, "Khārijite thought in the Umayyad Period", *Der Islam*, vol. 36, part 3 (1961), pp. 215–31; *idem*, *Islamic Political Thought*, Edinburgh, 1968. Cahen, "Points de vue sur la Révolution abbaside", *Revue Historique*, 1963, pp. 295–338.

4 B. Lewis, "The Regnal Titles of the First 'Abbāsid Caliphs", *Dr Zahir Husain Presentation Volume*, New Delhi, 1968, p. 17.

5 C. E. Bosworth, *Sīstān under the Arabs*, Rome, 1968, p. 48.

In considering the situation of the Arabs in Khurāsān, and the 'Abbāsid Revolution, Wellhausen was greatly influenced by the racial interpretation of G. van Vloten. The latter's opinion was that "the inveterate hatred of the subject population against its oppressor of a foreign race, Shī'ism, and the expectation of a liberator or a Messiah caused the Khurāsānians to embrace the cause of the House of the Prophet".[1] He explained that it was all the fault of the Arab rulers who failed to treat their conquered subjects in Khurāsān, who embraced Islam, as equals of their fellow Arab Muslims. This discrimination produced the renaissance of Iranian nationalism as a measure of self defence of the oppressed people against their oppressors. Van Vloten's main fault was that he made practically no attempt to understand the developments in Khurāsān before the 'Abbāsid Revolution, and therefore based his thesis on false assumptions which, naturally, lead to false conclusions.

Although Wellhausen accepted Van Vloten's conclusions without much argument, he did try to be more systematic about his work. He devoted a long chapter of his *Arab Kingdom* to the Arab tribes in Khurāsān and tried to explain their situation in that province.[2] Wellhausen's failure was due to the fact that he saw the Arab tribesmen only as influenced and motivated by their pre-Islamic tribal traditions and completely absorbed in an endless tribal strife. He neglected altogether the effect of the new circumstances of these tribesmen in the conquered land, particularly in Khurāsān. With this fixed idea in mind, Wellhausen could not see or understand the implications of the source material he himself utilized. In short, he tried to support Van Vloten's conclusions rather than to correct them.

D. C. Dennett recognized the failure of Van Vloten and Wellhausen and disagreed with their conclusions about the background and nature of the 'Abbāsid Revolution, but he himself failed to offer any explanation. Instead, he presented a rather confused account of the reign of Marwān ibn Muḥammad, the last of the Umayyads.[3]

In the new edition of the *Encyclopaedia of Islam*, Bernard Lewis followed the outdated conclusions of Van Vloten and Wellhausen,

[1] G. van Vloten, *Recherches sur la Domination Arabe*, Amsterdam, 1894, p. 1.
[2] Wellhausen, Ch. 8, pp. 396–491.
[3] Dennett, "Marwān".

although one cannot help feeling that he himself was not completely convinced by their arguments.[1]

Professor S. A. al-'Alī in an article about the settlement of the Arabs in Khurāsān and Professor A. al-Dūrī, writing about the taxation system there, could not completely free themselves from Wellhausen's influence. Although they tried to correct some of the details of his exposition, they generally accepted his main thesis.[2]

Dr F. Omar agreed with Dennett on "refuting the outdated ideas of Van Vloten and Wellhausen". Furthermore, he accepted my interpretation of the developments in Khurāsān which led to the Revolution. But strangely enough he added, "what remains to be done is to reconstruct and clarify the political nature of the 'Abbāsid movement and expose the important role played by the Arabs in the revolution".[3] In this attempt he reverted to Wellhausen's position and, in one contradiction after another, he based his argument on endless tribal strife among the Arabs all over the empire.

In my opinion the 'Abbāsid Revolution had as its objective the assimilation of all Muslims, Arabs and non-Arabs, in the empire into one Muslim community with equal rights for every member of this community. Those who took part in this Revolution certainly had a more universal interpretation of Islam than the relatively limited Umayyad Arab view. This Revolution took place in Khurāsān, more specifically in Merv, whose colonization, and the subsequent developments, led to the assimilation of many of the Arab tribesmen in the Merv oasis into the local Iranian population. It was these assimilated Arabs, who had lost their privileges as members of the Arab ruling class and who were also aggrieved by their subjection to the non-Muslim aristocracy of Merv, who were the main support of the 'Abbāsid Revolution. They were joined by some of the local Islamized population, *mawālī*, who could not have been very numerous since Islam was not yet widespread even in Merv itself. These two groups were in the same position and had no grievances against each other. Moreover, they were both from the section of the population that

[1] B. Lewis, "'Abbāsids", *Encyclopaedia of Islam*, New Edition, Leiden, 1954–.

[2] S. A. al-'Alī, "Istīṭān al-'Arab fī Khurāsān", *Bulletin of the College of Arts and Sciences*, Bagdād, 1958, pp. 36–83; A. al-Dūrī, "Niẓām al-Ḍarā'ib fī Khurāsān", *Majallat al Majma' al-'Ilmī al-'Iraqī*, vol. XI, 1964, pp. 75–87.

[3] F. Omar, "The 'Abbāsid Caliphate, 132–70/750–86", unpublished Ph.D. thesis, University of London, 1967, pp. 72–4.

would benefit most from the success of the Revolution and the demolition of the social structure in which all the privileges went to the Arab *muqātila*, who formed the ruling class, and to the predominantly non-Muslim Iranian aristocracy, who formed the local administration and continued to enjoy their pre-Islamic privileges under Arab rule. Undoubtedly, the Hāshimiyya secret organization and its persistent propaganda, in addition to the division and struggle for power between the Arab ruling classes, also contributed to the success of the Revolution, but any revolutionary movement in such circumstances could hardly have failed.

In this book I have tried to analyse the social and political background of the 'Abbāsid Revolution in Khurāsān in order to achieve a better understanding of this real Revolution which was, certainly, a turning point in the history of the development of the Islamic society. First, I have presented a picture of the situation in the East at the time of the Arab conquest. Secondly, I have tried to follow, as closely as possible, the Arab tribesmen in Khurāsān—the way they settled there; their relationship with the conquered people; their relationship with the central government; their activities, interests and their internal rivalries—from the time they arrived in Khurāsān until the Revolution. Finally I have discussed the Revolution, the nature and development of the ideology it adopted and the extent of its success in achieving its objectives. I have not attempted to discuss the arguments put forward by Van Vloten, Wellhausen and Dennett, because from the very beginning of this work I adopted a different approach, based on the sources, and it would have only confused the issues if I had tried to incorporate such a discussion.

SOURCES

Abu al-Ḥasan ʿAlī ibn Muḥammad al-Madā'inī, a client of Quraysh, 135–225/752–839, is the undisputed authority on the early history of the Arabs in Khurāsān. Although he is quoted in many Arabic sources, the most complete version concerning the events in Khurāsān is that preserved by Ṭabarī. Since the latter was not a contemporary of Madā'inī, he quoted him through different *rāwīs*. Among many others, the most frequently quoted were ʿUmar ibn Shabbah and Aḥmad ibn Zuhayr ibn Ḥarb. Though Ṭabarī in most cases is careful about mentioning the *isnād* through which these particular traditions were related to him, he sometimes omits it altogether.[1] The authorities of Madā'inī are often mentioned in the traditions ascribed to him, but again sometimes, apparently when the different versions of the particular traditions were in agreement, the authorities of Madā'inī are not mentioned and instead the tradition is related to Madā'inī, "after his teachers".[2] In some cases Madā'inī named some of his authorities but did not specify others.[3] If there was any doubt about the reliability of a certain tradition, for example when it was of exaggerated tribal origin, this tradition was traced to its origin, and other versions of the same tradition were given in addition, in such a way that it is clear to the reader why a certain version is the most reliable.[4] When these tribal versions were of any value, Madā'inī himself combined them with other versions, in order to give a complete picture of the event related in these traditions.[5] However, "by applying to the mass of Iraqi traditions the sound methods of criticism associated with the Medīnian school, he [Madā'inī] gained for his work such a reputation for trustworthiness that it became the principal source for the compilations of the succeeding period, and one whose general accuracy has been confirmed by modern investigation".[6]

A great number of the traditions related by Madā'inī have reached us through another important source. This is the *Kitāb*

1 Al-Ṭabarī, *Annales quos scripsit Abū Jaʿfar...at-Ṭabarī*, ed. M. J. de Goeje *et al.*, Leiden, 1879–1901, vol. II, pp. 1432, 1492.

2 *Ibid.*, pp. 1430, 1436.

3 *Ibid.*, p. 1286.

4 *Ibid.*, p. 1240.

5 *Ibid.*, pp. 1204–5.

6 H. A. R. Gibb, "Tārīkh", supplement of the *Encyclopaedia of Islam*, Leiden, 1939.

al-Futūḥ of Abū Muḥammad Aḥmad ibn Aʿtham al-Kūfī al-Kindī, preserved in two volumes in the Library of Ahmet III, Istanbul.

In the very first paragraph of the first volume, Ibn Aʿtham tells us about his authorities and then proceeds to tell us that he has combined all the traditions together in one single narrative. The paragraph begins, "Qāla Abū Muḥammad ibn Aʿtham al-Kūfī, ḥaddathanī Abū al-Ḥusayn ʿAlī ibn Muḥammad al-Qurashī, qāla ḥaddathanī ʿUthmān ibn Sulaym ʿan Mujāhid ʿan al-Shaʿbī, wa Abī Miḥṣan ʿan Abī Waʿil, wa ʿAlī ibn Mujāhid ʿan Abī Isḥāq. Qāla wa ḥaddathanī Nuʿaym ibn Muzāḥim qāla ḥaddathanī Abū ʿAbdillah Muḥammad ibn ʿUmar al-Wāqidī al-Aslamī."[1] Then Ibn Aʿtham continues, in the same way, to enumerate his authorities, who were al-Zuhrī, Abū Mikhnaf, Ṣāliḥ ibn Ibrāhīm, Zayd ibn ʿAbdirraḥman al-Wāqifī, and ʿAlī ibn Ḥanẓala al-Shāmī.

There is no doubt that the first name was that of Abū al-Ḥasan Muḥammad ibn ʿAlī al-Madā'inī al-Qurashī, who was a client of Quraysh. The reading Abū al-Ḥusayn is a mistake of the scribe. During the course of the narrative the name always occurs in its proper form as one of the most frequently mentioned authorities for significant traditions. Ibn Aʿtham states clearly that "He [Madā'inī] told me" (ḥaddathanī), which means that he was a contemporary of Madā'inī (135–225/752–839). We find another confirmation of this in a note written by Muḥammad ibn Aḥmad al-Mustawfī al-Harawī who translated *al-Futūḥ* into Persian in 596/1199. In this note he states clearly that the *Kitāb al-Futūḥ* was composed by Ibn Aʿtham al-Kūfī in 204/819.[2] This leaves no doubt about the date of Ibn Aʿtham and confirms that he was able to quote directly from the highest authority on the history of Khurāsān, Madā'inī, in his lifetime. This also makes Ibn Aʿtham a predecessor of al-Balādhurī (d. 279/892), thought to be the earliest writer to attempt to combine the materials derived from the *sīra*, the monographs and other sources into a connected historical narrative.[3] Thus Balādhurī did not introduce a new method but merely imitated the earlier work of Ibn Aʿtham.

1 Ibn Aʿtham, *Kitāb al-Futūḥ*, Istanbul manuscript, Library of Ahmet III, No. 2956, Vol. I, p. 1A.

2 Ibn Aʿtham, *al-Futūḥ*, Persian translation by Muḥammad ibn Aḥmad al-Mustawfī al-Harawī, Bombay, 1300/1882, p. 3; ʿAbdullah Mukhlis, "Tārīkh Ibn Aʿtham al-Kūfī", *Majallat al-Majmaʿ al-ʿIlmī al-ʿArabī*, vol. VI, part 3, March 1926, pp. 142–3.

3 Gibb, "Tārīkh".

As for the value of the material related by Ibn Aʻtham (we are concerned here with the early history of Khurāsān), his claim to be the earliest known source is very strong. Comparing the narrative of Ibn Aʻtham with the traditions of Madā'inī as related by Ṭabarī, we find further proof that Ibn Aʻtham was quoting the same authority. Although Ṭabarī gives us a more complete picture of the early history of Khurāsān, Ibn Aʻtham not only provides us with a means of checking the traditions related by the former, but also adds some additional details in his *Kitāb al-Futūḥ*. In most cases these details are of the utmost importance because they are concerned with the fiscal arrangements in Khurāsān, and in this work I have tried to make use of such new material. It should be mentioned that, apart from the new material derived from Ibn Aʻtham, the rest of the material concerning the early history of Khurāsān does not contradict the traditions of Madā'inī as related by Ṭabarī. However, we must not forget that Ibn Aʻtham was writing a "Book of Conquests", in contrast with Ṭabarī who was writing history proper; thus the latter's scope was wider in many respects and he remains the major source for the early history of Khurāsān, to which the *Futūḥ* of Iban Aʻtham serves as a complementary source.[1]

The *Futūḥ* of Balādhurī serves us in the same way as the *Futūḥ* of Ibn Aʻtham, but, in addition to Madā'inī, it quotes other authorities, such as Abū ʻUbayda, who are not quoted by the latter, thus adding new material and valuable remarks about the history of this period. Moreover, the discovery of the *Futūḥ* of Ibn Aʻtham does not detract from the value of the *Futūḥ* of Balādhurī as one of the most important sources for the history of the Arab conquests.[2] Undoubtedly Balādhurī gives the most comprehensive account of the advance of the Arab armies in the Sāsānian domains.

The *Ansāb al-Ashrāf* of Balādhurī is a unique source. Its value

[1] For further information on this source see M. A. Shaban, "Ibn Aʻtham al-Kūfī", *Encyclopaedia of Islam*, New Edition, Leiden, 1954–. In addition to the Istanbul manuscript there is a copy of only the first volume (327 Ar.) in the Chester Beatty Library, Dublin. Although it is badly worn in many places, it is of value because it contains a great deal of poetry not included in the Istanbul manuscript. Another copy of the first volume is No. 918 (572) in the Mingana collection at Selly Oak Colleges Library, Birmingham. It is in good condition although a few folios are missing from the beginning and the end. It is hoped that a critical edition, prepared by myself, will be published in the near future.

[2] F. Rosenthal, "Balādhurī", *Encyclopaedia of Islam*, New Edition, Leiden, 1954–.

for early Islamic history has been widely recognized. In contrast to other biographical collections it contains a wealth of historical information. In many cases, like that of the revolt of al-Mukhtār in Kūfa, it gives fuller traditions and more details than other sources.[1]

Ya'qūbī, in his history, tells us about his sources at the beginning of the second part, but he hardly ever mentions them in the narrative. In the case of Ya'qūbī this is a disadvantage, because he apparently quoted sources unknown to us, probably because he spent his youth in Khurāsān. However, the little additional information in Ya'qūbī does not contradict the material which we have from Ṭabarī, Balādhurī and Ibn A'tham, and in general Ya'qūbī confirms the traditions related by these authorities. It is to the credit of both Ibn A'tham and Ya'qūbī that, in spite of their Shī'a tendency, they did not attempt to present a biased picture of events in the early history of Khurāsān.[2]

Another source, which has recently come to light, is *Tārīkh al-Khulafā'* by an anonymous author of the eleventh century. Although the editor, P. Griyaznevitch, believes that it was written about 409–10/1015–17, there is a note in the book which reveals that it must have been written after 480/1087.[3] In spite of the author's repeated insistence that it is a concise, abridged account, the book contains a considerable number of traditions which correspond to those found in other proven sources. Its account of the revolt of al-Mukhtār is very similar to Balādhurī's account, and the traditions about the downfall of Qutayba are almost identical with those related by Ṭabarī and Ibn A'tham.[4] There is no doubt that the anonymous author relies on the same trustworthy authorities as his predecessors, and indeed this is clearly stated in the book. On the other hand, his eagerness to be concise is a serious shortcoming. His account of Qutayba's campaigns in central Asia is too brief to be of much use.[5] His narrative of the

[1] Al-Balādhurī, *Ansāb al-Ashrāf*, vol. v, ed. S. D. Goitein, Jerusalem, 1936, pp. 215–73. This source is still largely in manuscript form preserved in Suleymanniye Kütüphanesi, Reisulkuttap, in two big volumes no. 597–8.

[2] See C. Brockelmann, article "Ya'ḳūbī", in the *Encyclopaedia of Islam*, New Edition, Leiden, 1954–; H. A. R. Gibb, *The Arab Conquests in Central Asia*, London, 1923, pp. 11–14; also "Tārīkh; F. Rosenthal, *A History of Muslim Historiography*, Leiden, 1952, pp. 114–16.

[3] *Tārīkh al-Khulafā'*, anon., ed. P. Griyaznevitch, Moscow, 1967, p. 52 of the introduction and p. 53 A.

[4] *Ibid.*, pp. 101 A–104 B, 164 A–B.

[5] *Ibid.*, pp. 151 A–153 B.

reign of Hishām contains many mistakes due to his careless abridgement.[1] It is difficult to understand what is meant by the statement that the book "contains an independent version of the history of the Umayyads", unless it means that it has its own distinctive mistakes.[2] Furthermore, there is little justification for the assertion of the "general anti-Shī'ite trend of the work".[3] Also, one cannot fully agree with Griyaznevitch that it contains "fresh material of the utmost importance reflecting a peculiar tradition coming through a number of generations from a narrow circle of conspirers, ring leaders and active participants of the 'Abbāsid Revolution".[4] This is in fact an exaggerated statement, since all traditions in our sources claim to originate from eye-witnesses, if not from active participants in the event concerned and the 'Abbāsid Revolution is no different in this respect; in their accounts Ṭabarī and Mas'ūdī also quote active participants in the Revolution.[5] *Tārīkh al-Khulafā'* does add a little additional information about the organization of the Revolution, but even then, for the sake of brevity, it gives only the bare facts and omits vital details revealed elsewhere.[6]

In the library of the Institute of Higher Islamic Studies in Baghdād, there is a manuscript of a work entitled *Akhbār al-'Abbās wa Waladihi*, also by an anonymous author. According to Professor al-Dūrī it was composed around the middle of the ninth century.[7] I have been able to see only a part of this manuscript. Dr F. Omar tells us that it is "an annalistical work in biographical form concerned, as the title indicates, with al-'Abbās and his descendants".[8] He also believes that the part of *Tārīkh al-Khulafā'* concerned with the 'Abbāsids is a brief adaptation of the *Akhbār al-'Abbās* achieved by "quoting only the main authority instead of the whole chain of transmitters, and by combining different accounts and giving one well-digested account".[9] However, Dr Omar's statement that *Akhbār al-'Abbās* is "invaluable for the understanding of the organization of the 'Abbāsid movement in Khurāsān" is extravagant.[10] He himself had to rely on

1 *Ibid.*, pp. 197B–214A. 2 *Ibid.*, p. 53. 3 *Ibid.*, p. 52. 4 *Ibid.*, p. 53.
5 Ṭabarī, vol. III, pp. 49–50; al-Mas'ūdī, *Murūj al-Dhahab*, ed. C. Barbier de Meynard and P. de Courteille, Paris, 1861–77, vol. v, pp. 4–5.
6 Omar, "'Abbāsid Caliphate", p. 23.
7 A. al-Dūrī, "Ḍaw jadīd 'alā al-da'wa al-'Abbāsiyya", *Bulletin of the College of Arts and Sciences*, Baghdād, 1960, pp. 64–82.
8 Omar, "'Abbāsid Caliphate", p. 21.
9 *Ibid.*, p. 23. 10 *Ibid.*, p. 20.

Ṭabarī to give us the list of the *naqībs* of the Hāshimiyya in Merv, about which *Akhbār al-'Abbās* is not so reliable.[1] The most that can be said is that this source, like *Tārīkh al-Khulafā'*, gives some additional information about the organization of the 'Abbāsid Revolution.

Unfortunately, neither the *Rijāl* books nor the *Adab* books supply us with much information about this early period in Khurāsān. They are mostly concerned with the rest of the Umayyad empire and do not say much about Khurāsān except under the 'Abbāsids.

The Persian sources with regard to this period, namely the *Tārīkh-i-Sīstān* and the *Zayn al-Akhbār* of Gardīzī, are merely corrupt translations of Arabic sources. However, Gardīzī seems to have had access to an unknown valuable source which could have brought to light some new material, but he was hopelessly confused and confusing and it is almost impossible to make use of any of his material. The *Tārīkh-i-Sīstān* is a little better in this respect, particularly about the early Arab campaigns in this region and, as expected, agrees with the Arabic sources, adding very little to our knowledge of this early period. Finally, the *Tārīkh-i-Qumm* of Qummī is of value with regard to western Iran but, because of the unique development in Khurāsān, is not of much use for our purposes.

[1] *Ibid.*, pp. 89–90.

I

THE POLITICAL GEOGRAPHY OF KHURĀSĀN AND THE EAST

The first problem for a historian is to define the area of his interest in terms of geography and population. In some cases this requires very little effort and is comparatively easy. A historian of the British Isles, dealing with a relatively small and self-contained area with clearly defined English, Scottish and Welsh divisions, would not find much difficulty. But, for an Islamic historian, this is a difficult task to be undertaken with particular care at every turn of the immense area of space and time covered by Islamic history. Islam, practically from its beginning, brought together many peoples of different lands, with well-established cultures, traditions and political systems. The assimilation of all these elements, after a century of strife and conflicts, brought about the Islamic civilization with its easily recognizable features.

It was not only Sāsānian and Byzantine domains that contributed to the world of Islam; Khurāsān and the East (*al-Mashriq*) played a vital part in the formative years of the Islamic society. Yet this part has been underestimated by many scholars who, unfortunately, have not understood the political geography of the East. Khurāsān has been treated as an open-ended province to which Soghdiana was vaguely attached. It was assumed that, at the time of the Arab conquest, they were within the Sāsānian sphere of influence if not part of the Sāsānian empire. Almost one hundred years later, a revolution suddenly worked itself out there and spread to the rest of the Arab empire. Then, for nearly a century, the area fell into abeyance after which the so-called Persian dynasties (Tāhirids, Sāmānids, etc.) arose. Many of these apparently inexplicable historical developments would have been easier to understand if an effort had been made to establish the political geography of the East at the time of the Arab conquest. This is what I propose to do here.

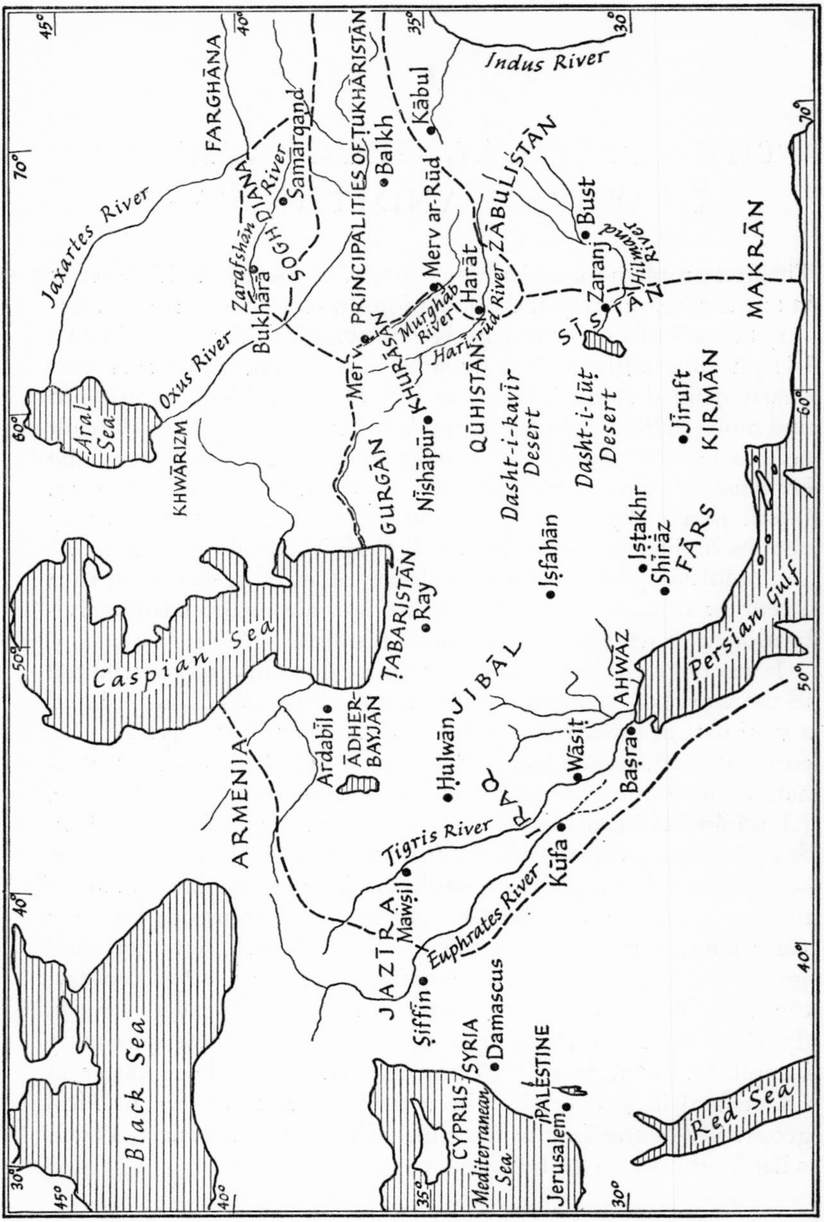
Black Sea
Caspian Sea
Aral Sea
Mediterranean Sea
Red Sea
Persian Gulf
Jaxartes River
Oxus River
Zarafshān River
Murghāb River
Harī-rūd River
Hilmand River
Indus River
Tigris River
Euphrates River
FARGHĀNA
SOGHDIANA
PRINCIPALITIES OF ṬUKHĀRISTĀN
KHURĀSĀN
KHWĀRIZM
GURGĀN
ṬABARISTĀN
QŪHISTĀN
ZĀBULISTĀN
SĪSTĀN
MAKRĀN
KIRMĀN
FĀRS
JIBĀL
AHWĀZ
ĀDHERBAYJĀN
ARMENIA
JAZĪRA
'IRĀQ
SYRIA
PALESTINE
CYPRUS
Dasht-i-kavīr Desert
Dasht-i-lūṭ Desert
Bukhārā
Samarqand
Balkh
Kābul
Merv
Merv ar-Rūd
Harāt
Bust
Zaranj
Nīshāpūr
Jīruft
Iṣṭakhr
Shīrāz
Iṣfahān
Ray
Ardabīl
Ḥulwān
Wāsiṭ
Baṣra
Kūfa
Mawṣil
Ṣiffīn
Damascus
Jerusalem
30°
35°
40°
45°
50°
60°
70°

1 *Khurāsān of the Sāsānians*

The geographical definition of Khurāsān has always been subject to political circumstances there, or rather to the strength of the power ruling over Iran. As the word Khurāsān means literally the land of the east, it was used sometimes to cover all the regions in the east of Iran, even including Transoxiana; while at other times it covered only part of Khurāsān as we know it now. Yāqūt, the Arab geographer, recognized this fact,[1] observing that the Arab geographers were misleading in their definition of Khurāsān because they included under this name all the lands which used to be under the Arab governors of Khurāsān.[2] However, it has been established that, at the time of the Arab conquest, the Murghāb River, or, more precisely, the lower part of the Murghāb from Merv ar-Rūd to the north of Merv, formed the eastern boundary of the Sāsānian empire.[3] Thus Khurāsān of the Sāsānians, at that time, was only the districts of Nīshāpūr, among which the districts of Qūhistan were counted,[4] and the two cities of Merv and Merv ar-Rūd with their immediate neighbourhood west of the Murghāb; indeed the last two cities were outposts of the eastern borders.[5] It is not without significance that though we have a very detailed account in the Arabic sources of the conquest of the districts of Nīshāpūr, yet, when these same sources describe the conquest of Merv and Merv ar-Rūd, they mention only one *rustāq* (district), at most, along with each of these cities.[6] In the narratives concerning the Arab conquest of Khurāsān, there is mention of an office holder who was probably the Sāsānian governor-general of Khurāsān. Ibn Khurdādhbeh alone mentions a *pādhūsbān* as the *spahbad* (general of the realm) of

[1] Yāqūt, *Mu'jam al-Buldān*, ed. F. Wüstenfeld, Leipzig, 1924, vol. II, p. 410.

[2] *Ibid.*, p. 409; Ibn Khurdādhbeh, *Kitāb al-Masālik wa'l' Mamālik*, ed. M. J. de Goeje, Leiden, 1889, p. 18.

[3] J. Marquart, "Eranšahr", *Abhandlungen der Königlichen Gesellschaft der Wissenschaften zu Göttingen*, vol. III, 1901, pp. 74–5; H. A. R. Gibb, *The Arab Conquests in Central Asia*, London, 1923, p. 1.

[4] Ya'qūbī, *Kitāb al-Buldān*, ed. M. J. de Goeje, Leiden, 1892, p. 278; al-Balādhurī, *Futūḥ al-Buldān*, ed. M. J. de Goeje, Leiden, 1866, pp. 403–5; Ibn Sa'd, *aṭ-Ṭabaqāt al-Kabīr*, ed. Sachau *et al.*, 1905–21, vol. 5, p. 33.

[5] Ibn Ḥawqal, *Sūrat al-Arḍ*, ed. J. H. Kramers, Leiden, 1938–9, vol. II, p. 434; E. Chavannes, *Documents sur les Tou-Kiue (Turc) Occidentaux*, St Petersbourg, 1903, p. 251.

[6] Balādhurī, *Futūḥ*, p. 406; al-Ṭabarī, *Annales quos scripsit Abū Ja'far...at-Ṭabarī*, ed. M. J. de Goeje *et al.*, Leiden, 1879–1901, vol. I, pp. 2897–8.

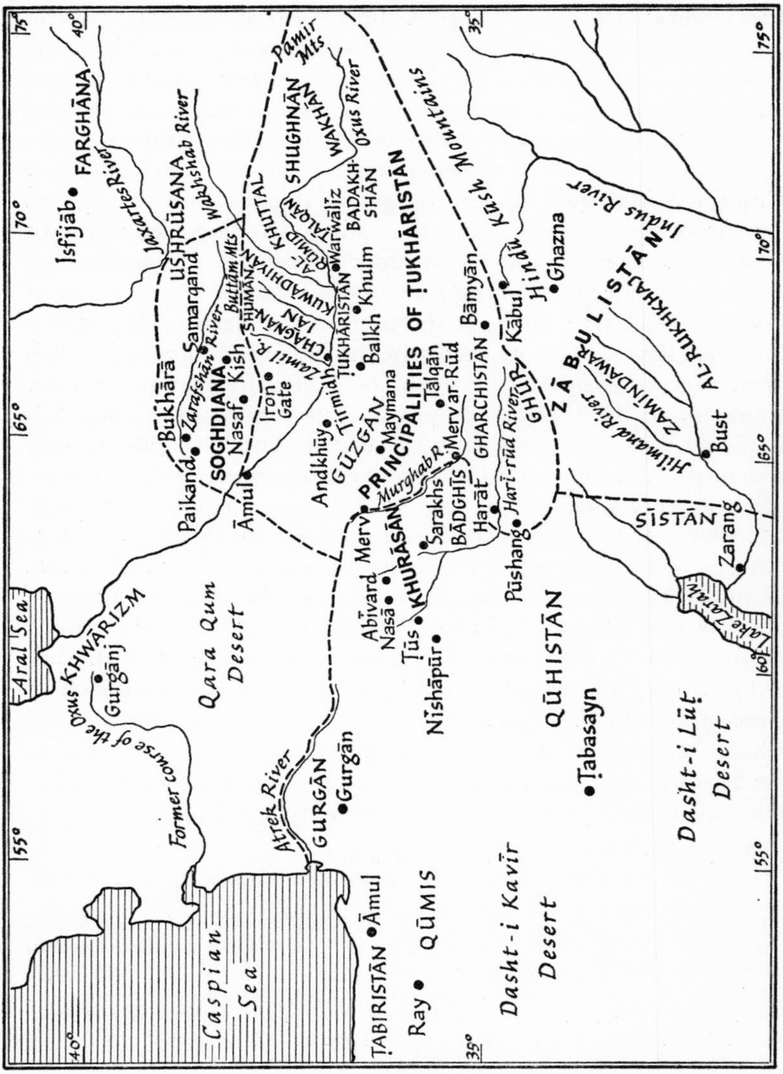

Khurāsān and the East

all of Khurāsān.[1] Other sources mention a *kanārang* as governor of Ṭūs,[2] together with the *marzbāns* (wardens of the marches) of the various districts of Khurāsān. Christensen suggests that the title of *kanārang* carries with it the connotation of a "governor of a province",[3] but Minorsky was able to identify it as the "Lord of the eastern March" who was "ruling in the remote Persian province co-terminous with the lands of the Hephthalites".[4] It is clear now that the *kanārang* was the title of the Sāsānian governor-general of Khurāsān, whose authority, as might be expected, diminished after the collapse of the Sāsānian central government in the west. As we find *marzbāns* in Sarakhs and Abīvard, so we find *marzbāns* in Merv and Merv ar-Rūd. These *marzbāns*, who were chosen from the local nobility, were charged with the administration of their districts; and, because Merv and Merv ar-Rūd were frontier outposts, their *marzbāns* had also the military obligation of defending these frontiers. The *kanārang* also had the military duty of defending the countryside, frequently exposed to the raids of the Hephthalites from Bādghīs,[5] and for this reason he resided in Ṭūs which occupied a central position, a fact which caused the Arab chroniclers to identify him with this city.[6] With the collapse of the central government of the Sāsānians each *marzbān* acted as an independent representative of his district before the new invaders. Most of them offered no resistance to the Arabs, and were only too glad to conclude peace treaties, assuring the continuation of their authority under the new régime. In Khurāsān of the Sāsānians, as in the rest of the empire, the *dihqāns* who formed the local nobility held the upper hand, and their principal function was the allocation and collection of taxes.[7] According to the Sāsānian system, they, as well as the warriors, the priests and the civil servants, were exempted from the poll tax. The burden of the taxes fell heavily on the peasantry, and they also had to serve in the infantry in the army. In the cities the bourgeoisie were in a better situation; they paid the poll tax but they did not have to serve in the army.[8]

[1] Ibn Khurdādhbeh, p. 18.

[2] Balādhurī, *Futūḥ*, p. 405; Ṭabarī, vol. I, p. 2886.

[3] A. Christensen, *L'Iran sous les Sassanides*, Copenhagen, 1936, p. 102, note 3.

[4] V. Minorsky, *Iranica*, Publications of The University of Teheran, vol. 775, Teheran, 1964, p. 262.

[5] Marquart, "Eranšahr", pp. 74–5.

[6] Balādhurī, *Futūḥ*, p. 405; Ya'qūbī, *Tārīkh*, ed. M. Houtsma, Leiden, 1883, vol. II, p. 129.

[7] Christensen, *L'Iran*, p. 107.

[8] *Ibid.*, pp. 315–16.

When trying to follow the Arab conquest of Khurāsān, it is important to keep in mind the fact that the Murghāb was the easternmost border of the Sāsānian empire, because the Arabs must have realized that once they had conquered the "small" Khurāsān of the Sāsānians and advanced east of the Murghāb they would be in conflict with completely different sovereigns, if not peoples. Although these peoples were mostly of Iranian origin, their independent historical development had led to different social, political and cultural backgrounds. The Arabs must have realized, then, that they were opening up new fronts against enemies who proved by their resistance to the conquerors that they had better-organized armies than the remnant forces of the Sāsānian empire. The choice of Merv to be the garrison town for the Arab armies, and later the capital of the Arab governors, is the best indication that the Arabs recognized this fact. In the beginning their intention, as heirs of the Sāsānian empire, was probably to maintain the Murghāb as their eastern border while raiding the areas to the east to keep their armies busy. As it turned out later, following the same pattern as the previous conquerors from the west, they were compelled to advance not only to the Oxus but even further to the Jaxartes, bringing under Arab domain the lands in which had flourished previously the Greco-Bactrian, the Kushan and the Hephthalite empires. In contrast to the previous conquerors, the Arabs were able to integrate these areas into their empire, and in due course they became great centres of Islamic civilization.

2 *The Hephthalites ("Hayāṭila")*

Although the Chinese sources throw some light on the history of these regions yet, in spite of much research done in this field, it is still to some extent a matter of speculation. From the earliest times there had been successive waves of emigration of nomadic tribes of Iranian origin from central Asia westwards to settle down in the area rightly called "Outer Iran".[1] These nomads were soon assimilated to sedentary life, though some of them were not fully assimilated and led a semi-nomadic life. We are concerned here with the last wave of these nomads, mainly the Hephthalites, known in the Arabic sources as the *Hayāṭila*.

[1] R. Grousset, *The Civilizations of the East. The Near and Middle East*, London, 1931, p. 133.

It is generally accepted that they take their name from their eponymous ancestor, or perhaps from the ruling dynasty. They probably appear for the first time in the fourth century, among the armies of the later Kushans, helping them against the Sāsānians. Soon after, they became the successors to the Kushan empire in the east. The ethnic origin of the Hephthalites is difficult to determine. In spite of the theories constructed on the basis of suggested etymologies of one or two words, the fact remains that we have no sources for the history of eastern Iran in this period. While most scholars are inclined to accept the Hephthalites as of Iranian origin, a few suggest a Turkish origin.[1] R. N. Frye concludes that

> One may well expect Altaic, i.e. Hunic elements among the Hephthalites, but again the evidence points primarily to Iranians. It is possible that some of the early rulers were Huns, but there were still many Iranians in Central Asia, and the people of eastern Iran among whom the Hephthalites settled were also Iranian, so we may consider the Hephthalite empire in eastern Iran and north-west India as basically an Iranian one.[2]

Although one may not agree with R. Ghirshman in all his suggestions about the history of the Hephthalites, he offers a plausible interpretation of this difficult and obscure subject. He convincingly points out one factor which distinguishes the Hephthalite empire from the empires of Bactria and the Kushans, and which had a great influence on the history and development of this area. In contrast to the two previous empires, which in the course of their expansion southwards had to stop for some time to the north of the Hindū-Kūsh, the Hephthalites occupied the areas to the north and to the south of these mountains at much the same time. It seems that Hephthalite tribes were divided into two major divisions—the northern tribes, who kept the name Hephthalites, and the southern tribes, whose tribal name was the Zābu-

[1] For further discussions of the history of the Hephthalites see: W. M. McGovern, *The Early Empires of Central Asia*, Chapel Hill, 1939, Supplementary notes, pp. 471–83; R. Ghirshman, *Les Chionites–Hephthalites*, Le Caire, 1948; F. Altheim–R. Stiehl, *Geschichte der Hunnen. II Die Hephthaliten in Iran*, Berlin, 1960; K. Enoki, "On the nationality of the Ephthalites", *Memoirs of the Research Department of the Toyo Bunko*, 18, Tokyo, 1959, pp. 1–58; G. Widengren, *Xosrau Anosurwan, les Hephthalites et les peuples Turcs*, Orientalia Succana, i, 1952; A. D. H. Bivar, *Hayātila*, *Encyclopaedia of Islam*, New Edition, Leiden, 1954–.

[2] R. N. Frye, *The Heritage of Persia*, London, 1962, p. 227.

lites, from whom the area of Zābulistān took its name. These southern Hephthalites, the Zābulites, expanded successfully south-eastwards into India, while the northern tribes, the Hephthalites, had to go westwards for their expansion, and they clashed with the Sāsānians, inflicting on them a series of defeats beginning in A.D. 484 with a battle in which the Sāsānian king Peroz lost his life. After a period of half a century of fighting, the final victory rested with the Hephthalites, and they became virtually the masters of Persia, from whom for half a century they exacted a heavy annual tribute in cash. The Hephthalite empire in the first half of the sixth century A.D. extended over Soghdiana, the Oxus basin and the lands to the north and south of the Hindū-Kūsh.

There is ample evidence that the trade which flourished under the Kushans continued under the Hephthalites and became one of their major sources of income; and the Soghdians also continued to play a major role in this trade. Though the Sāsānian influence on the life and culture of the Hephthalites cannot be denied, Buddhism was still the predominant religion of the whole empire. However, because of the religious tolerance of these people, other religions were found among them, like Zoroastrianism, Manichaeism and even Christianity. At the time of Yuan Chwang, the Chinese pilgrim, Buddhism was very strong south of the Iron Gate, though north of it among the Soghdians Zoroastrianism was gradually taking its place.

Finally the Sāsānians had to seek the alliance of the rising new power beyond the Jaxartes, namely the western Turks, to rid themselves of Hephthalite domination. The two allies were able to defeat the Hephthalites in A.D. 563–568. This resulted in the partition of their empire between the two victors, and for a brief moment the Oxus became the boundary between the Iranians and the Turks. The Sāsānians were not able to hold their newly acquired lands for very long, and with their gradual weakening and the rising power of the Turks, the latter were able to extend their suzerainty southwards to include the Hephthalite lands north of the Hindū-Kūsh.[1] Apparently the Hephthalites of the south were able to escape the fate of their brethren in the north, to meet their final destruction later at the hands of the Muslims, but not until after a stubborn resistance which lasted well over two hundred years.

[1] R. Ghirshman, *Les Chionites–Hephthalites*, pp. 67–133.

3 *The Principalities of Ṭukhāristān*

The defeat of the Hephthalites to the north of the Hindū-Kūsh did not mean their disappearance from the scene. They continued to live side by side with the previously settled population and were probably more closely assimilated into it. In some places where they were not fully assimilated and the semi-nomadic element was dominant, they were able to form their own principalities, probably encouraged by the Turks, and they continued to give the Sāsānians much trouble on their north-eastern frontiers.[1] In fact, on his way to India in A.D. 630 Yuan Chwang found that all the Hephthalite territories south of the Iron Gate were divided up into twenty-seven principalities with separate chiefs.[2] These came under Turkish suzerainty, but, because of the lack of a strong central government and the frequent internal conflicts among the Turks, they enjoyed a semi-independent status.[3] The oldest son of the Jābghū of the western Turks was appointed as a general in command, with the title of Shād, and had his residence near Warwālīz,[4] possibly with the principality of Huo (Qunduz) and the city of Balkh under his governorship.[5]

From A.D. 630, when the Chinese government started its intrigues against the western Turks, until A.D. 658, when they were destroyed by the Chinese, there was a period of near-anarchy in this region. A son of the former Shād founded the dynasty of the Jābghūs of Ṭukhāristān which ruled over the district we know as Ṭukhāristān proper. The chiefs in the other principalities, and probably others who seized the opportunity to form new principalities, recognized the new Jābghū as their suzerain, though his authority could hardly have been anything but nominal.[6] The Chinese sources inform us that in A.D. 661 the government of China, after formally annexing the territories between Khotan and Persia, tried to reorganize them into sixteen governments under Chinese suzerainty. But this attempt failed because China had to devote all its energy to check the dangerous advances of Tibet in central Asia. If Turkish interference in the administra-

[1] Gibb, *Arab Conquests*, p. 3; Ghirshman, *Les Chionites–Hephthalites*, p. 96.
[2] T. Watters, *On Yuan Chwang's travels in India*, London, 1904–5, vol. I, p. 102.
[3] Chavannes, *Documents*, pp. 263–4, 299.
[4] Watters, vol. I, p. 106; Gibb, *Arab Conquests*, p. 8.
[5] Watters, pp. 75–6, 108–9.
[6] Gibb, *Arab Conquests*, p. 8; Watters, vol. I, p. 270.

tion of the subject territories was limited to the appointment of military governors and the collection of tribute, Chinese interference was practically nothing more than diplomatic manœuvres, and thereafter these principalities enjoyed an even greater measure of independence, only linked together by their acceptance of the nominal suzerainty of the Jābghū of Ṭukhāristān.[1]

Among the principalities, Ṭukhāristān occupied a predominant position, yet it seems rather difficult to define what Ṭukhāristān was. Gibb draws our attention to the fact that the name Ṭukhāristān is used very loosely, in the Arabic records, with misleading effects.[2] Barthold suggests that it was used in two different senses: the first and narrower sense defines the area east of Balkh and west of Badakhshān south of the Oxus; the second and larger sense defines the area east of Balkh on both sides of the Oxus.[3] The Chinese sources provide a wider definition than even Barthold's larger sense. Yuan Chwang, speaking about the land of the Tu-hou-lo (Ṭukhārā), defined it as reaching on the east to the Tsung-ling, on the west to Persia, on the south to the great mountains (the Hindū-Kūsh) and on the north to the Iron Gate; the river Oxus flowed through the middle of it from east to west.[4] Balādhurī used the word Ṭukhāristān in a similar sense, indicating that the lands immediately to the east of the Murghāb were considered at the time of the Arab invasion as part of Ṭukhāristān.[5]

In spite of much research on the Ṭukhārā people and Ṭukhāristān, no satisfactory suggestion has been made.[6] It is beyond the scope of this book to decide the origin of the Ṭukhārā people, but it seems that they were Iranians who emigrated to this region in earlier times, and at the time of the Arab invasion formed a part of the settled population. As Gibb observed, they were "noted in the Chinese annals for their commercial enterprise".[7] In this work Ṭukhāristān is used to mean the principality of that name, i.e. the district which lies east of Balkh and west of Badakhshān to the south of the Oxus, in contrast to the Principalities of Ṭukhāristān which means the principalities under the suzerainty of the Jābghū of Ṭukhāristān at the time of the Arab invasion.

1 Chavannes, *Documents*, pp. 263, 264, 274, 287, 299; Gibb, *Arab Conquests*, pp. 7–9.
2 Gibb, *Arab Conquests*, p. 8.
3 W. Barthold, "Ṭukhāristān", *Encyclopaedia of Islam*, Leiden, 1939.
4 Watters, vol. 1, p. 102.
5 Balādurī, *Futūḥ*, p. 406.
6 See the excellent note by W. M. McGovern (*Early Empires*, pp. 479–83) on Dahia and Tachari.
7 Gibb, *Arab Conquests*, p. 2.

Among the Principalities of Ṭukhāristān, the various Hephthalite principalities had an important place, but a difficulty arises when we try to define their location or number. It is certain, from the later activities of Nēzak, that Bādghīs was a Hephthalite principality or at least part of one. Bādghīs was associated with Harāt and Pūshang, which makes it a principality of considerable size. Since, when Nēzak made peace with Qutayba ibn Muslim, he made stipulations in regard to Bādghīs alone,[1] it is tempting to conclude that there was more than one principality in this district of Harāt, Pūshang and Bādghīs. It could be argued that this peace was made long after the Hephthalites had been reduced to the sole principality of Bādghīs, but it is more probable that there were numerous principalities in this region which were subjugated by the Arabs in different stages.

From the list of the titles of the kings of Khurāsān and the East provided by Ibn Khurdādhbeh,[2] we gather that the prince of Nasā (Yahūdiyya of Gūzgān)[3] used to have the title of *abrāz*, the prince of Gharchistān had the title of *barāz-bandeh* and the prince of Harāt, Pūshang and Bādghīs was called *barāzān*.[4] On certain coins which have been identified as Hephthalite coins belonging to the second half of the seventh century A.D., the word BRZ was found on the obverse.[5] It is possible to conclude that *barāz* or *abrāz* was the title of the princes of the Hephthalite principalities, *barāz-bandeh* was the title of the lesser princes subject to the *barāz*, and *barāzān* was simply the plural of *barāz*.

The principality of Nasā (Yahūdiyya) was one of many principalities formed around the different towns in the district of Gūzān, in which the Gūzān-khudā,[6] the most powerful prince, held the supreme authority. In the area of Harāt, Pūshang and Bādghīs there were many principalities with separate princes each of whom was a *barāz*, and of whom Nēzak Ṭarkhān later distinguished himself as the leading Hephthalite prince against Arab domination. Gharchistān was a lesser principality under a weaker prince subject to a more powerful *barāz*, probably from the district of Gūzgān. Thus, in the area west of Balkh extending south-west to include all of Gūzgān, the upper course of the Murghāb south of Merv ar-Rūd to Gharchistān, and then extend-

[1] Ṭabarī, vol. II, pp. 1184–5.
[2] Ibn Khurdādhbeh, p. 39.
[3] Marquart, "Eranšahr", p. 67.
[4] Ibn Khurdādhbeh, p. 40.
[5] Ghirshman, *Les Chionites–Hephthalites*, p. 23.
[6] Ibn Khurdādhbeh, p. 39.

ing west to reach the middle course of the Harī-rūd River, there were a number of Hephthalite principalities, ruled by their own princes but subject to the nominal suzerainty of the Jābghū of Ṭukhāristān.

From the information that has reached us, particularly in the Chinese annals, sometimes supplemented by the Arabic sources, most of the rest of the principalities can be identified as follows:

(1) Shūmān, which also includes Akhrūn. Its prince was said to be of Turkish origin in the Chinese sources.[1]

(2) al-Qūmid (Karātegin) in the Surkhāb valley to the north-east of Ṭukhāristān. Its prince was also a Turk.[2]

(3) al-Khuttal. Its prince was called *as-Sabal*, according to Arabic sources.[3]

(4) Ṭukhāristān, which included the towns of Baghlān, Khulm, Siminjān and its capital Warwālīz.

(5) Badakhshān.

(6) Kuwādhiyān.

(7) Wakhān.

(8) Ṭālqān.

(9) Chaghāniān.

All these last five principalities, though they were under separate princes, seem to have had a closer relationship with Ṭukhāristān. Yuan Chwang on his way back from India in A.D. 644 spoke about the king of Houh, who was a Turk and ruled over the small states south of the Iron Gate, moving about from one to another.[4] It is possible that the princes of these principalities had formed with the Jābghū of Ṭukhāristān some sort of defensive military alliance. This is also indicated by the preservation of the office of Shād as late as A.D. 710. Gibb identified him as the king of Chaghāniān (Chaghān Khudā) and not as the Jābghū himself.[5]

(10) Shughnān to the north of Wakhān. It was divided into five autonomous valleys, but all under one prince. The people there were nomads who used to raid the merchants on the road to Tibet via Wakhān.[6]

(11) Tirmidh. Under the rule of the Tirmidh-Shāh.[7]

1 Chavannes, *Documents*, p. 275.
2 *Ibid.*, p. 278.
3 Ibn Khurdādhbeh, p. 39; Tabari, vol. II, p. 1224.
4 Watters, vol. II, pp. 270–7.
5 Ṭabarī, vol. II, p. 1224; Gibb, *Arab Conquests*, p. 9.
6 Chavannes, *Documents*, p. 163.
7 Ṭabarī, vol. II, p. 1147.

(12) Āmul. To the west of the Oxus.[1]

These two principalities were mainly cities with strong fortresses to control the main trade routes at the crossings of the Oxus.

(13) Bāmyān, north of the main range of the Hindū-Kūsh. Its prince was called Shēr-Bāmyān.[2] This principality was at the southern end of the lands which were under the suzerainty of the Jābghū of Ṭukhāristān. It controls an important road between the Oxus and the Indus valleys.

The kingdom of Zābulistān (ar-Rukhkhaj) with its capital Ghazna where the king, Zunbīl or Rutbīl, resided is mentioned in the Chinese sources as under the suzerainty of the Jābghū.[3] However this must be considered as the sort of exaggeration often found in these sources, particularly when we notice that it is mentioned in connection with events of the year A.D. 718, when it could not possibly have been the case. This kingdom had always defended its independence with great zeal and proved its military strength even when the Arabs penetrated western Sīstān and concentrated their attacks against it.

In addition to the Principalities of Ṭukhāristān already mentioned, there may have been others which it has not been possible to identify under the names given in the Chinese sources,[4] but most probably they were minor principalities or perhaps formed parts of the bigger principalities.

It must be mentioned that the city of Balkh does not seem to have held the pre-eminence it had in earlier times or the importance it was given later by the Arab historians and geographers.[5] According to Yuan Chwang, at the time of his journey to India in A.D. 630 it was thinly populated and was part of the governorship of Qunduz.[6] Warwālīz seems to have taken its place as the seat of government, and the only explanation is that this city, from a military point of view, was easier to defend than Balkh.

The mass of the population in the Principalities of Ṭukhāristān were Iranians who had come in the successive waves of

[1] Marquart, "Eranshahr", pp. 310–11.

[2] Ibn Khurdādhbeh, p. 39.

[3] Marquart, "Eranšahr", pp. 250, 287–9; in *Tārīkh-i-Sīstān*, Teheran, A.H. 1314, p. 92, note 2. M. Bahar prefers Zimbīl; Ibn Khurdādhbeh, p. 39, calls him Rutbīl, the king of Sijistān, ar-Rukhkhaj and Bilād ad-Dāwar; Chavannes, *Documents*, p. 291; see also C. E. Bosworth, *Sīstān under the Arabs*, Rome, 1968, p. 34.

[4] Watters, vol. II, pp. 267–74.

[5] Ya'qūbī, *Buldān*, p. 287.

[6] Watters, vol. I, pp. 108–9.

nomadic emigration. When they settled down in the seat of the old Bactrian Hellenistic civilization, they were gradually assimilated and are known to us under different names—Ṭukhārā, Khushans or Hephthalites. Under the Kushan empire, Buddhism became the predominant religion and it continued to be so until it was replaced by Islam. Because the Hephthalites were the last to come to this region, assimilation had not been completed among them, particularly among those who had settled in the rich pasture lands of Gūzgān and around Harāt and Bādghīs,[1] and who posed the greatest problem to the Arabs at the time of the invasion. It is to be expected that in all these petty principalities the political institutions were different from those in the Sāsānian domain. These small princes were probably nothing more than military lords who imposed their authority over the local population by virtue of their arms. Certainly the expenditure involved in maintaining separate courts and armies must have created a heavy burden on their people, and these people would have been only too happy to see a chance for a change in their desperate conditions. Such conditions, added to the political disunity of the area, were naturally in favour of the Arab invasion.

4 *Soghdiana*

Moving northwards through the Iron Gate, we come to the rich cultivated lands of the Zarafshān River. In spite of the great differences between the Oxus and the Zarafshān valleys in almost every respect, we do find in Soghdiana a political disunity not dissimilar to that south of the Iron Gate. The country was divided into a number of small independent principalities, but, though each had its own prince, all the princes belonged to what is known in Chinese sources as the Shao-wu clan. They formed together what Gibb aptly described as "a loose confederacy in a manner strikingly reminiscent of the Hellenic city-states".[2]

Between A.D. 605 and 611 the king of Samarqand, the chief city of Soghdiana, who was the head of the Shao-wu clan, married a princess from the Turkish royal family.[3] Whether this was done for reasons of policy or ambition, he ended up by being a vassal of the western Turks. It is not clear what the origin of

[1] Gibb, *Arab Conquests*, p. 14, note 6.
[2] *Ibid.*, p. 5.
[3] Chavannes, *Documents*, p. 135.

the Shao-wu clan was, but it is clear that during their long rule—about six or seven hundred years—all these princes had fully identified themselves with their Iranian subjects. Also, in contrast with the princes of Ṭukhāristān, their authority was much limited by the great power of the *dihqāns* and the rich merchants, and, as suggested by Gibb, "the 'kingship' was not a real monarchy but rather the primacy in an oligarchical system".[1]

The Soghdians were famous for their commercial enterprise, and they were highly interested in the Chinese silk trade, the centres of which were at Samarqand, Paykand and Kish, and they worked as intermediaries between east and west. Sūq as-Soghd (the market of the Soghdians) was one of the most ancient quarters of the city of Merv.[2] The population of the cities, as well as of the countryside, was of Iranian elements reinforced by immigrants from Sāsānian dominions. Gibb singles out the merchant families of Paykand as probably being Kushans.[3] In Samarqand, probably not all the people were Zoroastrians, but they were evidently not Buddhists at the time of Yuan Chwang's visit.[4] However, among the Soghdians Christianity and Manichaeism lived side by side with Zoroastrianism.

To conquer and establish their rule in the lands to the east of the Sāsānian empire the Arabs had to fight for almost a century against these peoples, who were of Iranian origin, not, as Arabic sources wrongly describe them, Turks. In fact, the Turks did not come to their help against the Arabs until the rise of the Turgesh power in 98/716,[5] and even then their resistance to the Arab armies did not last more than twenty years, since they were finally dispersed in 119/737.

[1] Gibb, *Arab Conquests*, pp. 5, 6.

[2] Ibn Khurdādhbeh, p. 178; Ibn al-Athīr, *al-Lubāb Fī Ma'rifat al-Ansāb*, Cairo, A.H. 1357, vol. I, p. 37.

[3] Gibb, *Arab Conquests*, p. 5.

[4] Watters, vol. I, p. 95.

[5] Chavannes, *Documents*, pp. 284–5.

2

THE ARAB CONQUEST OF KHURĀSĀN

I 'Abdullah ibn 'Āmir

There is general agreement in the Arabic sources that the conquest of Khurāsān was started in the reign of the *Amīr al-Mu'minīn* 'Uthmān ibn 'Affān under the able generalship of the newly appointed governor of Baṣra, 'Abdullah ibn 'Āmir (29–35/649–55). The only tradition which does not agree with this is related to us by Sayf. According to him, after the battle of Qādisiyya (16/637), *Amīr al-Mu'minīn* 'Umar ibn al-Khaṭṭāb gave instructions to advance towards Khurāsān, and Aḥnaf ibn Qays was entrusted with the conquest of this province, to which he proceeded in the year 18/639. Yet Ṭabarī himself informs us that the conquest of Aḥnaf was in the year 22/643, after the Battle of Nihāvand (21/642).[1] This tradition can easily be explained in two ways. First, it could be a confusion with the later activities of Aḥnaf ibn Qays as a lieutenant of 'Abdullah ibn 'Āmir in the year 32/652.[2] Second, it could have been an attempt to magnify the role of Aḥnaf, chief of Tamīm, in the conquest of Khurāsān, in which he did play an important role, but only under 'Abdullah ibn 'Āmir.

In the *Futūḥ al-Buldān* of Balādhurī, we find the most detailed and comprehensive accounts of the advance of the Arab armies eastwards in the provinces of the Sāsānian empire, and it is supported in general by the authorities of Ṭabarī and Ya'qūbī. The Battle of Nihāvand (21/642) marks the final break up of the Sāsānian imperial army, and the defence of the provinces was left to the *marzbāns* and the local rulers.[3] Between the year 21/642 and the time Ibn 'Āmir arrived at Baṣra (30/650), the Arab armies of Kūfa and Baṣra, supported by fresh troops from the Arabian peninsula, were busy raiding and conquering the western part of the Sāsānian domains in Iran. The troops of Baṣra under Abū

[1] Ṭabarī, vol. I, pp. 2569, 2682–4. [2] *Ibid.*, p. 2907.

[3] Balādhurī, *Futūḥ*, pp. 302–5; Christensen, *L'Iran*, p. 500.

Mūsā al-Ash'arī invaded most of the provinces of Ahwāz, Jibāl and Fārs. 'Ammār ibn Yāsir, governor of Kūfa, was instructed by 'Umar ibn al-Khaṭṭāb to send expeditions to Rayy in the Jibāl province, and the next governor of Kūfa, al-Mughīra ibn Shu'ba, conquered Ādharbayjān. Some of the expeditions went as far as Ṭabaristān and Gīlān and made peace treaties with the *spahbad* of these provinces. Another expedition penetrated into Qūmis and met no resistance.[1] The furthest point to the east reached by the Baṣran armies at that time was Ṭabasayn, which Balādhurī described as the doors of Khurāsān.[2] It is reported that one of the expeditions of the troops of Abū Mūsa, governor of Baṣra, raided Ṭabasayn. These expeditions certainly did not result in the final conquest of these provinces: some of them were no more than raids, while others were simply marches meeting no resistance. Some areas, such as Rayy, had to be reconquered several times during this period. Iṣṭakhr was not conquered at this time, though the whole province of Fārs was subjugated by Abū Mūsa.[3]

It was not until after the arrival of 'Abdullah ibn 'Āmir as governor of Baṣra that an organized campaign was planned to extend Arab rule eastwards to reach Khurāsān. 'Uthmān was confronted with increasing tensions in Iraq as a result of the continuous pressure of the influx of Arab tribesmen into the two garrison towns, Kūfa and Baṣra. His solution to this problem was to open new fronts in new territories to consume the energies of these tribesmen. In 29/649 he appointed two new governors to Kūfa and Baṣra, both Qurayshites from his own clan: Sa'īd ibn al-'Āṣī to Kūfa and 'Abdullah ibn 'Āmir to Baṣra. The latter was only twenty-five years of age. Though they were his relatives, their appointment was not, as widely interpreted, an indication of 'Uthmān's nepotism. He was, primarily, trying to assert his power over the increasingly autonomous province. He thought that as head of the clan of Umayya he could, perhaps, exercise more authority over his younger clansmen than over other independent-minded leaders, and thus be able to carry out his plan of bringing the tribesmen into line with his policies.

When Ibn 'Āmir arrived at Baṣra, he immediately set out for the province of Fārs and conquered the city of Iṣṭakhr. He was able

[1] Balādhurī, *Futūḥ*, pp. 309–16; Ṭabarī, vol. I, p. 2659.
[2] Balādhurī, *Futūḥ*, p. 403.
[3] *Ibid.*, pp. 318–20.

to pacify the whole province in 30/650, though with some difficulty, which compelled him to use severe measures. From Fārs he sent an expedition into Kirmān, but it was not successful.[1] It seems that he then went back to Baṣra, where he organized a new army, and in the year 31/651 he started towards Khurāsān.[2]

We are told of another expedition which was organized from Kūfa for the same purpose and at the same time. It, too, was a large expedition under the command of the governor of Kūfa, Sa'īd ibn al-'Āṣī. One explanation given by our sources is that Knāzik (*kanārang*), the *marzbān* of Ṭūs, had written to the two governors inviting both of them to invade Khurāsān, promising help and expecting to be rewarded by the Arabs. Another explanation was that 'Uthmān himself had ordered both expeditions, instigating competition between the two governors.[3] As for the first explanation, it seems that the *kanārang*, who was really the governor of the whole province, was alarmed by the increasing raids from the Hephthalite principalities of Harāt and Bādghīs, which were taking advantage of the sudden collapse of the Sāsānian empire, and was actually seeking the help of the Arabs against these enemies who had been a continuous threat to his province. The second explanation does not contradict the first, but both put together would suggest that the two governors, to whom the *kanārang* had written, saw the chance and realized that Khurāsān was ready to fall to the Arabs. They therefore both asked permission from 'Uthmān to conquer this province, and he ordered them both to advance by two different routes. Thus Sa'īd ibn al-'Āṣī, with the troops of Kūfa, took the northern route through Qūmis, and 'Abdullah ibn 'Āmir, with the troops of Baṣra, took the southern route through Kirmān.

Meanwhile, the unfortunate king, Yazdgird III, after wandering around from one city to another seeking support against the Arabs, reached Merv in the year 31/651. At first Mahūyeh, the *marzbān* of Merv, received him with due respect, but soon, weary of Yazdgird's financial demands and jealous for his independence, he sought the alliance of Nēzak Ṭarkhān, the Hephthalite prince of Bādghīs, against his sovereign. Nēzak rushed to Merv, where

[1] Ya'qūbī, *Tārīkh*, vol. II, p. 192; Balādhurī, *Futūḥ*, pp. 334, 389, 390, 391; Ṭabarī, vol. I, p. 2862.

[2] Ibn Sa'd, vol. V, p. 32; Balādhurī, *Futūḥ*, pp. 334, 391; Ṭabarī, vol. I, pp. 2884–5.

[3] Ṭabarī, vol. I, p. 2836: Balādhurī, *Futūḥ*, p. 334; Ya'qūbī, *Tārīkh*, vol. II, p. 192.

he and Mahūyeh were able to defeat Yazdgird with his small retinue. The latter had to flee for his life, and was killed ignominiously in the neighbourhood of Merv.[1] This episode provides us with ample proof of the decadence of the Sāsānian empire and the great confusion in Khurāsān on the eve of the arrival of the Arabs.

In the narratives of this event, we also find that Mahūyeh was sometimes called *barāz*, *abrāz*, or *abī barāz*.[2] Though Mahūyeh was given in Ibn Khurdādhbeh's list as the title of the prince of Merv, it was most probably his personal name, a factor which strengthens our belief that *barāz* was used along with his name, Mahūyeh, as a sort of title.[3] Since *barāz* was the title of a Hephthalite prince, this suggests that the Hephthalites, trying to take advantage of the situation at the time, and particularly encouraged by the brief alliance with the *marzbān* of Merv, conferred on him the title given to their princes, in an attempt to control the important crossroads at Merv. However, we do not find any trace of them at Merv when the Arabs took the city, in the same year. Tha'ālibī tells us that in the same month that Yazdgird was killed, Nēzak quarrelled with Mahūyeh and killed him. Then he left the city to be taken by the Arabs.[4] But we know that Mahūyeh was still living at least until the year 36/656.[5] However, the fact remains that Nēzak left Merv after Yazdgird's death, probably to meet the Arabs halfway in Qūhistān.

2 *Peace treaties*

'Abdullah ibn 'Āmir, advancing by way of Kirmān, reached Ṭabasayn where, according to some sources, he made a peace treaty with its people or, according to other sources, he confirmed the treaty concluded at a previous date by one of Abū Mūsā al-Ash'arī's generals.[6] From Ṭabasayn Ibn 'Āmir advanced towards Nīshāpūr, following his advanced guard which was met

[1] Ṭabarī, vol. I, pp. 2863–88; al-Tha'ālibī, *Ghurar Akhbār Mulūk al-Furs wa Siyarihim*, ed. H. Zotenberg, Paris, 1900, pp. 782–4; Christensen, *L'Iran*, p. 500; Balādhurī, *Futūḥ*, pp. 315–16.

[2] Ṭabarī, vol. I, pp. 2876, 2877, 2879, 2882, 2888.

[3] Ibn Khurdādhbeh, p. 39.

[4] Tha'ālibī, p. 748.

[5] Ṭabarī, vol. I, p. 3249.

[6] Ya'qūbī, *Tārīkh*, vol. II, p. 192; Balādhurī, *Futūḥ*, p. 403; Ibn al-Faqīh, *Kitāb al-Buldān*, ed. M. J. de Goeje, Leiden, 1885, p. 318.

by the Hephthalites of Harāt, who, alarmed by the appearance of the Arabs in their neighbourhood, went out to check them. However, Aḥnaf was able to defeat them, and continued his march towards the city of Nīshāpūr where he was joined by Ibn 'Āmir.[1] There, he was met by some resistance and was obliged to besiege the city for several months, during which period he sent various expeditions to raid the different districts of Nīshāpūr. Sometimes he himself led such expeditions. As the winter was closing in, he had to intensify his attacks on the city. Finally, after the Arabs had captured certain parts, the *marzbān* of the city concluded a peace treaty with Ibn 'Āmir, promising to pay a tribute (*wazīfa*) of 700,000 or one million dirhams.[2]

Once Nīshāpūr had fallen to the Arabs, the other cities of Khurāsān, realizing that they would probably be next, preferred to send emissaries suing for peace, all of them agreeing to pay tribute to the Arabs. Thus the *dihqān* of Nasā agreed to pay 300,000 dirhams or, according to another tradition, as much as the land-tax would yield. The *'azīm* (chief) of Abīvard promised Ibn 'Āmir a tribute of 400,000 dirhams. Zādhūyeh, the *marzbān* of Sarakhs, surrendered to 'Abdullah Ibn Khāzim when the city was under siege, after obtaining a safe-conduct for a hundred persons; yet Ibn Khāzim killed the *marzbān* and entered his city by force of arms. The *marzbān* of Ṭūs, the *kanārang,* offered to pay a tribute of 600,000 dirhams. The *'azīm* of Harāt concluded a peace treaty with the Arabs, after agreeing to pay a tribute of one million dirhams. Finally, the *marzbān* of Merv, Mahūyeh, sued for peace, and his tribute was relatively large—between one and two million dirhams in addition to 200,000 *jarībs* of wheat and barley.[3] Madā'inī in general seems to agree with Balādhurī, except for the statement that after the city of Nīshāpūr fell to Ibn 'Āmir, the *kanārang* remained in possession of the eastern half of the province, and Ibn 'Āmir had to make peace with him in order to advance to Merv.[4]

Among these peace treaties concluded with the different *dihqāns*, the treaties of Harāt and of Merv deserve some attention. The treaty of Harāt, with Pūshang and Bādghīs, stipulated that the sum of the tribute should be "divided equally on the land".

[1] Ṭabarī, vol. I, p. 2885; Balādhurī, *Futūḥ*, p. 403.
[2] Balādhurī, *Futūḥ*, pp. 403–4; Yāqūt, *Buldān*, vol. IV, p. 487; vol. I, p. 280.
[3] Balādhurī, *Futūḥ*, pp. 404–5.
[4] Ṭabarī, vol. I, p. 2886.

Also the word *jizya* was used to signify what was obviously a tribute.[1] According to the treaty of Merv, it was left to the *dihqāns* to decide how the burden of the tribute would be divided. It is specifically mentioned that the Muslims, i.e. the Arabs, had nothing to do with the allocation of taxes; they simply received the money. In both treaties, the *dihqāns* were made responsible to the Arabs for the tribute. Another important feature in the treaty of Merv was that the inhabitants had to make room for the Arabs in their houses.[2] These treaties were the basis for the relationship between the Arabs, as rulers, and the subject people, and it will be seen later that they played a major role in the social and political development in Khurāsān.

Altogether, therefore, Ibn 'Āmir and his troops from Baṣra were able, in a matter of months, to bring most of Sāsānian Khurāsān under Arab domination. As for the troops from Kūfa led by Sa'īd ibn al-'Āṣī, who were advancing towards Khurāsān by way of the northern route, they reached as far as Qūmis where, learning of Ibn 'Āmir's success and seeing no advantage in going any further, they returned to Kūfa.[3]

In the year 32/652 Ibn 'Āmir sent an expedition against the last stronghold of the Sāsānians in Khurāsān—Merv ar-Rūd. This expedition, led by his best lieutenant al-Aḥnaf ibn Qays, first reduced the only *rustāq* (district) mentioned in the sources along with the city of Merv ar-Rūd, known thereafter as Rustāq or Qasr al-Aḥnaf. A peace treaty was concluded and a tribute of 300,000 dirhams was imposed on the *rustāq*. Aḥnaf then advanced to his main task and laid siege to the city. After some fighting, Bādhām, the *marzbān* of Merv ar-Rūd, sued for peace. The fight which the people of this city put up against the Arabs must have been very strong, because the Arabs were satisfied with the relatively small tribute of 60,000 dirhams offered by the *marzbān*. They granted him further concessions by allowing him to keep the lands which were given to his ancestors by the Sāsānian kings and by exempting him and members of his family from any taxes. The Arabs also promised to keep the marzbānship in his family. In return for these concessions the Arabs stipulated that the *marzbān* and his horsemen (*asāwira*) must support the Arabs

[1] Balādhurī, *Futūḥ*, pp. 405–6.
[2] *Ibid.*, p. 405; Ya'qūbī, *Tārīkh*, vol. II, p. 193.
[3] Balādhurī, *Futūḥ*, pp. 334–5; Ṭabarī, vol. I, pp. 2836–7.

against any enemy if they were asked to do so. At the same time the Arabs would also help the *marzbān* against the enemies of his people.[1]

Balādhurī quotes Abū 'Ubayda as stating that the Turks were supporting the people of Merv ar-Rūd against the Arabs. Of course, these were the Hephthalites, most probably of Gūzgān. This may explain why the next move by the Arabs was particularly against Gūzgān, Fāryāb and Ṭālqān. Aḥnaf again led this expedition, of 4,000 Arabs supported by 1,000 non-Arab Muslims, and Madā'inī specifically mentions that Aḥnaf did not wish to ask for the help of the infidels of Merv ar-Rūd, probably because he did not trust them. The Arabs camped in Qasr-al-Aḥnaf, a day's march to the north of Merv ar-Rūd, on the east side of the Murghāb. The armies of Gūzgān, Faryāb and Ṭālqān, numbering 30,000 men, supported by the army of Chaghāniān, advanced to meet the Arabs. The battle did not seem to go very much in favour of the Arabs. However, the enemy dispersed, some of them remaining at Gūzgān, while the Arabs withdrew to Merv ar-Rūd.

Aḥnaf sent an expedition, apparently exclusively of Tamīmites, led by al-Aqra' ibn Ḥābis, to Gūzgān, which was able to defeat the Gūzgānites and entered Gūzgān by force. Meanwhile, Aḥnaf himself advanced from Merv ar-Rūd towards Balkh, and on the way he made peace treaties with Ṭālqān and Fāryāb. Arriving at Balkh, he besieged the city, whereupon the people of the city offered to pay a tribute of 400,000 or 700,000 dirhams. Aḥnaf left his cousin to collect the tribute and he advanced towards Khwārizm, but as winter was approaching he returned to Balkh.[2]

Abū 'Ubayda mentioned a tradition that Ibn 'Āmir might have crossed the river (Oxus) and made peace treaties with the people on its eastern side. Barthold and Gibb accepted this tradition and believed it to be supported by the statement in the Chinese sources that the Arabs raided Māyamurgh in Soghdiana in 33/654. This is hardly possible since we know that Ibn 'Āmir was not in Khurāsān in 33/654, and there is no trace of Ibn 'Āmir's leading any expedition to the east of the Murghāb in the whole campaign. Furthermore, the date in the Chinese sources seems to be confused, because they mention in the same year the attack on Persia and the

[1] Balādhurī, *Futūḥ*, p. 406; Ṭabarī, vol. 1, pp. 2887–90.
[2] Ṭabarī, vol. 1, pp. 2897–903; Balādhurī, *Futūḥ*, pp. 406–8.

death of Yazdgird at the hands of the Arabs. It is certain that the Arab armies did not attempt to cross the Oxus at that time and did not try to advance beyond Balkh.[1]

During that time, while the greater part of the Baṣran troops of 'Abdullah ibn 'Āmir were busy in Khurāsān, a group were making progress in another part of the eastern provinces of the Sāsānians. When Ibn 'Āmir was on his way to Khurāsān he conquered parts of the province of Kirmān; but he left Mujāshi' ibn Mas'ūd as-Sulamī in Kirmān with orders to continue the conquest whilst he continued his march with the main part of the Baṣran army. Ibn Mas'ūd as-Sulamī was able to conquer most of the province, but many people fled, leaving their lands and houses. These were divided among the Arabs, who cultivated the land and paid the tithes due on it.[2]

At the same time Ibn 'Āmir sent another expedition to Sīstān, led by ar-Rabī' ibn Ziyād al-Ḥārithī. After occupying a few villages, Rabī' reached his main objective and laid siege to the city of Zarang, whose *marzbān* asked for peace, offering 1,000 slaves and 1,000 golden cups. Rabī' accepted and entered the city, where he stayed with his troops for more than two years, after which period he left a cousin in charge of his troops and returned to Ibn 'Āmir. Soon after, the Arabs were driven out of the city.[3] It is not surprising to find no mention of any resistance to the Arabs from Zābulistān or its king Zunbīl, since Zarang had been in the Sāsānian domain and since the Arabs made no attempt to advance eastwards in the Bilād ad-Dāwar, confining themselves to western Sīstān.

Al-Aḥnaf ibn Qays, having achieved the purpose of his expedition, returned from Balkh to Nīshāpūr, where Ibn 'Āmir had his headquarters. The Arabs seemed to be in control of practically all the Sāsānian domains in the east. Furthermore, they had neutralized, though temporarily, any danger to their position there from the Hephthalite principalities.

Ibn 'Āmir saw no reason for remaining in Khurāsān, and he left, apparently to report to 'Uthmān and then to return to Baṣra in time for the following year's campaign. The Arab plan, then,

[1] Balādhurī, *Futūḥ*, p. 408; W. Barthold, *Turkestan down to the Mongol invasion*, G.M.S., London, 1928, p. 6; Gibb, *Arab Conquests*, p. 15, p. 28, note 1; Ṭabarī, vol. I, p. 2905; Chavannes, *Documents*, p. 172, note 1; Ya'qūbī, *Tārīkh*, vol. II, p. 193.

[2] Balādhurī, *Futūḥ*, pp. 391–2.

[3] *Ibid.*, pp. 392–4.

was to send an expedition every year from Baṣra to raid those areas which had not made peace treaties with them, and to carry their conquests as far as possible to the east. At the end of the campaign, in the autumn, they would return to Baṣra, leaving in Khurāsān a garrison of 4,000 men to secure the area for their return.[1] This garrison would stay in the district of Merv, where provision had been made for them to be quartered in the houses of the local population. There was no plan at that time for the Arabs to settle permanently in Khurāsān.

3 *The structure of the Arab army*

A brief description of the structure of the army of ʿAbdullah ibn ʿĀmir would help us to solve some of the problems we meet in reconstructing the history of this period. The army of Baṣra was recruited from the tribesmen who had recently emigrated to that garrison town (*miṣr*) and enlisted in the *dīwān*. It was natural that these tribesmen should carry on their old tribal traditions, bearing the name of their original clan (*ʿashīra*) or tribe, with whom they might have severed their relationship by emigrating to the *miṣr*. Each clan, or even a tribal grouping from related clans, would have its own chief acting as its military commander. Though the clan was the basic unit in the army, the numbers in each clan varied because of the continuous influx of immigrants into the *miṣr*.[2]

Our sources do not indicate exactly which clans formed the population of Baṣra at this early stage of its development, but, from reviewing the names of the tribal chiefs which occur in the narratives of this expedition, we can infer to some extent which clans formed part of the army of Ibn ʿĀmir. There were a certain number of clans belonging to the tribe of Tamīm, all under the undisputed leadership of Al-Aḥnaf ibn Qays. It seems that these clans, though numerous, were individually small in size, explaining why they should prefer to gather under the bigger tribal name of Tamīm.[3] This is the only tribal grouping which appears in our sources at this early period. The other chiefs mentioned

[1] Ṭabarī, vol. I, pp. 2904–6.

[2] S. A. al-ʿAlī, *al-Tanẓīmāt al-Ijtimāʿiyya wal Iqtiṣādiyya fī al-Baṣra*, Baghdad, 1953, pp. 33–45.

[3] Balādhurī, *Futūḥ*, p. 406; Ṭabarī, vol. I, pp. 2897, 2902, 2903; Yaʿqūbī, *Buldān*, pp. 279, 291; Ibn Saʿd, vol. V, p. 33, vol. VII, part I, p. 66.

were leaders of their own clans or combinations of related clans which were too small to form independent units. In this respect, there were tribesmen from the clans of Azd, Bakr, Madhhij and Qays.[1] The last group seems to have been of a considerable size, and its leadership was the subject of dispute between Qays ibn al-Haytham and ʿAbdullah ibn Khāzim, who were both from the Qaysite clan of Sulaym.[2]

The only non-Arab element in the army of Ibn ʿĀmir were the one thousand men, mentioned as non-Arab Muslims, among Aḥnaf's troops in his battle against the Hephthalite principalities. These men were not from the people of Khurāsān but from the *asāwira* of Baṣra, who were previously members of the Sāsānian army and then joined the Arab *muqātila* of Baṣra.[3] As they were allies of Tamīm, it is not surprising to find them with Aḥnaf ibn Qays, the chief of Tamīm.

According to Madā'ini, ʿAbdullah ibn ʿĀmir, upon leaving Khurāsān, appointed Qays ibn al-Haytham as-Sulamī to be in charge of the province. Yaʿqūbī, to some extent supported by Balādhurī, asserts that Ibn ʿĀmir divided Khurāsān between four different tribal chiefs.[4] These two statements can now be reconciled in this way: When ʿAbdullah ibn ʿĀmir left Khurāsān, with the bulk of his army, he left behind a garrison of which the majority was the Qaysite group of Sulaym, supported by other clans from Tamīm, Azd and Khuzāʿa. Since the Qaysite group was the biggest, it was natural that its chief, Qays ibn al-Haytham, should be responsible for the whole garrison, particularly in case of any military operation, though we should remember that this garrison was not meant to take the initiative in any military operation particularly in the winter. In order that the other tribal chiefs should share in the responsibility and the honour, they were charged with collecting the tribute from certain parts of the province assigned to them, from which they would have to distribute the stipends—*ʿaṭā'*—to their men, and deliver the rest to Qays ibn al-Haytham, who was supposed to send it to the governor in Baṣra.[5]

[1] Balādhurī, *Futūḥ*, pp. 368, 381, 392–4, 402–6, 408; Ṭabarī, vol. I, pp. 2887, 2888, 2897, 2903;Yaʿqūbī, *Buldān*, pp. 279, 291; Ibn Saʿd, vol. V, pp. 32–3; Yāqūt, *Buldān*, vol. II, p. 131, vol. IV, p. 265.

[2] Ṭabarī, vol. II, p. 65.

[3] Balādhurī, *Futūḥ*, pp. 373–4; al-ʿAlī, *Tanẓīmāt*, p. 69.

[4] Ṭabarī, vol. I, p. 2905, Yaʿqūbī, *Tārīkh*, vol. II, p. 193; Balādhurī, *Futūḥ*, pp. 375, 408.

[5] Ṭabarī, vol. II, p. 65.

4 *Uprisings in Khurāsān*

The situation in Khurāsān did not remain as peaceful as the Arabs anticipated. Soon after Ibn 'Āmir left the province, in the winter of 32/653, a general insurrection broke out. According to Madā'inī, it was headed by Qārin, probably a member of the Sāsānian noble family known by that name,[1] who was supported by the people of Qūhistān, and the Hephthalites of Harāt and Bādghīs.[2] It seems that, following this, a general rising occurred in the whole province. Yāqūt reported that the family of the *kanārang*, which was related to the Sāsānian royal family, drove the Arabs out of Nīshāpūr. He also mentioned that Nēzak took part in this revolution and occupied Balkh.[3] In spite of the great number of the followers of Qārin, mentioned as 40,000 men, which is probably an exaggeration, the relatively small garrison of Khurāsān—4,000 Arabs—was able (so it is reported by Madā'inī) to defeat his army or at least to hold out until it was rescued by the arrival of Ibn 'Āmir with the rest of his army from Baṣra in 33/653.[4] He succeeded, in a short period, in pacifying the province, and then returned to Baṣra.

According to Madā'inī, Ibn 'Āmir did not come to Khurāsān that year, probably because of the explosive conditions in Madīna, and Ibn Khāzim was credited with the effective role in quelling the Qārin insurrection, after the failure of his opponent, Qays ibn al-Haytham, to deal with it. Ibn 'Āmir then confirmed Ibn Khāzim as the leader of the Arab garrison in Khurāsān.[5] However, the succession of the Arab chiefs in Khurāsān, from this time until the establishment of Umayyad rule in 41/661, is not made clear in our sources, probably because of the continuous rotation of the clans forming the garrison there, to avoid keeping the Arab tribesmen away from their homes in Baṣra, *tajmīr al-bu'ūth*.

In the last uneasy years of the reign of 'Uthmān, and during the period of the civil war between 'Alī and Mu'āwiya, the Arabs were preoccupied with their own internal affairs, and it was to

[1] Christensen, *L'Iran*, pp. 98–9.
[2] Ṭabarī, vol. I, p. 2905.
[3] Yāqūt, *Buldān*, vol. II, p. 411.
[4] Ṭabarī, vol. I, p. 2907. This is the assertion of Ṭabarī himself, apparently on the authority of Wāqidī.
[5] *Ibid.*, pp. 2905–6. Ṭabarī gives different versions of this tradition, by Madā'inī, all of which agree that it was Ibn Khāzim who pacified the province.

be expected that the recently subjugated peoples would take advantage of this situation to liberate themselves. Although Khurāsān was no exception, there does not seem to have been any all-out effort to drive the Arabs from the province after the suppression of the Qārin insurrection. We hear only of local movements. The city of Nīshāpūr is said to have revolted.[1] Merv seems to have risen, and even the *marzbān* Māhūyeh, who had concluded the peace treaty with the Arabs, had to leave the city. He appeared in Iraq in 36/656–7, seeking the support of *Amīr al-Mu'minīn* 'Alī and confirming this peace treaty.[2] According to Madā'inī, 'Alī, after the Battle of the Camel, was able to send an expedition to Khurāsān in 37/658, which entered the city of Nīshāpūr after a short siege, and then proceeded to Merv where it reinstated Māhūyeh.[3] According to Balādhurī, the situation in Khurāsān continued to be unstable until the death of 'Alī.[4]

The Arabs were able, because of the weak resistance of the local population rather than their own efforts, to maintain their authority as far as Merv, but the Hephthalite principalities, particularly those of Harāt, Pūshang and Bādghīs, were able to regain the status they had prior to the arrival of the Arabs, and to stop paying tribute to them.[5] The Chinese sources add that in A.D. 655 there was an attempt, supported by the army of Ṭukhāristān, to reinstate Peroz, the son of Yazdgird, as titular king of Persia, but this episode is not confirmed by the Arabic sources.[6]

5 *Re-establishment of Arab authority*

When the civil war ended and Mu'āwiya was recognized as the first Umayyad *Amīr al-Mu'minīn* (41/661), the central government was able to devote more attention to re-establishing Arab authority in those parts of the empire where it had been badly shaken. 'Abdullah ibn 'Āmir was restored as governor of Baṣra, with Khurāsān and Sīstān included in his governorship. He assigned the garrison of Khurāsān to Qays ibn al-Haytham with instructions

[1] Ṭabarī, vol. I, pp. 3249, 3350, 3389; Dīnawarī, *al-Akhbār aṭ-Ṭiwāl*, ed. V. Guirgass, Leiden, 1888, p. 163.

[2] Ṭabarī, vol. I, p. 3249; Balādhurī, *Futūḥ*, p. 408; Ya'qūbī, *Buldān*, pp. 213–14.

[3] Ṭabarī, vol. I, pp. 3249, 3350, 3389–90.

[4] Balādhurī, *Futūḥ*, p. 409. Unfortunately, Balādhurī does not specify his source at this point.

[5] *Ibid.*, p. 409.

[6] Gibb, *Arab Conquests*, p. 16; Chavannes, *Documents*, p. 172.

to collect the tribute only from those who had kept their peace with the Arabs and not to interfere with those who had revolted.[1]

In the meantime, he prepared an expedition under the leadership of ʿAbdurraḥman ibn Samura, who was also a Qurayshite, and including such famous leaders as ʿUmar ibn ʿUbaydillah ibn Maʿmar, ʿAbdullah ibn Khāzim, Qaṭariyy ibn al-Fuja'a and al-Muhallab ibn Abi Ṣufra. It is rather surprising to find that such a big army was sent, not to Khurāsān, but to Sīstān. An explanation may be found if we accept Chavannes' suggestion that Zarang was the centre of the provisional government of Persia under Peroz mentioned in the Chinese sources,[2] since the Arabs may have considered Sīstān as the centre of agitation in the east.

Though the reports about this expedition in the Arabic sources are confused with the earlier expedition of 31–2/651–2, it is still possible to follow its advance. First, Zarang was recaptured and a tribute of two million dirhams and 2,000 slaves was imposed on the city. Then the Arabs, opening a new front against Zunbīl, king of Zābulistān, advanced eastwards, conquering towns like Khwāsh, Bust, Khushshak and Razān. They besieged the city of Kābul for a few months and finally entered it. As a reward, Muʿāwiya made Sīstān a separate governorship and appointed as governor Ibn Samura, who stayed there until he was replaced by ar-Rabīʿ ibn Ziyād al-Ḥarithī in 45/665.[3]

Yaʿqūbī is the only one of our sources who reports that this expedition of Ibn Samura was sent to Khurāsān, where it recaptured Balkh, and then advanced south to Kābul, where Ibn Samura concluded a peace treaty. He then returned, leaving Khurāsān to Ibn Khāzim.[4] There is also a report in Balādhurī that Qays ibn al-Haytham advanced directly to Balkh, destroyed its famous shrine of Nawbahār and accepted the plea of the people of the city for peace.[5] But from Madā'inī we learn that Balkh was not recaptured until after 51/671 by Rabīʿ ibn Ziyād, and it is particularly pointed out that Balkh had revoked its peace treaty with the Arabs soon after the time of Aḥnaf ibn Qays.[6] Since we also know that the instructions to Qays ibn al-Haytham were that he should not interfere with any people who had revolted,[7] it

[1] Ṭabarī, vol. II, pp. 15, 17. Balādhurī, *Futūḥ*, p. 409.
[2] Chavannes, *Documents*, p. 279.
[3] Balādhurī, *Futūḥ*, pp. 396–7.
[4] Yaʿqūbī, *Tārīkh*, vol. II, p. 258.
[5] Balādhurī, *Futūḥ*, p. 409.
[6] Ṭabarī, vol. II, pp. 155–6.
[7] Balādhurī, *Futūḥ*, p. 409.

would seem that Ya'qūbī and Balādhurī were quoting an exaggerated Qaysite tradition, which is particularly noticeable in references to 'Abdullah ibn Khāzim. On the other hand, the situation in the east would not have allowed a direct advance to Balkh.

Although we are not clear about the situation in the Hephthalite principalities of Gūzgān, it seems that it was only those principalities in the west around Ṭālqān and Fāryāb that had continued to recognize their peace treaties with the Arabs; the rest of these Hephthalite principalities seem to have revolted until they were reconquered by al-Ḥakam ibn 'Amr (45–50/665–70). As for the Hephthalite principalities of Harāt, Pūshang and Bādghīs, it seems that when they realized that peace had been restored in the Arab lands, they preferred to resume their peace treaties with the Arabs. Ibn Khāzim, who appeared again as the leader of the Arab garrison in Khurāsān in 43/663, accepted their pleas and, naturally, their tribute.[1]

The following year, the new garrison was under the leadership of 'Abdullah ibn Abī Shaykh al-Yashkurī. Late in the same year 'Abdullah ibn 'Āmir was removed from his governorship because of his limited administrative ability. The huge numbers of tribesmen immigrating into Baṣra had aroused jealousies between the different tribes and caused some tensions. Mu'āwiya took the unusual step of appointing the Azdite, al-Ḥārith ibn 'Abdillah, as governor of Baṣra, but this did not remedy the situation, and in four months he was removed in favour of the strong and able Ziyād ibn Abī Sufyān, whose terms of appointment in 45/665 included Khurāsān and Sīstān.[2]

6 *The plan of Ziyād ibn Abī Sufyān*

Wellhausen believes that in 45/665 Ziyād "divided Khurāsān into four independent districts: Marw, Abrshahr (Nisabur), Marwrudh (with Faryab and Taliqan) and Herat (with Badghis, Qadis and Bushang), but united them in 47/667 under Ḥakam b. 'Amr al-Ghifari".[3] Gibb, agreeing with this opinion, says that

[1] *Ibid.*, p. 409; Ya'qūbī, *Tārīkh*, vol. II, p. 264.

[2] Ṭabarī, vol. II, pp. 67–8.

[3] J. Wellhausen, *Das Arabische Reich und sein Sturz*, Berlin, 1902, *The Arab Kingdom and its Fall*, tr. M. G. Wier, Calcutta, 1927, p. 415.

> after an experimental division of the province under tribal leaders, a policy obviously dangerous and quickly abandoned, Ziyād, realizing the danger of allowing Persian nationalism a free hand in the East, backed up by the resources of Ṭukhāristān, centralized the administration at Merv, and organized a preventive campaign. In 47/667 his lieutenant al-Ḥakam b. ʿAmr al-Ghifārī opened a series of campaigns directed to the conquest of Lower Ṭukhāristān and Gharjistān.[1]

This belief is apparently based on a statement by Madā'inī,[2] which was also quoted by Balādhurī.[3]

The report of a division of Khurāsān among tribal leaders, making them responsible only for the collection of the tribute from certain parts of the province, has already been referred to.[4] The report of this later division under Ziyād should be taken as referring to the same measure. In fact, Madā'inī, in another version of the same tradition, states that Ziyād appointed al-Ḥakam ibn ʿAmr to Khurāsān in 45/665, assigning to different districts the tribal leaders, all of whom were subordinated to al-Ḥakam and made responsible for the collection of the tribute.[5] Yaʿqūbī and Ibn Aʿtham do not mention this division of Khurāsān either before al-Ḥakam or during his governorship.[6] The appointment of al-Ḥakam took place either in 45/665 or in 47/667 and his death is mentioned in 47/447 and 50/670.[7] The dates concerning the appointments and events between 45/665 and 51/671 are confused in our sources, though they all agree that in 51/671 ar-Rabīʿ ibn Ziyād al-Ḥārithī was appointed to Khurāsān,[8] and this appointment marked a new Arab policy in this part of the empire.

When Ziyād was appointed to Baṣra in 45/665, his first preoccupation was naturally that increasingly important garrison town,[9] and he found little time to introduce any new policy in Khurāsān. He may have appointed al-Ḥakam ibn ʿAmr in 45/665 as governor of Khurāsān and to lead a new expedition there,

1 Gibb, *Arab Conquests*, p. 16.
2 Ṭabarī, vol. II, p. 79.
3 Balādhurī, *Futūḥ*, p. 409.
4 Yaʿqūbī, *Tārīkh*, vol. II, p. 193; Balādhurī, *Futūḥ*, p. 408; see also above, p. 25.
5 Ṭabarī, vol. II, p. 81.
6 Yaʿqūbī, *Tārīkh*, vol. II, p. 264; Ibn Aʿtham, *Kitāb al-Futūḥ*, Istanbul manuscript, Library of Ahmet III, No. 2956, vol. I, pp. 169 B, 170 A.
7 Ṭabarī, vol. II, pp. 81, 84, 85, 109.
8 *Ibid.*, vol. II, p. 155; Balādhurī, *Futūḥ*, p. 410; Ibn al-Athīr, *al-Kāmil fī at-Tārīkh*, ed. C. J. Tornberg, Leiden, 1866–71, vol. III, p. 408.
9 Ibn Aʿtham, *Futūḥ*, vol. I, p. 169 B.

but al-Ḥakam was not able to assemble a new army and advance into Khurāsān until 47/667. Meanwhile, the leaders of the garrison of Khurāsān were responsible for collecting the tribute there, and probably sent it to Baṣra to help al-Ḥakam ibn ʻAmr recruit his army.

Al-Ḥakam appeared in Khurāsān in 47/667, advancing eastwards to re-establish Arab authority among the Principalities of Ṭukhāristān. He was able to bring the Hephthalite principalities of Gūzgān and Gharchistān into line, though it is reported that he sometimes met with strong resistance.[1] It is said that he had crossed the River Oxus, but only to make his prayers and cross back,[2] then he returned to Merv. When he reported his conquests to Ziyād, the latter wrote to him, on Muʻāwiya's instructions, to set aside all the gold and silver from the booty to be sent to the treasury in Damascus. Al-Ḥakam publicly rejected these instructions and set aside only the fifth of the booty (*ghanā'im*) to be sent to Ziyād and divided the rest among the Muslims.[3] It is not clear from our sources whether al-Ḥakam undertook more expeditions, or whether he died in 47/667 or 50/670. He was succeeded by another man of the same calibre, who was also one of the companions of the Prophet (*ṣaḥāba*). This was Ghālib ibn Fuḍāla (or Abdillah) al-Laythī who continued the task of al-Ḥakam among the Principalities of Ṭukhāristān.[4]

Meanwhile, Ziyād ibn Abī Sufyān was busy in Baṣra carrying out his administrative reorganization. He divided Baṣra into five big tribal divisions, each called *khums* (fifth) and comprising several clans. The *akhmās* were Tamīm, Bakr, Azd, ʻAbdulqays and Ahl al-ʻĀliya. When in 50/670 Kūfa was added to Ziyād's governorship, he similarly divided it into *arbā*ʻ (quarters). The heads of these divisions were appointed by the government from the highly regarded men in the tribes. In the new organization, each clan formed an independent unit with regard to the distribution of the *ʻaṭā'*, and the records of the *dīwān* were revised, omitting the names of the dead and adding instead some of the names of the newcomers. The result was that a great number of

[1] Ṭabarī, vol. II, pp. 81–4, 109–11; Yaʻqūbī, *Tārīkh*, vol. II, p. 264.

[2] Ṭabarī, vol. II, p. 156.

[3] *Ibid.*, vol. I, p. 110; Ibn al-Athīr, *Kāmil*, vol. III, p. 391; Ibn Aʻtham, *Futūḥ*, vol. I, p. 170 A.

[4] Ṭabarī, vol. II, p. 85; Ibn Aʻtham, *Futūḥ*, vol. I, p. 170 A; al-ʻAlī, *Tanẓimāt*, pp. 287–95.

tribesmen were not included in the *dīwān* of Baṣra and Kūfa.[1] This inspired Ziyād to transfer 50,000 families from the two *miṣrs* to Khurāsān to settle permanently there, securing the conquests already made and providing the forces needed for their further extension. Balādhurī and Madā'inī agree that the number of families transferred was 50,000 but Madā'inī adds that half of them were from Baṣra and the other half from Kūfa.[2] Al-'Alī doubts Madā'inī's claim, arguing that in the governorship of Qutayba in 96/715 there were only 10,000 men from Kūfa, and there is no evidence in our sources that the Kūfans had withdrawn from Khurāsān after the time of Ziyād ibn Abī Sufyān.[3] Yet the fact remains that, for the first time, the tribesmen of Kūfa were employed in the conquests in Khurāsān.

According to Ibn A'tham, Ghālib ibn Fuḍāla (Abdillah) did not have much success in fighting against the Principalities of Ṭukhāristān, so Ziyād in 51/671 appointed as governor of Khurāsān ar-Rabī' ibn Ziyād al-Ḥārithī, who led this expedition of 50,000 men from Baṣra and Kūfa to settle there. He advanced directly towards Balkh where he made a peace treaty with the people of the city who had revolted after Al-Aḥnaf ibn Qays had made peace with them. Ar-Rabī' then turned to the remnants of the army of the Hephthalite principalities of Bādghīs, Harāt and Pūshang, pursued them into Qūhistān and defeated them, but Nēzak was able to survive until he met his death at the hands of Qutayba many years later.

During his governorship of Khurāsān (51–3/671–3) ar-Rabī' ibn Ziyād was able to re-establish Arab authority as far as Balkh in the east, and his son, 'Abdullah ibn ar-Rabī', who succeeded him for a few months in 53/673, extended it to the bank of the Oxus and made peace treaties with Āmul and Zamm. Both ar-Rabī' and his son made Merv their base and they always returned to it after their expeditions.[4] No mention is made in our sources of any Arab tribesmen being left behind in any other part of Khurāsān. The statements in the Arabic sources concerning the

[1] Ṭabarī, vol. I, p. 2405; al-'Alī, *Tanẓimāt*, pp. 36–41, 287–95; H. Lammens, *Etudes sur le Siècle des Omayyades*, Beyrouth, 1930, pp. 127–32. For further details about Baṣra, see the excellent work of al-'Alī, *Tanẓimāt*.

[2] Ṭabarī, vol. II, p. 81; Balādhurī, *Futūḥ*, p. 410.

[3] Ṭabarī, vol. II, p. 1291; Balādhurī, *Futūḥ*, p. 423; al-'Alī, *Tanẓimāt*, p. 32.

[4] Ṭabarī, vol. II, p. 161; Ibn A'tham, *Futūḥ*, vol. I, p. 170A; Balādhurī, *Futūḥ*, p. 410; Ṭabarī, vol. II, pp. 156–61.

settlement of the people from Kūfa and Baṣra are surprisingly brief. Madā'inī says only that they moved their families and settled in Khurāsān.[1] Ibn al-Athīr does not elaborate this point, and says simply that they made Khurāsān their home.[2] Balādhurī, who is always particular about the settlement of the Arabs in certain towns in Western Persia, *tamṣīr*, does not mention any *tamṣīr* in Khurāsān; however, he specifies in this case that they were settled on the near side of "the River", *dūn al-Nahr*.[3] Ibn A'tham is more definite, saying that they stayed in Merv and that from there they went on expeditions to the different parts of Khurāsān.[4]

In all the Arabic biographical notes, geographical works and historical narratives, only two men belonging to those 50,000 Kūfans and Baṣrans are named, and, as might be expected, this is because they were companions of the Prophet. They are Burayda ibn al-Ḥuṣayb al-Aslamī and Abū Barza 'Abdullah ibn Naḍla al-Aslamī, who both settled in Merv, died there, the first dying in 62 or 63/681 or 682, and were buried in a village of Merv called Fanī (Fanīn).[5] We also know that al-Ḥakam ibn 'Amr al-Ghifārī, the governor of Khurāsān who died between 47/667 and 50/670, was buried in the same village in the house of Khālid ibn 'Abdillah al-Ḥanafī, the brother of Khulayd, one of the early leaders who played an important role in the conquest of Khurāsān.[6] There are some few names of Arabs who were likely to have lived in one or another of the villages of Merv, like Būzan Shāh, Mehrigān, Jundāfarqān, Sīnān, Fanīn, Dārijeh, Jārūsa, Bursānjird and Darwāzaq.[7] The names of the men mentioned in this connection do not permit us to infer their tribal affiliations.

It is clear therefore that when these 50,000 Arab families came to Khurāsān they were settled in the different villages of the oasis

[1] Ṭabarī, vol. II, p. 156.
[2] Ibn al-Athīr, *Kāmil*, vol. III, p. 408.
[3] Balādhurī, *Futūḥ*, pp. 329, 332, 333, 410.
[4] Ibn A'tham, *Futūḥ*, vol. I, p. 170A.
[5] Balādhurī, *Futūḥ*, p. 410; Ibn al-Athīr, *Kāmil*, vol. III, p. 408; Ibn Sa'd, vol. VII, part I, pp. 3–4, vol. 7, part II, p. 100; Yāqūt, *Buldān*, vol. I, p. 777, vol. IV, p. 511; al-Dhahabī, *Tārīkh al-Islām*, Cairo, vol. II, 1367, p. 386. Ibn al-Athīr, *Lubāb*, vol. II, p. 225.
[6] Yāqūt, *Buldān*, vol. IV, p. 511; Ṭabarī, vol. II, p. 155.
[7] Yāqūt, *Buldān*, vol. I, pp. 565, 757, vol. II, pp. 11, 129, 570, 572, vol. III, p. 220, vol. IV, p. 700; Ibn al-Athīr, *Lubāb*, pp. 112, 206, 240, 417.

of Merv, probably with their kinsmen who had been there among the garrison of Khurāsān, making the best possible use of the treaty of Merv which stipulated that the people of Merv would make room for the Arabs in their houses. Neither ar-Rabīʿ ibn Ziyād nor Ziyād ibn Abī Sufyān lived long enough to carry out Ziyād's plan completely and it was left mostly to Ziyād's sons to follow up the execution of his policy.

3

THE CENTRAL GOVERNMENT AND THE TRIBESMEN

1 *Khurāsān, a separate governorship*

The settling of 50,000 Arab families in Khurāsān was certainly a major step and marked the beginning of a new aggressive policy in this part of the empire. Although Ziyād ibn Abī Sufyān died in 53/673, Mu'āwiya secured the continuation of his policy by the appointment of Ziyād's son to Khurāsān. 'Abdullah ibn ar-Rabī', who died in 53/673 before the death of Ziyād, had left Khulayd ibn 'Abdillah al-Ḥanafī, one of the tribal leaders, in charge of the province.[1] Mu'āwiya made Khurāsān a separate governorship and appointed 'Ubaydullah ibn Ziyād as governor. He was only twenty-five years old at that time. He immediately left for Khurāsān in the autumn of 53/673, where he began to prepare an expedition.[2]

In the following spring of 54/674 he crossed the Oxus, raided Paykand and probably reduced Bukhārā to tributary status.[3] Since the Arab conquests in Transoxiana are fully described in H. A. R. Gibb's work *The Arab Conquests in Central Asia*, there does not seem to be any need for further discussion, except in so far as the conquests reflect on the situation in Khurāsān. The important thing here is to notice that the army of Ibn Ziyād was about 24,000 strong,[4] almost half the Arab army in Khurāsān at that time. There is no indication, in our sources, that Ibn Ziyād made any attempt to move any of the Arab tribesmen from the Merv oasis to settle in other parts of Khurāsān. This is understandable, since such a move would have defeated his own purpose of having these *muqātila* in close proximity, ready for the yearly campaign in Transoxiana.[5] Merv was not made a *miṣr*, and at this stage the Arabs were kept deliberately outside the city and were only allowed to live in the surrounding villages.[6]

[1] Ṭabarī, vol. II, p. 161.
[2] *Ibid.*, pp. 166–8; Balādhurī, *Futūḥ*, p. 410.
[3] Gibb, *Arab Conquests*, pp. 17–19.
[4] Balādhurī, *Futūḥ*, p. 410.
[5] Ṭabarī, vol. II, p. 394.
[6] Ibn al-Athīr, *Lubāb*, vol. I, p. 569; Ibn 'Abd Rabbih, *al-'Iqd al-Farīd*, Beirut, 1951–4, vol. II, p. 65.

The local administration in the different districts of Khurāsān was left in the hands of the *dihqāns*, although in some places Ibn Ziyād had appointed certain tribal chiefs as "residents" along with the native rulers. We only know about one case, related by Abū-'Ubayda and quoted in *al-Aghānī*, which illustrates very well the Arab chiefs' grasp of administration in the conquered lands, and it would seem appropriate to quote it at length. Abu-'Ubayda relates that:

> 'Ubaydullah ibn Ziyād appointed Ḥāritha ibn Badr (al-Ghuddānī from Tamīm) to Nīshāpūr. He stayed there for a few months, and then returned to Ibn Ziyād, who asked him, "What brought you back without being recalled?" He answered, "I have extracted all your *kharāj*, and I have brought it with me, and I have nothing else to do there, so why should I stay there?" Ibn Ziyād said, "Were those my instructions? Go back and give them back the *kharāj*, and take it only in instalments over the whole year, because this is more kind to the subject people and to yourself. Watch not to push them too hard so that they would have to sell their products, or their cattle." So, he returned and gave them back the *kharāj* and stayed there for the whole year taking the *kharāj* in instalments.[1]

This particular appointment was a favour from 'Ubaydullah ibn Ziyād to an old friend of the house of Ziyād, but in a political sense it was a means of reconciling the tribal leaders to Umayyad rule, and making them share the responsibility of the government while at the same time giving them some training in the art of ruling. It was also a source of financial support to these tribal leaders, necessary to strengthen their authority over their tribesmen. Not only were these appointments, since the time of Ziyād ibn Abī Sufyān, salaried,[2] but also at their election the tribal leaders, because of their appointments, became the recipients of the annual gifts on the occasions of the *naurūz* and *mihrjān*, according to an old Sāsānian tradition which was continued under the Arabs in Khurāsān.[3] Moreover, they could retain parts of the income from their districts and not deliver it to the governor, a

[1] Al-Isfahānī, *al-Aghānī*, vol. XXI, ed. R. E. Brunnow, Leiden, 1888, p. 39, also p. 22; Ibn 'Abd Rabbih, vol. 30, p. 106; Ibn Ḥazm, *Jamharatu Ansāb al-'Arab*, E. Levi-Provencal, Cairo, 1948, p. 214.

[2] Ya'qūbī, *Tārīkh*, vol. II, p. 279.

[3] *Ibid.*, p. 259; Ṭabarī, vol. I, p. 2903; Ibn Qutayba, *'Uyun al-Akhbār*, Cairo, 1925–30, vol. I, pp. 52–60; al-'Ali, *Tanẓīmāt*, p. 197.

practice which came to be rather the rule than the exception. On taking up these appointments tribal leaders were not accompanied by any number of their followers.[1]

2 *Aslam ibn Zur'a, a representative of the tribesmen*

'Ubaydullah ibn Ziyād did not lead more than one expedition into Transoxiana, and in the year 55/675 he was transferred to Baṣra. The same year he went back there, leaving Aslam ibn Zur'a al-Kilābī in charge of the province.[2] Aslam, who was a tribal leader from Qays, did not make any conquests nor did he lead any expeditions.[3] There is no reason given in the sources why the Arab army in Khurāsān should have stayed inactive in the year 55/675 until the arrival, the following year, of the new governor, Sa'īd ibn 'Uthmān ibn 'Affān. He was appointed by Mu'āwiya only for *al-ḥarb* (military administration), the responsibility of *al-kharāj* (fiscal affairs) having been assigned to Isḥāq ibn Ṭalḥa, who died on the way to Khurāsān.[4] Although some traditions claim that Sa'īd ibn 'Uthmān became responsible for both *al-ḥarb* and *al-kharāj* in Khurāsān,[5] it is probable that Aslam ibn Zur'a became responsible for *al-kharāj*.[6] He seems to have posed a problem for the central government, one which went beyond his functions as a tribal leader and was related to the revenue of the province.

From the *Futūḥ* of Ibn A'tham we gather some valuable information which may throw light on this problem. We remember that in the governorship of al-Ḥakam ibn 'Amr al-Ghifārī, Ziyād ibn Abī Sufyān and Mu'āwiya tried to interfere with the distribution of the booty (*ghanīma*). Al-Ḥakam flatly and publicly rejected this interference, sending to Ziyād only the legitimate one-fifth. Naturally, the income from the tribute in Khurāsān was sent to Baṣrā, since the *muqātila* in Khurāsān were members of the *dīwān* there and Khurāsān itself was part of the governorship of Baṣra.[7] When Khurāsān was made a separate governorship, it was required, like all the other provinces, to send part of its

1 Al-Isfahānī, *Aghānī*, vol. XXI, p. 39.
2 Ṭabarī, vol. II, p. 171.
3 *Ibid.*, p. 172.
4 *Ibid.*, p. 178; Ibn Qutayba, *al-Ma'ārif*, ed. F. Wustenfeld, Göttingen, 1850, p. 120.
5 Ṭabarī, vol. II, p. 178.
6 Balādhurī, *Futūḥ*, p. 413; Balādhurī, *Ansāb al-Ashrāf*, vol. V, ed. S. Goitein, Jerusalem, 1936, p. 118.
7 Ṭabarī, vol. II, p. 65.

income to the central treasury in Damascus, and it is reported that when 'Ubaydullah ibn Ziyād left Khurāsān to be governor of Baṣra, he carried with him the money and the booty (*al-amwāl wal ghanā'im*).[1] This was not acceptable to the Arabs in Khurāsān, since they considered themselves responsible for a frontier (*thaghr*) and costly expeditions. But Mu'āwiya, encouraged by the money which Ibn Ziyād had brought him, when he appointed the new governor also appointed with him a representative of the central government with complete authority over the finances of the province to strengthen the *Amīr al-Mu'minīn*'s grip on the greater part of the income there. To this the tribesmen objected, and when the central government's representative died before reaching Khurāsān, Aslam ibn Zur'a took over his position as a representative of the tribesmen vis-à-vis the central government. Aslam had very strong Qaysite support in the capital, and Mu'āwiya, who was at that time seeking the support of the tribesmen in making his son, Yazīd, his heir, had to give way and let the storm pass. Sa'īd ibn 'Uthmān had to accept Aslam ibn Zur'a as his partner in Khurāsān, and was finally obliged to leave the province altogether to Aslam, who became governor there from 57/677 to 59/679.[2]

When Sa'īd ibn 'Uthmān went to Khurāsān, he was accompanied by such capable military leaders as al-Muhallab ibn Abī Ṣufra,[3] and an army of 4,000 men. The governor of Baṣra, on instructions from Mu'āwiya, gave him four million dirhams which he distributed among his men. It is interesting to note that the 4,000 men who formed Sa'īd's army were selected from those who were in jail and the troublesome elements in Baṣra.[4] Again, it is reported that Sa'īd persuaded a group of highway robbers from Tamīm to accompany him on his expedition.[5] Arriving in Khurāsān, Sa'īd, after fully preparing his army, "carried the Arab arms more deeply into Transoxiana, defeated the Soghdians in the open field and reduced their city. Taking fifty young nobles as hostages, he retired from Soghd and subsequently occupied Tirmidh, an important fortress on the Oxus controlling the main north and south trade route, having presumably marched through

[1] Ibn A'tham, *Futūḥ*, vol. I, p. 171 A.
[2] Ṭabarī, vol. II, p. 180; Balādhurī, *Futūḥ*, p. 413; Balādhurī, *Ansāb*, vol. V, p. 118; Ya'qūbī, *Tārīkh*, vol. II, p. 282.
[3] Ṭabarī, vol. II, p. 178.
[4] Ibn A'tham, *Futūḥ*, vol. I, p. 167 A.
[5] Ṭabarī, vol. II, p. 178; al-Iṣfahānī, *al-Aghānī*, vol. XIX, Cairo, 1285, pp. 163–6.

the Iron Gate."[1] After this campaign the disagreement between Sa'īd and Aslam threatened to break out openly; Aslam was left in Khurāsān, and for two years he did not undertake any expeditions.

3 *Attempts to reconcile the tribesmen to the growing power of the central government*

Mu'āwiya's problem, then, was to restore order in Khurāsān and keep the Arab tribesmen there in line with his policy. Thus in 59/679 he appointed another son of Ziyād, 'Abdurraḥman ibn Ziyād, as governor of Khurāsān, with the primary objective, not of undertaking new expeditions this time, but of re-establishing Umayyad authority over the Arab tribesmen. 'Abdurraḥman sent ahead of him another strong Qaysite leader who was well acquainted with the province, Qays ibn al-Haytham as-Sulamī. On his arrival at Khurāsān he arrested Aslam ibn Zur'a and extracted from him 300,000 dirhams.[2]

Ibn Ziyād stayed in Khurāsān for two years, during which time he was busy establishing the central government's rights to the income of the province and collecting tribute. His success was such that in two years he was able to set aside twenty million dirhams (probably an exaggerated figure), which was given to him by the *Amir al-Mu'minīn* as a reward for his efforts.[3] During his governorship Ibn Ziyād did not undertake any expeditions, bu he was able to achieve the purpose of his appointment. When Mu'āwiya died and his son Yazīd succeeded him, he appointed, in 61/681, Salm ibn Ziyād as governor with the purpose of leading more expeditions into Transoxiana.

Salm first stopped at Baṣra, where he assembled a hand-picked force of probably 2,000 men from the best fighters and the *ashrāf*; and in Ṭabarī's narratives we find echoes of the eagerness of the people there to join Salm on his expedition. He also had with him a great number of leaders from different tribes including such veretans as al-Muhallab ibn Abī Ṣufra, 'Abdullah ibn Khāzim as-Sulamī, Ṭalḥa ibn 'Abdillah al-Khuzā'ī and 'Umar ibn 'Ubay-

[1] Gibb, *Arab Conquests*, pp. 19–20.

[2] Ṭabarī, vol. II, p. 189; Balādhurī, *Futūḥ*, p. 413; Ibn al-Athīr, *Kāmil*, vol. III, p. 430; Ibn Qutayba, *'Uyūn*, vol. I, p. 197.

[3] Ṭabarī, vol. II, p. 189; Balādhurī, *Ansāb al-Ashrāf*, vol. IV B, ed. M. Schloessinger, Jerusalem, 1938, p. 75; Ya'qubī, *Tārīkh*, vol. II, p. 281.

dillah ibn Maʿmar at-Taymī.[1] His first action when he arrived at Merv was of great political significance. He arrested Qays ibn al-Haytham and humiliated him and his son.[2] This was as much an appeal to the supporters of Aslam ibn Zurʿa as a declaration of a change in the policy which Qays ibn al-Haytham had advocated under ʿAbdurraḥman ibn Ziyād, that of sending part of the income of the province to Damascus.[3]

Salm was very active in his raids in Transoxiana, and, in contrast with the other expeditions when the men used to return to Merv for the winter, he stayed, probably in Samarqand, for one winter. This action on the side of Salm provoked a stronger resistance from the combined forces of Bukhārā and Samarqand. Nevertheless, Salm was able to defeat them through the ability of his general, al-Muhallab, and the booty taken in this battle was very rewarding to the Arab tribesmen.[4] Ibn Aʿtham, following his usual habit of reporting the arrangements in regard to booty, informs us that Salm set aside one-fifth for Yazīd and divided the rest among the tribesmen.[5] According to Madā'inī, Salm sent Yazīd's share along with the *marzbān* of Merv,[6] an action indicating that Salm was making an effort to appeal to the local population of Khurāsān. It is not surprising, then, to find reports of the popularity that Salm had enjoyed during his stay there.[7]

4 *The situation in Sīstān*

Salm ibn Ziyād's governorship also included Sīstān,[8] and we must go back a little to explain how this came about. When Ziyād ibn Abī Sufyān was appointed to Baṣra in 45/665, Khurāsān and Sīstān were parts of his governorship.[9] He appointed ar-Rabīʿ ibn Ziyād al-Ḥārithī to Sīstān and then replaced him by ʿUbaydullah ibn Abī Bakra who remained there until Ziyād's death in 53/673. During this period, the fierce resistance of

1 Ṭabarī, vol. II, p. 393; Yaʿqūbī, *Tārīkh*, vol. II, p. 300; Ibn Aʿtham, *Futūḥ*, vol. I, pp. 231B, 232A.

2 Ṭabarī, vol. II, p. 392.

3 Ibn Aʿtham, *Futūḥ*, vol. I, p. 232B.

4 Gibb, *Arab Conquests*, pp. 21–2; Ṭabarī, vol. II, p. 394; Yaʿqūbī, *Tārīkh*, vol. II, p. 300; Ibn al-Athīr, *Kāmil*, vol. IV, p. 83; Balādhurī, *Futūḥ*, p. 413.

5 Ibn Aʿtham, *Futūḥ*, vol. I, p. 232B.

6 Ṭabarī, vol. II, p. 394.

7 *Ibid.*, p. 489; Ibn al-Athīr, vol. IV, p. 128; al-Dhahabī, vol. II, p. 368.

8 Ṭabarī, vol. II, p. 392.

9 *Ibid.*, p. 74.

Zunbīl continued until finally he agreed to pay a tribute of one million dirhams.[1] After Ziyād's death, Mu'āwiya made Sīstān a separate governorship, appointing to it 'Abbād, one of Ziyād's sons, who remained there until Mu'āwiya's death in 61/681.[2] During his long governorship, the situation in Sīstān was quiet, and no rebellions or expeditions are reported in our sources.

Yazīd added Sīstān to the governorship of Salm ibn Ziyād, and the latter appointed his brother, Yazīd ibn Ziyād, to this region,[3] apparently to lead an expedition against Zunbīl of Zābulistān. This expedition was disastrous for Yazīd ibn Ziyād's army; he himself was killed in the battle, his brother, Abū 'Ubayda, was captured and the Arabs lost a great number of men. Salm sent an expedition from Khurāsān, led by Ṭalḥa ibn 'Abdillah al-Khūza'ī, to rescue his brother and pacify the region. He ransomed Abū-'Ubayda and the other Arab captives for half a million dirhams and was able to restore order in Sīstān by diplomacy more than force.[4] He died there very shortly before *Amīr al-Mu'minīn* Yazīd's death in 64/683, and the civil war (64–73/684–92) that followed had its effect even in this remote part of the Arab empire.

5 *Khurāsān during the second civil war*

When the news of the death of *Amīr al-Mu'minīn* Yazīd and the establishment of 'Abdullah ibn al-Zubayr in al-Ḥijāz arrived in Baṣra, the tribesmen there agreed to pay their allegiance to the Umayyad governor, 'Ubaydullah ibn Ziyād, until agreement could be reached on an *Amīr al-Mu'minīn*.[5] In Khurāsān a similar agreement was reached in regard to Salm ibn Ziyād, in spite of his unsuccessful attempt to conceal the news about the confusion at the heart of the empire.[6] However, the two brothers chose different paths. While 'Ubaydullah continued his support of the Umayyads, Salm turned to the rising power of the rival *Amīr al-Mu'minīn* 'Abdullah ibn al-Zubayr.[7] Salm apparently tried actively

[1] Balādhurī, *Futūḥ*, p. 397; *Tārīkh-i-Sīstān*, anon., ed. M. Bahār, Teheran, 1314, pp. 91–9.

[2] Balādhurī, *Futūḥ*, p. 397; *Tārīkh-i-Sīstān*, p. 95.

[3] Ṭabarī, vol. II, p. 392; Balādhurī, *Futūḥ*, p. 397; *Tārīkh-i-Sīstān*, p. 100.

[4] Balādhurī, *Futūḥ*, pp. 397–8; *Tārīkh-i-Sīstān*, pp. 100–4.

[5] Ṭabarī, vol. II, p. 433.

[6] *Ibid.*, p. 488; Ya'qūbī, *Tārīkh*, vol. II, p. 301.

[7] Balādhurī, *Futūḥ*, pp. 413–14; Balādhurī, *Ansāb*, vol. V, p. 188; Ya'qūbī, *Tārīkh*, vol. II, p. 323.

to persuade the tribesmen to support Ibn al-Zubayr, but in a place like Khurāsān, where the position of the Arabs depended on their strength and unity, this policy proved to be dangerous. Only two months passed before Salm was no longer acceptable to the Arab tribesmen and had to leave Khurāsān for al-Ḥijāz, where he joined Ibn al-Zubayr.[1]

The Arab tribesmen, being without any kind of governmental authority around which to rally, and having neither a recognized *Amīr al-Mu'minīn* nor a legitimate representative of the central government in Khurāsān, naturally congregated around their chiefs, forming big tribal groups. Politics became identified with tribal interests and jealousies, and each tribal group pressed only for what seemed to be in its own interests. The reports in Ṭabarī, that Salm appointed certain tribal chiefs to certain parts of Khurāsān, or appointed others as his successors, should not be taken seriously,[2] because, as Balādhurī points out, Salm himself, after leaving Khurāsān, no longer had the authority to do so.[3] Moreover, these reports may be tribal traditions trying to legitimize the subsequent actions of their heroes.

Presumably what happened was that Salm, in his attempts to secure the province for Ibn al-Zubayr, had made certain deals with the chiefs who were ready to support his cause. Among these chiefs 'Abdullah ibn Khāzim of Qays was the most powerful and vehement supporter of Ibn al-Zubayr, as a result of a co-ordinated Qaysite effort.[4] On going to join Ibn al-Zubayr, Salm left with Ibn Khāzim 100,000 dirhams, which admittedly was not of great importance, and he appointed him as his successor or rather representative in Khurāsān, probably until such time as the appointment could come from Ibn al-Zubayr himself.[5]

Although the reports of Ṭabarī are rather confusing, yet they agree in general with Ya'qūbī and Balādhurī, and the latter gives a clearer version of the situation. Ibn Khāzim established himself in Merv without much difficulty at the beginning,[6] but when, six months later, he received his appointment from Ibn al-Zubayr, serious opposition was aroused.[7] Sulaymān ibn Marthad, from Rabī'a, and his followers took up arms, and when Sulaymān

[1] Balādhurī, *Futūḥ*, p. 414.
[2] Ṭabarī, vol. II, pp. 489–90.
[3] Balādhurī, *Futuḥ*, p. 414.
[4] Ṭabarī, vol. II, p. 433.
[5] Balādhurī, *Futuḥ*, p. 414; Ṭabarī, vol. II, p. 489.
[6] Ṭabarī, vol. II, p. 490; Balādhurī, *Futūḥ*, p. 414.
[7] Balādhurī, *Futūḥ*, p. 414.

was killed in battle his men, led by his brother, fled to Ṭalqān where Ibn Khāzim followed and defeated them. When he returned to Merv, all the tribesmen belonging to Rabī'a in Khurāsān gathered in Harāt under the leadership of Aws ibn Tha'laba, probably intending to remain under the city's protection until the conclusion of the struggle.[1] They were not so much for the Umayyads as they were against Ibn al-Zubayr, who represented to them a Qaysite (Muḍarite) domination.[2] Ibn Khāzim, who was determined to establish Ibn al-Zubayr's authority over all Khurāsān, promptly advanced to Harāt and besieged it. It took him a whole year to defeat Rabī'a and to enter Harāt, and it is reported that 8,000 from Rabī'a were killed in this battle. Having entered Harāt, he placed his son Muḥammad in charge of the city with a strong garrison of Tamīm tribesmen.[3]

Another group of tribesmen from Azd, who did not want to take part in this struggle between Muḍar (Qays and Tamīm) and Rabī'a, left Merv for a fortress in the countryside, near Nīshāpūr.[4] When the Hephthalites, taking advantage of the Arabs' internal difficulties, raided and penetrated as far as Nīshāpūr, they attacked these Azdites, who probably formed a small group. The Azdites asked Ibn Khāzim for help and he sent a Tamīmite expedition which drove back the Hephthalites.[5] It seemed as if Ibn Khāzim would be able to gain control over the whole province, but this was only a temporary probability.

Since the whole situation was now dominated by the tribal feelings and jealousies of the Arabs, tribal feuds were bound to break out at the slightest provocation, or for no reason at all. These jealousies showed themselves very strongly in Tamīm, who had supported Ibn Khāzim in his fight against Rabī'a, and who apparently expected too much as a reward.[6] Ibn Khāzim considered himself a legitimate governor appointed by the *Amīr al-Mu'minīn* Ibn al-Zubayr, but Tamīm did not consider him more than a tribal chief and expected him to act as such. First, Tamīm turned against Ibn Khāzim's son in Harāt, killed him and renounced

[1] Ṭabarī, vol. II, pp. 489–91; Balādhurī, *Futūḥ*, p. 414; Ya'qūbī, *Tārīkh*, vol. II, p. 301.

[2] Balādhurī, *Futūḥ*, p. 414; Ṭabarī, vol. II, pp. 491–3.

[3] Balādhurī, *Futūḥ*, pp. 414–15; Ṭabarī, vol. II, pp. 491–6; Ya'qūbī, *Tārīkh*, vol. II, p. 401.

[4] Ṭabarī, vol. II, p. 493.

[5] Balādhurī, *Fūtuḥ*, p. 414; Ṭabarī, vol. II, p. 493.

[6] Ṭabarī, vol. II, pp. 593; Balādhurī, *Futūḥ*, p. 415.

his father.[1] Second, to avoid any concentrated attack by Ibn Khāzim's followers, they divided themselves into different contingents, occupying the citadel of Ṭūs and the city of Nīshāpūr.[2] The fight dragged on for more than two years.[3]

6 *Tamīm gains supremacy in Khurāsān*

'Abdulmalik ibn Marwān, the new Umayyad *Amīr al-Mu'minīn*, tried to gain Ibn Khāzim to his side by recognizing him as governor of Khurāsān, and promising to keep him there for seven years. Ibn Khāzim's answer was to make 'Abdulmalik's messenger eat his letter.[4] 'Abdulmalik turned to Tamīm and in 72/691 appointed one of their chiefs, Bukayr ibn Wishāḥ, as governor of Khurāsān.[5] Finally, those of Tamīm who remained in Merv itself rose against Ibn Khāzim, and with Tamīm in Harāt, Ṭūs and Nīshāpūr, Ibn Khāzim had no chance.[6] He, in turn, sent his son Mūsā to seek refuge in a fortress somewhere. After wandering in Transoxiana, Mūsā was able to settle in the strong fortress of Tirmidh.[7] When Ibn Khāzim's position became desperate he tried to follow his son to Tirmidh, but he was killed in battle in a small village near Merv in 72/691.[8]

Khurāsān was thus restored to the Umayyads by the support of Tamīm, who, as a result, were virtually in control of the province with the governor appointed from amongst them. But the tribal tendencies and the desert traditions were too deep-rooted in these Arab tribesmen to allow them to live peacefully with each other. In spite of the victory of Tamīm, two factions of the tribe turned against one another and inter-tribal war again threatened the peace in Khurāsān.[9] To remedy this situation 'Abdulmalik was advised to put an end to tribal jealousies by appointing a Qurayshite, who would keep himself above the factions and reunite the Arabs in Khurāsān. Consequently, the

[1] Ṭabarī, vol. II, pp. 593–5; Balādhurī, *Futūḥ*, p. 415.
[2] Balādhurī, *Futūḥ*, p. 415; Ibn al-Athīr, *Kāmil*, vol. IV, pp. 171–2.
[3] Ṭabarī, vol. II, pp. 595–6.
[4] Ṭabarī, vol. II, p. 831; Balādhurī, *Futūḥ*, p. 415.
[5] Ṭabarī, vol. II, p. 832; Balādhurī, *Futūḥ*, p. 415.
[6] Ṭabarī, vol. II, pp. 832–3; Balādhurī, *Futūḥ*, p. 415.
[7] Ibn al-Athīr, *Kāmil*, vol. II, pp. 402–3; Balādhurī, *Futūḥ*, pp. 417–18; Ṭabarī, vol. II, p. 1145.
[8] Ṭabarī, vol. II, pp. 832–4; Balādhurī, *Futūḥ*, p. 415.
[9] Ṭabarī, vol. II, p. 860; Balādhurī, *Futūḥ*, p. 416.

Qurayshite Umayya ibn ʿAbdillah ibn Khālid ibn Asīd was appointed as a governor of the troubled province in 74/694.[1] Following the same policy as the earlier Umayyads, ʿAbdulmalik kept Khurāsān as a separate governorship but with Sīstān included.[2]

The new governor's problem was to bring the factions of Tamīm together under his leadership, but the indignant Bukayr ibn Wishāḥ, the ex-governor of the province, made it very difficult for Umayya.[3] His rival, Baḥīr ibn Warqā', did not make it any easier either by his continuous intriguing against Bukayr.[4] The latter was leading a group of Tamīm who did not want to submit any longer to the central authority, but wanted the tribal traditions to prevail, with the chiefs having the right to "eat" the province, as one of their leaders expressed it.[5] Baḥīr's faction, probably only for the sake of rivalry, was for co-operation with the central government represented by the governor of Khurāsān.[6] Umayya tried by peaceful means, through generosity and appointment to important positions, to get Bukayr to co-operate with him.[7]

In 77/696 the governor felt that the situation in Khurāsān was stable enough to allow him to reactivate the old Umayyad policy of engaging the Arab tribesmen in expeditions in Transoxiana. He could not have been more wrong, because he had hardly left Merv when Bukayr revolted and renounced him. Umayya, who was heading towards Bukhārā, had to abandon his expedition and return quickly to Merv, where he was able to defeat Bukayr and granted him generous peace terms.[8] Bukayr, defeated in the field, resorted to intrigues against Umayya, who finally had to order him to be killed to stabilize the province. Baḥīr was more than happy to carry out the execution order himself.[9]

The reports of Ṭabarī and Balādhurī that Umayya led other expeditions in Transoxiana are rather doubtful, or they may only be variants on this expedition of 77/696,[10] since Umayya did not

1 Ṭabarī, vol. II, pp. 859–60; Balādhurī, *Futūḥ*, p. 416.
2 Ṭabarī, vol. II, p. 1028; Balādhurī, *Futūḥ*, p. 399.
3 Ṭabarī, vol. II, p. 1022.
4 Ṭabarī, vol. II, p. 862; Balādhurī, *Futūḥ*, p. 416; Ibn Aʿtham, *Futūḥ*, vol. II, p. 47B; Ibn Ḥazm, p. 207.
5 Ṭabarī, vol. II, pp. 1023–4.
6 *Ibid.*, pp. 861–2.
7 *Ibid.*, pp. 1022–3.
8 *Ibid.*, pp. 1025–8.
9 *Ibid.*, pp. 1030–1; Balādhurī, *Futūḥ*, pp. 416–17; Yaʿqūbī, *Tārīkh*, vol. II, p. 324.
10 Gibb, *Arab Conquests*, p. 24; Ṭabarī, vol. II, p. 1031; Balādhurī, *Futūḥ*, p. 417.

stay long in Khurāsān after the suppression of Bukayr's revolt. 'Abdulmalik, annoyed at his governor for not sending him anything more than "two old horses" from Khurāsān,[1] and disappointed by the failure of his policy in Khurāsān, in 78/697 dismissed Umayya, adding the province to the governorship of his able adherent al-Ḥajjāj,[2] and a completely new policy was introduced in Khurāsān.

7 *Seeds of assimilation*

In the period from 64/683 to 78/697, i.e. during the governorships of Ibn Khāzim, Bukayr and Umayya, there were certain new features in the Arab situation in Khurāsān which became especially clear in the last years of Umayya's governorship, though they may have had their origin in developments in Khurāsān in the time of Ibn Khāzim. The tradition of Madā'inī, as narrated by Ṭabarī, concerning events in the year 77/696–7 is indeed very rich.[3]

One point to be noted is that, for the first time, certain groups of Arab tribesmen, who were in disagreement with Ibn Khāzim's policy, tried to settle in various parts of Khurāsān other than Merv. It may be inferred that they tried to settle in the cities and towns where they would be protected by citadels. Ṭālqān, Harāt, Merv ar-Rūd, Ṭūs and Nīshāpūr are the towns mentioned.[4] But it should not be thought that the Arabs settled permanently in these cities. They went there only to seek refuge in the citadels, and once the situation in Merv was stabilized they returned. Even the city of Merv opened its doors to the Arabs, and at the end of this period we have reports about Arabs living in the city itself for the first time. When Umayya returned from Transoxiana in 77/696 because of the Tamīmite revolt, the actual fighting took place in the city, and some of Umayya's men had their families within its walls. After the revolt Umayya himself was reported to have been present in the city.[5]

We also learn from the same reports of certain villages around

[1] Ibn 'Abd Rabbih, vol. xiv, p. 45; Ibn A'tham, *Futūḥ*, vol. ii, p. 58b.
[2] Ṭabarī, vol. ii, p. 1032; Ya'qūbī, *Tārīkh*, vol. ii, p. 330; Balādhurī, *Futūḥ*, p. 417.
[3] Ṭabarī, vol. ii, pp. 1022–31.
[4] Ṭabarī, vol. ii, pp. 490, 491, 493, 593, 696; Ya'qūbī, *Tārīkh*, vol. ii, p. 301; Balādhurī, *Futūḥ*, pp. 415, 416.
[5] Ṭabarī, vol. ii, pp. 1026–8.

Merv, like Bāsān and Buwayna, which belonged to Arab clans[1] who had apparently stayed there long enough to acquire land. In spite of the fact that a great number of the tribesmen took part in the war, there were others who were not involved, either because they considered it as *fitna* (misguided strife) or because their tribes were not involved at all since only Muḍar and Rabī'a were the major antagonists. For these neutralists it was a period of inactivity because the expeditions against the unbelievers stopped for more than thirteen years. It is to be expected that these tribesmen practised some trade or bought lands from the local population. This explains the remark in this tradition that certain Tamīmites complained to their leader Bukayr that the governor Umayya had supported the *dihqāns* in extracting the taxes from them.[2] This tax was probably the land tax which was supposed to be paid by the original owners of the land to help pay the tribute to the Arabs, and for the collection of which the *dihqāns* were responsible. But the Tamīmite tribesmen, as Muslims and Arabs, saw themselves as tax-exempted citizens.

The long stay of some of the Arab tribesmen in close proximity to the local population helped to start the process of assimilation between the two peoples. Although the tribal warfare in Ibn Khāzim's time involved only the Arab tribesmen, and the local population is not mentioned anywhere in our sources as taking part in what they must have considered a purely Arab affair, yet in the events of 77/696–7 we hear for the first time about converts from Khurāsān, including such prominent figures as Thābit ibn Quṭba and his brother Ḥurayth, both clients of Khuzā'a, who were taking a great interest in Arab affairs. The presence of these two men in Umayya's army sent to Transoxiana and then against Bukayr would indicate that they were accompanied by some of their followers. When Bukayr captured Thābit in the battle near Merv, he let him go free, probably trying to appeal to his supporters.[3] Bukayr made another move to rally the Iranians to his side by promising all converts remission from the *kharāj*.[4] Though Bukayr's revolt failed, his action made both the Arabs and the Iranians aware of the problems which might occur as a result of widespread conversion.

During this period of almost fourteen years, the Arabs were

[1] *Ibid.*, p. 1026.
[2] *Ibid.*, p. 1029.
[3] *Ibid.*, pp. 1023, 1026–7.
[4] *Ibid.*, p. 1024.

deprived of the rich booty of Transoxiana, and the princes of this region, who had become tributary to the Arabs, were able to regain their independence, thus depriving the Arabs of another source of income.[1] But it is surprising to learn from Madā'inī that the Arabs borrowed money for the expedition to Transoxiana in 77/696 from the Soghdian traders in Merv.[2] In other words, these Soghdian traders in Merv were helping to finance the Arab expeditions to the Soghdian lands which had just regained their independence and ceased to be Arab tributaries. We can only conclude that these traders were interested in maintaining the tributary status of these Soghdian principalities, or rather in maintaining peaceful co-existence between them and the Arabs, so that they would not be considered as part of *dār al-ḥarb* (enemy territory). Consequently the duties imposed on their trade would be only 5 per cent instead of the 10 per cent which the people from *dār al-ḥarb* had to pay,[3] thus stimulating the flow of trade between Transoxiana and Merv.

It is clear from our sources that during this period the princes of Transoxiana regained their independence, but the situation is not as clear regarding the principalities south of the Oxus. Except for the rather unimportant raids across the countryside around Nīshāpūr, which were probably launched by the Hephthalites of Bādghīs, there does not seem to have been any serious trouble for the Arabs from that area at this time. It is possible that some of these principalities may have stopped paying tribute but, as Gibb points out, on the gradual restoration of order under Umayya they again recognized Arab suzerainty, at least in name.[4]

8 *Mūsā ibn 'Abdillah ibn Khāzim*

There were two other problems which Umayya failed to solve —Mūsā, the son of 'Abdullah ibn Khāzim, who had taken refuge in the stronghold of Tirmidh, and Sīstān, which was part of his governorship. As for Mūsā, his

[1] Gibb, *Arab Conquests*, pp. 22–3.

[2] Ṭabarī, vol. II, p. 1022.

[3] Al-'Alī, *Tanẓīmāt*, p. 123; al-Māwardī, *al-Aḥkām al-Sulṭāniyya*, Cairo, Subayḥ, pp. 132, 141; Ibn Sallām, *al-Amwāl*, Cairo, A.H. 1353, pp. 16, 538–9; Yahyā ibn Ādam, *al-Kharāj*, ed. T. E. Juynboll, Leiden, 1896, p. 125; Abū-Yūsuf, *al-Kharāj*, Cairo, A.H. 1302, p. 76; Ibn Sa'd, vol. VII, part 1, p. 151.

[4] Gibb, *Arab Conquests*, p. 23.

exploits were worked up in popular story into an epic of adventure, in which legend has almost overlaid historical fact...But in truth his actual exploits were sufficiently amazing...For fifteen years he remained in secure possession of his stronghold, a refuge for the disaffected from all sides, and a standing example of the helplessness of the rulers across the river.[1]

He started out from Merv with 200 horsemen and, after trying to find refuge in Bukhārā, Samarqand and Kish, he ended up in Tirmidh. Either by trickery or force, or both, he was able to occupy this stronghold on the Oxus, which controlled the route from Balkh into Transoxiana, and drive out the prince, the Tirmidh-Shāh. When 'Abdullah ibn Khāzim was killed, 400 of his followers joined Mūsā. Feeling that he was established in his fortress, he started raiding the areas around Tirmidh, probably in Chaghāniān. Naturally this alarmed the population of this area, to such an extent that they finally responded to the pleas of the Tirmidh-Shāh and sent an army to besiege Mūsā in Tirmidh. It is not clear from our sources who attacked Mūsā at this time; they are referred to simply as Turks, in the usual manner of the Arabic sources.

Meanwhile Bukayr ibn Wishāḥ made no moves against Mūsā. When Umayya went on his expedition to Transoxiana, it is reported he was planning to attack Tirmidh on his way back, but the revolt in Merv obliged him to return hurriedly. In 78/697, after he had suppressed this revolt, he sent a Khuzā'ite force which attacked Tirmidh at the same time as it was attacked by the "Turks". Mūsā, with his few followers, was able to defeat them all and, reportedly, some of the Khuzā'ite force joined him.[2] It was not until seven years later that the governor of Khurāsān was able to deal with and defeat Mūsā.

9 *Unrest spreads to Sīstān*

In Sīstān, Umayya had another problem and also another failure. *Amīr al-Mu'minīn* Yazīd's death in 64/683, followed almost immediately by the death of Ṭalḥa ibn 'Ubaydillah, the governor of Sīstān under Salm ibn Ziyād, meant there was no governor there. Though Ṭalḥa had appointed a tribal chief from Rabī'a,

[1] *Ibid.*, p. 24.

[2] Ṭabarī, vol. II, pp. 1145–51; Balādhurī, *Futūḥ*, pp. 411–12, 417–18.

a Yashkurite, to take his place, he was not recognized by the other chiefs, particularly those of Muḍar, and each one of them quickly established himself in one of the different towns which had been under Arab rule.

When Ibn al-Zubayr recognized ʿAbdullah ibn Khāzim as governor of Khurāsān, he also sent ʿAbdulʿazīz ibn ʿAbdillah ibn ʿĀmir as his governor for Sīstān. He was accepted by a certain group of Tamīmites led by Wakīʿ ibn Abī Sūd (about whom we shall hear later as governor of Khurāsān), but another group of Tamīmites rejected him and fought against him.[1] This feud was accelerated by the arrival from Khurāsān of some of the tribesmen who were defeated there by Ibn Khāzim.[2] Zunbīl tried to take advantage of this situation, but his action united the Arab forces against him. They were able to defeat him, and Zunbīl was killed in the battle.[3]

When the danger from Zunbīl was past, the two Tamīmite groups again turned against each other, but the final victory rested with the group of Wakīʿ ibn Abī Sūd that supported Ibn al-Zubayr's governor, who stayed there until Ibn al-Zubayr was killed.[4] After this the Tamīmites who had fled from Khurāsān returned to the governorship of Bukayr.[5] When ʿAbdulmalik appointed Umayya to Khurāsān in 74/693–4, he included Sīstān in his governorship. Umayya sent his son, ʿAbdullah, at the head of an expedition to Sīstān. It was successful at the beginning, but soon the new Zunbīl was able to regain his strength and defeated the Arabs. According to some reports ʿAbdullah himself was killed. Umayya was dismissed before taking any more action in Sīstān, and it too was added to the governorship of al-Ḥajjāj.[6]

10 *The need for a new policy in the East*

In short, Muʿāwiya's policy in Khurāsān, which aimed at the gradual assertion of the central authority over the Arab tribesmen, proved, at least, to have required more time for its implementation.

[1] Balādhurī, *Futūḥ*, p. 398; *Tārīkh-i-Sīstān*, pp. 103–5.
[2] Ṭabarī, vol. II, p. 596, 1026.
[3] Balādhurī, *Futūḥ*, p. 398; *Tārīkh-i-Sīstān*, p. 106.
[4] Balādhurī, *Futūḥ*, p. 398; *Tarīkh-i-Sīstān*, p. 107; Ibn Qutayba, *Maʿārif*, p. 212.
[5] Ṭabarī, vol. II, p. 1026.
[6] Balādhurī, *Futūḥ*, p. 399; Yaʿqūbī, *Tārīkh*, vol. II, p. 324; *Tārīkh-i-Sīstān*, pp. 107–8.

Perhaps the maintenance of the tribal structure in Khurāsān, and the attempt to balance the authority of the tribal chiefs with the authority of an appointed Qurayshite governor, was not enough to make them forget their deep-rooted traditions. Furthermore, it helped to bolster the tribal relationships which Islam was trying so hard to replace with the relationship based on membership of one Muslim community. The almost continuous engagement of the tribesmen in yearly campaigns helped to postpone the time when the weakness of this policy would become evident rather than to ensure its success.

At the first indication of a weakening in the central authority, as happened after the death of *Amīr al-Mu'minīn* Yazīd, the tribesmen seized the opportunity to regain the ground they had lost to it. Ibn Khāzim's movement, which was at first a struggle between two parties who were both in varying degrees against the strong authority of the Umayyad government, took the form of tribal warfare between Muḍar and Rabī'a: Muḍar openly against the Umayyads and for the rather loose relationship to the régime of Ibn al-Zubayr, and Rabī'a, which was the minority party, not so much for the Umayyads as against the rise of the rival régime, which it saw as a threat to the unity of the Muslim community.

When this struggle ended with the victory of Muḍar, the more extreme elements in this party, who were in the majority, wanted more independence and more assertion of tribal traditions. Tamīm, which represented the majority of Muḍar in Khurāsān, rose in arms against Ibn Khāzim when he tried to assert his authority as governor of Khurāsān. Then again they revolted against Umayya ibn 'Abdillah when he tried to restore the authority of the previous Umayyad governors over the tribesmen in Khurāsān. Umayya was able to bring the revolution to an end, but it was only a temporary halt.

The situation in Khurāsān alarmed *Amīr al-Mu'minīn* 'Abdulmalik to such an extent that he introduced a new policy in this province to bring the tribesmen in line with the rest of the community. The failure of Umayyad policy at this first stage in Khurāsān, which resulted in these tribal outbreaks, had another important result. In spite of the disturbances which accompanied the civil strife in Khurāsān, the circumstances which prevailed there during this period helped to bring together the Arab conquerors and the conquered Iranian population and started the process of assimilation of these two peoples. The problems of these two assimilation movements—the assimilation of the tribesmen into the Muslim community and the assimilation of the Arab population to the Iranian population—determined the history of Khurāsān in the following few decades.

4

AL-ḤAJJĀJ AND THE EAST

1 *Al-Muhallab's Azd to balance Tamīm*

It is of great importance to notice that the Khawārij movements which spread all over Iraq and western Persia during Ibn al-Zubayr's and 'Abdulmalik's times did not extend to Khurāsān. Although tribesmen from Tamīm played a major role in the Khawārij uprisings, yet we do not find any traces of Khārijism among the Tamīm of Khurāsān. Naturally, the tribesmen in all the Empire belonged to the same tribal groups, but each of these had developed its own interests where it had settled. The tribal relationship, though it is important in understanding all the events of that time, was not the major factor in the conflicts within the Arab Muslim community. These conflicts took the form of struggles between the different tribal groups, but these groups represented the different parties promoting the different interests of the Arab tribesmen. To be sure, there were tribal outbreaks sometimes; after all, the Arab tribesmen were not to be expected to forget their ancient tribal traditions overnight; but to consider the history of this period solely in terms of tribal jealousies is certainly a mistake. The legends of ancient alliances between certain tribes or antagonisms between others do not withstand critical study.[1] The reasons for the conflicts between the different tribal groups must be sought in their interests rather than in legendary animosities. The Arab tribesmen in Iraq and in Khurāsān might have had similar reasons for revolting, mainly the tendency of some of these tribesmen not to submit to the authority of the central government, but, because of the different circumstances which surrounded them, their risings took different forms and followed different political paths from the very beginning until the 'Abbāsid Revolution.

Having finished with the Khawārij uprisings, 'Abdulmalik ibn Marwān was free to turn to the troublesome province of Khurāsān. As governor of Iraq, Al-Ḥajjāj had proved that he was the man

[1] Wellhausen, pp. 396–413.

to deal with such difficult problems, so ʿAbdulmalik turned the province over to him and made it part of his governorship. He also gave him control of the other difficult eastern region, namely Sīstān. Being responsible for more than half of the empire, al-Ḥajjāj was, naturally, granted enough power to cope with the many problems and also had the full support of *Amīr al-Mu'minīn*. For the rest of ʿAbdulmalik's reign (65–86/685–705) and practically throughout that of al-Walīd I (86–96/705–15), al-Ḥajjāj remained in his post, first as governor of Iraq (75/694) and then as governor of Iraq and the East (78–95/697–714). He carried out a bold imperial policy, supported by the might of the Syrian army (*jund*) wherever necessary and whenever possible. Of course, in Iraq the presence of the Syrian army was both necessary and possible. The two garrison towns, Kūfa and Baṣra, were demilitarized, Syrian troops brought to Iraq and eventually stationed in Wāsiṭ, a town built by al-Ḥajjāj especially for this purpose. Obviously there were not enough Syrian troops to be dispatched and settled in all corners of the empire. However, the demilitarization of Kūfa and Baṣra, and the victory over the Khawārij, left al-Ḥajjāj with a substantial number of tribesmen in Iraq, whom he decided to use to further the Arab conquests in Khurāsān and Sīstān. For Sīstān he probably had in mind a plan similar to that of Ziyjād ibn Abī Sufyān, i.e. to settle Arab tribesmen there, who would eventually bring Zābulistān into the Islamic domains, and from there strike deep into India. Al-Ḥajjāj did not realize the difficulties involved in campaigning in the mountainous regions to the east of Sīstān. He also underestimated the military strength of the Zunbīls of Zābulistān. As we shall see, his plans there resulted in a major disaster and a serious revolt, namely that of Ibn al-Ashʿath.

As for Khurāsān, al-Ḥajjāj turned to al-Muhallab ibn Abī Ṣufra, the hero of the wars against the Khawārij, and appointed him as his governor for Khurāsān.[1] Al-Ḥajjāj certainly deviated from the former policy of appointing a Qurayshite to rule over the tribal chieftains and instead appointed a tribal chief as a governor. He must have realized that the problem in Khurāsān was the predominance of Tamīm, with its unruly tendencies, so he decided to balance it with another tribe which had just distinguished itself in the battlefield, particularly against Tamīm.

[1] Ṭabarī, vol. II, p. 1032.

Although al-Muhallab was the chief of al-Azd, his followers were not exclusively from that tribe. True, they were mainly Azdites, but they were supported by another group, probably bigger in numbers, from Rabīʿa.[1] We do not have enough information to enable us to tell which clans of Rabīʿa were included with Azd. Only Taghlib is mentioned as part of al-Muhallab's followers as allies (*aḥlāf*) along with the more general names of Bakr and Rabīʿa.[2] This suggests that some tribesmen from certain clans of Rabīʿa, but who did not belong to the clans of the two *akhmās* of Baṣra, Bakr and ʿAbdulqays,[3] might have found it easier to enlist in the *dīwān* to ally themselves with al-Azd and join Muhallab's campaigns. Naturally, Muhallab would welcome such allies as they added to his prestige and strength. Thus, he was used to the idea of leading Arab tribesmen from other tribes besides his own, a talent which was much needed in Khurāsān.

With the resources of Iraq supporting the new governor in Khurāsān and the formidable reputation of al-Ḥajjāj, control over the tribesmen in Khurāsān was assured. As a distinguished military leader, al-Muhallab would also be able to keep these tribesmen engaged in the battlefield and further the conquests in central Asia. The incorporation of Khurāsān into the governorship of al-Ḥajjāj would also mean the incorporation of the treasury of this province into his treasury, and thus would eliminate any possible problems about the distribution of the income from Khurāsān, and eventually would enable al-Ḥajjāj to extract as much as he wanted from that income.

Arriving in Khurāsān in 79/698, al-Muhallab proceeded with the preparations for a big expedition. His army was composed of his followers, some of the tribesmen of Khurāsān and a group from the local population of Khurāsān led by Thābit and Ḥurayth ibn Quṭba, both clients of Khuzāʿa.[4] In the year 80/699 he advanced towards Transoxiana, leaving his son al-Mughīra at Merv in charge of the administration. Al-Muhallab then secured the crossing of his army at Zamm, the ruler of which became a Muslim and joined Muhallab's army.[5] He established his head-

[1] Al-Iṣfahānī, *al-Aghānī*, Cairo, 1285, vol. XIII, pp. 58–9, vol. XV, p. 20, vol. XIX, p. 107; al-Jāhiẓ, *al-Maḥāsin wal Aḍdad*, ed. Van Vloten, Leiden, 1898, p. 12; al-Tanūkhī, *al Mustajād*, ed. Kurd ʿAlī, Damascus, 1946, p. 206; al-Dīnawarī, pp. 282, 288.

[2] Ṭabarī, vol. II, p. 1082.

[3] Al-ʿAlī, pp. 39, 292–5.

[4] Ṭabarī, vol. II, pp. 1032, 1078, 1080.

[5] *Ibid.*, p. 1078.

quarters around Kish of Soghdiana and started a long siege of the city which continued for two years, at the same time sending his sons on various expeditions in the neighbouring areas, but these had little success.[1] In 82/701 his son al-Mughīra died and he came to terms with Kish and began the return journey to Merv, but he died near Merv ar-Rūd.[2]

The traditions represent al-Muhallab as heartbroken at the death of his son and give this as the reason for his abandoning the expedition. Nevertheless, from a remark by Madā'inī, we understand that al-Muhallab returned because of a conspiracy in his army which involved some tribesmen from Muḍar.[3] The prominent figure in this Muḍarite conspiracy was 'Abdulmalik ibn Abī-Shaykh al-Qushayrī, who was probably one of the tribal leaders who revolted in Sīstān after *Amīr al-Mu'minīn* Yazīd's death in 64/683 and who apparently later came to Khurāsān.[4] At the same time, Baḥīr ibn Warqā', the Tamīmite chief, was killed in revenge for Bukayr ibn Wishāḥ, and this incident took place in Muhallab's camp in Transoxiana.[5] We also know that a serious revolution, led by Ibn al-Ash'ath, against al-Ḥajjāj, broke out in Sīstān near the end of 81/700.[6] All these indications of unrest within his army and close to the borders of his governorship were enough to persuade al-Muhallab to return to Merv to put his own house in order before trying to make any military advances in Transoxiana.

Unfortunately, we do not have any details about the Muḍarite conspiracy, but the recurrence of the name Muḍar may help to throw some light on this problem, because it would signify a common action between the major divisions of Muḍar, i.e. Tamīm and Qays. It is possible that some tribesmen from Qays who were sympathetic to their kinsmen in Tirmidh, and who were supported by other members of Qays recently arrived from Sīstān, tried, while they were in Transoxiana and close to Tirmidh, to instigate an uprising against the new governor, al-Muhallab, and in favour of Mūsā ibn 'Abdillah ibn Khāzim who had become the symbol of resistance to the authority of the central government. Other tribesmen from Tamīm who were alarmed by the arrival

[1] Gibb, *Arab Conquests*, p. 25; Ṭabarī, vol. II, pp. 1040–1; Ya'qūbī, *Tārīkh*, vol. II, p. 330; Balādhurī, *Futūḥ*, p. 417.

[2] Ṭabarī, vol. II, pp. 1077–82.

[3] *Ibid.*, p. 1080.

[4] *Tārīkh-i-Sīstān*, p. 104; Ṭabarī, vol. II, p. 1042.

[5] Ṭabarī, vol. II, p. 1050.

[6] *Ibid.*, pp. 1054–9.

of the *parvenu* al-Muhallab and his strong followers, jealous for their predominance in Khurāsān,[1] and divided amongst themselves on the issue of Bukayr and Baḥīr, may have joined the restless Qaysites in a united action against al-Muhallab. The latter, alarmed by this dangerous movement within his army in enemy territory, arrested the leaders of the conspiracy and returned to his base.[2]

It is significant that in his governorship al-Muhallab, far from taking any action against Mūsā in Tirmidh, went out of his way to avoid this rebel, and secured another crossing of the Oxus at Zamm. Al-Muhallab may have realized that there were strong feelings in Muḍar in support of Mūsā, and since he was not yet well established in Khurāsān, he preferred to set aside this problem for a time, rather than to antagonize this group by staging an attack on Tirmidh.

Before his death in 82/702 al-Muhallab appointed his son Yazīd to succeed him and al-Ḥajjāj promptly confirmed his appointment as governor of Khurāsān.[3] It was not to be expected that Yazīd's record of campaigns would be very impressive. According to Madā'inī he raided Bādghīs where he encountered the Hephthalites of Nēzak,[4] and, according to Balādhurī, another raid was reported in Khwārizm.[5] More important was the arrival from Sīstān of the remnants of the rebel troops of Ibn al-Ash'ath at Harāt and their successful attempt to capture the city. First Yazīd, who was not sure about the attitude of the tribesmen of Khurāsān, was reluctant to move against this new threat, but finally he had to advance to Harāt and was able to drive them out of the city, whereupon some of them joined Mūsā in Tirmidh.[6] This rebel was becoming more and more of a real threat to the governor's authority in Khurāsān. By this time, Mūsā had gathered around him 8,000 Arab tribesmen from the dissatisfied elements from all the Arab tribes.[7] He was also joined by Ḥurayth ibn Quṭba and his brother Thābit who played an important role which deserves special attention.

[1] Al-Dhahabī, vol. III, p. 122.

[2] Ṭabarī, vol. II, p. 1042.

[3] *Ibid.*, p. 1082.

[4] *Ibid.*, p. 1129.

[5] Balādhurī, *Futūḥ*, p. 417.

[6] Ṭabarī, vol. II, pp. 1105–10; Balādhurī, *Futūḥ*, p. 417.

[7] Ṭabarī, vol. II, p. 1152.

2 *Thābit and Ḥurayth ibn Quṭba, representatives of the Soghdian traders in Merv*

These two brothers were clients of Khuzā'a,[1] but in spite of this fact they had great influence on some members of this tribe. It is even reported that there were Khuzā'ite Arabs among their followers, which is certainly remarkable at this early stage in Khurāsān.[2] We first hear about the two brothers as leaders in Umayya's expedition to Transoxiana in 77/696, and they were also on his side against Bukayr's revolt (see above, p. 47). Bukayr captured Thābit in this struggle, but he set him free because, according to Madā'inī, he owed him a favour.[3] The two brothers again took part in al-Muhallab's expedition to Kish in the year 80/699, and when he had to abandon the siege of that city, he left Ḥurayth there to collect the tribute and then to follow him to Merv. Ḥurayth, for a reason not explained in our sources, accorded favourable treatment to the prince of Kish, of which al-Muhallab disapproved, and when Ḥurayth joined him on his way back to Merv, he was humiliated and was ordered to be beaten by al-Muhallab. The two brothers then fled with 300 of their Arabs and Iranian followers (*shākiriyya*) to join Mūsā in Tirmidh.[4]

When Yazīd succeeded his father, al-Muhallab, he confiscated their property and maltreated their family in Merv. If we accept Yazīd's action as foolish retaliation,[5] it is difficult to understand Muhallab's attitude towards these two brothers, who certainly enjoyed some influence, particularly as it does not fit with the character of al-Muhallab as a great leader. He was not the man to take action which might antagonize the local Iranian population of Khurāsān, especially when the situation there was so precarious that it forced him to abandon his expedition. Apparently in Khurāsān the influence of these two brothers was negligible and our sources certainly give no indication that they enjoyed any great influence in the province itself, or that they had any followers among the Iranian population there. Furthermore, there was apparently no reaction in Khurāsān when they were both killed.

From all the activities of Thābit and Ḥurayth, particularly

[1] *Ibid.*, pp. 1023, 1026, 1080.

[2] *Ibid.*, pp. 1155, 1157–8.

[3] *Ibid.*, pp. 1023–6.

[4] *Ibid.*, pp. 1080–2, 1152; Barthold, *Turkestan*, p. 180.

[5] Gibb, *Arab Conquests*, p. 26.

after joining Mūsā, it is evident that their interest lay in Transoxiana. From our sources, we learn that they enjoyed great prestige and influence among the people and the princes of Transoxiana.[1] They were engaged in trade activities between Khurāsān and Transoxiana even in the midst of their struggle, later, against Mūsā.[2] Moreover, they were surrounded by *chākirs*, in the same fashion as the princes of Soghdiana.[3]

We have mentioned earlier that there were Soghdian traders in Merv who helped to finance Umayya's expedition to Transoxiana, and it is reported specifically that Bukayr and his followers were the borrowers of the money from these traders, when Bukayr was supposed to lead Umayya's expedition.[4] We also know that Bukayr owed Thābit a great favour.[5] It is highly probable that these two brothers were the leaders of the Soghdian traders in Merv. If this is true, their activities could easily be explained by their interest in the trade between Soghdiana and Khurāsān.

As has been suggested, these brothers, motivated by their trade interests, first helped to finance the expeditions to Transoxiana to restore some sort of peaceful relationship between the Arabs and the principalities of Transoxiana, under which the trade could flow more easily.[6] Then they themselves took part in these expeditions, particularly when the arrival of al-Muhallab promised a more stable government in Khurāsān. But when they realized that elements of dissension still existed among the Arab tribesmen and were threatening to explode even on the battlefield, they started thinking about other schemes to secure their trade. They saw Mūsā in Tirmidh successfully defying the authority of the Arab governors of Khurāsān while his power was gradually increasing, and they decided to use him for their own purposes.

Using their influence with the princes of Transoxiana they were able to form an alliance between Mūsā, on one side, and the princes of Bukhārā, Samarqand, Chaghāniān and Khuttal, on the other. Nēzak, the Hephthalite prince of Bādghīs, joined the alliance to strengthen his own position against the Arabs in Khurāsān.[7] They tried to persuade Mūsā to drive Yazīd ibn al-Muhallab out of Khurāsān but, because of the reluctance of Mūsā's followers to ally themselves with the infidels against their

[1] Ṭabarī, vol. II, p. 1152.
[2] *Ibid.*, p. 1157.
[3] *Ibid.*, p. 1082.
[4] *Ibid.*, pp. 1022–3.
[5] *Ibid.*, p. 1026.
[6] See above, p. 48.
[7] Ṭabarī, vol. II, pp. 1152–3.

kinsmen, they agreed to form an Arab principality in Tirmidh to protect the trade route and at the same time resist the Arab attacks against Transoxiana. In return for these services, they agreed to pay tribute to Mūsā instead of Yazīd, the governor of Khurāsān. Mūsā's followers, who were not in favour of such an alliance with the infidels, started pressing Mūsā to break with Thābit and Ḥurayth, the organizers of the alliance, and, as Madā'inī points out, "their state of affairs became unstable".[1]

The allies realized that the alliance was not working out and turned against each other. Mūsā was soon attacked by the princes of Transoxiana, but he was able to repel the attack, though Ḥurayth was wounded in the battle and died two days later.[2] This attack confirmed the beliefs of Mūsā's followers and they turned strongly against Thābit, who had to flee to the fortress of Ḥashshūra (Khushwāragh), where he was joined by some of his followers from the *'ajam* (probably his *chākirs*) and many Arabs.[3] Thābit's position was very strong among the Khuzā'ites of Khurāsān, who had supported him all through this episode.[4] But it is important to notice that there were other members of this tribe who were fighting against their brothers on Mūsā's side. These Khuzā'ite supporters of Mūsā were newcomers to Khurāsān, among the remnants of Ibn al-Ash'ath's forces.[5] This is a striking example of the difference in the interests of members of the same tribe and the gradual weakening of tribal feelings among the Arabs settled in Khurāsān. It is significant that when Abū Muslim came to Khurāsān, about forty years later, he too was supported by Khuzā'ites from the beginning of his movement.[6]

Thābit, who was now isolated against Mūsā, asked for help from his friends, the princes of Transoxiana, and they all came to besiege Mūsā in Tirmidh.[7] There is an interesting report by Madā'inī about Thābit's attempts to bribe some of Mūsā's followers with the money he was receiving from his trade with Balkh, still active up to that time[8]—the typical attitude of a merchant who knew too well the price of his opponents. During the siege of Tirmidh, Thābit was assassinated by one of Mūsā's men, and the leadership of the campaign against Mūsā passed to Ṭarkhūn,

1 *Ibid.*, p. 1153.
2 *Ibid.*, p. 1154.
3 *Ibid.*, p. 1155; Wellhausen, p. 425.
4 Ṭabarī, vol. II, pp. 1155, 1157–8.
5 *Ibid.*, p. 1158.
6 *Ibid.*, pp. 1953–4.
7 *Ibid.*, pp. 1156–9.
8 *Ibid.*, pp. 1156–7.

the prince of Samarqand, though Thābit's own followers were led by an Arab called Ẓuhayr.[1] Before Yazīd was recalled by al-Ḥajjāj, a sort of truce was declared between Mūsā and his antagonists, and each party, presumably even Thābit's party, went home.[2] Yazīd, the governor of Khurāsān, was not able to take any part in these events, partly because of the arrival of those followers of Ibn al-Ash'ath at Harāt but mostly because of his precarious position due to the attitude of the Muḍar party in Khurāsān. This was illustrated by the fact that he was not able to take any action against a certain house from Tamīm, Banū al-Ahtam, who were active in their resistance to the policy of the governor of Khurāsān, and whom al-Ḥajjāj himself had ordered Yazīd to prosecute.[3]

3 *Al-Mufaḍḍal ibn al-Muhallab, a transitional governor*

By that time, al-Ḥajjāj had realized that his policy of bringing al-Muhallab and his followers to Khurāsān had had the effect of driving the Muḍar party to the other extreme, and that it had even strengthened the tribal solidarity between Qays and Tamīm. A change of policy in Khurāsān had become mandatory, and al-Ḥajjāj had to look for another governor who would be acceptable to Muḍar and at the same time could carry out his master's policy. In Qutayba ibn Muslim he found his man. He was from Qays but from the weak clan of Bāhila. Thus he would not have much tribal support and would have to depend on the support of the central authority; and at the same time it would not look like a victory for Qays, i.e. Muḍar, because the appointment had not gone to one of their prominent leaders. Meanwhile, al-Ḥajjāj, who did not want to antagonize the followers of the Muhallabite family, took the ingenious step of transferring the governorship of Khurāsān to al-Mufaḍḍal, the weaker brother of Yazīd. It does not seem that Yazīd objected at all to al-Ḥajjāj's action; on the contrary, he is said to have reaffirmed at the time his obedience to the central authority.[4]

Al-Mufaḍḍal stayed in office for nine months in 85/704, during which period he was able to achieve what his father and brother

[1] *Ibid.*, pp. 1158–9.
[2] *Ibid.*, p. 1160.
[3] *Ibid.*, p. 1161; al-Iṣfahānī, *Aghānī*, vol. XIII, p. 61.
[4] Ṭabarī, vol. II, pp. 1141–4.

could not achieve, namely put an end to Mūsā's rebellion in Tirmidh. This seems strange, because the situation in Khurāsān could not have changed enough to justify such an undertaking, but certainly Mūsā's position was much weaker than it had ever been before. Al-Mufaḍḍal, probably willing to prove himself and to impress al-Ḥajjāj, decided to run the risk against Mūsā and prepared an expedition for this purpose under the leadership of 'Uthmān ibn Mas'ūd, a member of the Banū al-Ahtam of Tamīm, who have been mentioned before as a disobedient element.[1] In other words, Mufaḍḍal sent the tribesmen from whom he feared most in Khurāsān against Mūsā, who, because of his weakening position, had ceased to be of any attraction to the rebellious tribesmen. To guarantee their behaviour, he ordered his brother Mudrik, who was stationed at Balkh, to join the expedition. He also announced in the city of Merv that whoever joined 'Uthmān ibn Mas'ūd would be listed in the *dīwān*.[2] It is not clear, from the narrative, whether this was meant to persuade the Arabs or the Iranian converts to join the army, but, since it is difficult to conceive of any Arab tribesmen who were not already enlisted in the *dīwān* in Khurāsān, this move was probably intended to persuade the Persian converts to join the Arab armies. Arriving at Tirmidh, Ibn Mas'ūd and Mudrik, acting in concert with the princes of Transoxiana, with whom they struck an alliance against Mūsā, defeated the latter, who was killed.[3] It is said that 'Uthmān ordered all the Arab followers of Mūsā to be killed in cold blood, while setting free the few non-Arabs found in the citadel, but it seems that this was an exaggeration on the part of the narrators.[4]

Al-Mufaḍḍal is also credited with two other expeditions, one against Bādghīs and the other against Shūmān and Akhrūn, but, because of his short term in office, these expeditions, if they ever took place, must have been minor raids.[5] From an important remark with regard to these expeditions we learn that al-Mufaḍḍal did not have a treasury and used to distribute whatever he received among the people.[6] It would seem that al-Ḥajjāj was not able to extract any part of the income of Khurāsān during the governor-

[1] *Ibid.*, p. 1161; Balādhurī, *Futūḥ*, p. 419; see above p. 61.
[2] Ṭabarī, vol. II, pp. 1161–2.
[3] *Ibid.*, pp. 1162–3; Baladhūrī, *Futūḥ*, p. 419; Gibb, *Arab Conquests*, p. 27.
[4] Ṭabarī, vol. II, p. 1163.
[5] *Ibid.*, p. 1144; Balādhurī, *Futūḥ*, p. 417.
[6] Ṭabarī, vol. II, p. 1144; Ibn al-Athīr, *Tārīkh*, vol. IV, p. 402.

ship of al-Muhallab and his two sons, except, according to Ibn A'tham, the one-fifth of the booty; this, however, was very little since there were few expeditions.[1] The reports in Ṭabarī that al-Ḥajjāj arrested Yazīd ibn al-Muhallab and his brothers and charged them with a fine of six million dirhams are undoubtedly partly invented and to a great extent exaggerated, particularly since their Azdite origin is clear in Ṭabarī's narrative.[2] These traditions were probably an attempt to furnish a background for Yazīd's later revolt after the death of 'Umar II. However, even according to these reports, this arrest did not take place until shortly before al-Ḥajjāj's death in 95/714;[3] probably it was an all-out effort to suppress the increasing opposition to his policy.[4]

There is no indication in our sources that al-Muhallab or his sons had tried to settle any of the Arab tribesmen in any part of Khurāsān. Merv, including the city itself, continued to be their base, and we only hear about two small garrisons in Harāt and Balkh, which were stationed there for defence purposes. Except for the small group of followers of Ḥurayth ibn Quṭba, al-Muhallab's army consisted at first entirely of Arab tribesmen. After entering Zamm, he introduced a new feature. He invited the prince there, who had become a Muslim, and presumably his small local army, to join the Arab army.[5] Al-Mufaḍḍal, following his father's precedent, called on the *mawālī* (Iranian converts) of Merv to join his army and in return be enlisted in the *dīwān*,[6] i.e. receive the pension which hitherto had been an exclusive Arab privilege.

4 *Qutayba ibn Muslim, an empire builder*

In spite of the success of al-Mufaḍḍal against Mūsā in Tirmidh, al-Ḥajjāj, who was determined to change his policy in Khurāsān and who, not without reason, did not trust the Muhallabites with the execution of his policy, dismissed al-Mufaḍḍal and sent his man Qutayba ibn Muslim to Khurāsān. Qutayba's governorship, which lasted for ten years (86–96/705–15), was one of the outstanding periods in the history of Khurāsān under the Umyyads.

[1] Ibn A'tham, *Futūḥ*, vol. II, p. 90A.
[2] Ṭabarī, vol. II, p. 1208.
[3] *Ibid.*, p. 1217.
[4] See below, p. 74.
[5] Ṭabarī, vol. II, p. 1078.
[6] *Ibid.*, p. 1161.

It was distinguished both from the military and from the organizational point of view. However, the later developments in Khurāsān leave a great doubt as to whether the policy so carefully conceived by al-Ḥajjāj and so faithfully implemented by Qutayba for a whole decade was necessarily the wisest. Since Qutayba's conquests are best described by H. A. R. Gibb,[1] we shall try here to explain his organization of the province which certainly enabled him to achieve on the battlefield what no other Umayyad governor of Khurāsān was able to achieve.

When Qutayba arrived in Khurāsān in 86/705 he was not accompanied by any fresh troops from Iraq.[2] We are told that by the end of his governorship in 96/715 the Arab *muqātila* in his army numbered 47,000 men divided as follows: from Baṣra, Ahl al-'Āliya 9,000, Bakr 7,000, Tamīm 10,000, 'Abdulqays 4,000 and Azd 10,000, and from Kūfa 7,000.[3] But we also know that in the year 95/714 he was joined by a Kūfan army, which was withdrawn from India at al-Ḥajjāj's orders to be sent to Khurāsān under the leadership of Jahm ibn Zaḥr al-Ju'fī,[4] and which probably formed the greater part of the 7,000 men from Kūfa mentioned in 96/715. He was also supported by another army from Iraq itself which was sent by al-Ḥajjāj later in the same year, 95/714.[5] This would mean that when Qutayba arrived in Khurāsān, the number of Arab tribesmen was much less than 47,000 men. From the very beginning of his governorship, Qutayba applied the policy of using the local population in the conquered lands to support his army. We are told that in his first campaign in 86/705, immediately following his arrival at Khurāsān, he was joined by the *dahāqīn* of Balkh.[6] In this campaign, he secured the road for the following expeditions into Transoxiana and received the submission of the king of Chaghāniān, the king of Akhrūn and Shūmān and the king of Kiftān (Kifyāin). He was also probably able to suppress a minor revolt in Balkh. He then returned to Merv, leaving his army behind to undertake minor raids.[7]

The purpose of his early return was to reorganize the Arab tribesmen in Khurāsān. He took as a model the organization of

[1] Gibb, *Arab Conquests*, pp. 29–57.
[2] Ṭabarī, vol. II, pp. 1178–9.
[3] *Ibid.*, pp. 1290–1; Ibn A'tham, *Futūḥ*, vol. II, p. 151B.
[4] Ṭabarī, vol. II, pp. 1257, 1290.
[5] *Ibid.*, p. 1267.
[6] *Ibid.*, p. 1181; Balādhurī, *Futūḥ*, p. 419.
[7] Gibb, *Arab Conquests*, pp. 31–2; Balādhurī, *Futūḥ*, p. 419; Ṭabarī, vol. II, pp. 1180–1.

Baṣra and divided the Arab tribesmen into five different tribal groups: Azd, Tamīm, Ahl al-'Āliya, Bakr and 'Abdulqays; and it is under Qutayba that we hear about such a division for the first time.[1] He also made peace with the Hephthalite prince of Bādghīs, Nēzak, on condition that the latter would join the Arab expeditions, and in the following campaigns (87–90/716–19) against Bukhārā, Nēzak was singled out for his devotion in the fight on the Arab side.[2] In these campaigns of 87–90/716–19 Qutayba concentrated his attacks against the oasis of Bukhārā. In addition to the rich booty his army was able to capture, particularly from the city of Paykand, the centre of the Chinese trade, Qutayba was finally rewarded by the conquest of the city of Bukhārā itself. The city agreed to pay a tribute of 200,000 dirhams, and an Arab garrison was stationed in the citadel.[3]

In these campaigns Qutayba was supported not only by Nēzak but also by the powerful Ḥayyān an-Nabaṭī and his followers.[4] All through Qutayba's governorship, Ḥayyān appears to have held a prominent position in his campaigns and to have acted as his chief negotiator, particularly with the Soghdians.[5] The only time the number of Ḥayyān's followers is specified is with the numbers of the Arab tribesmen in the year 96/715. They are said to have been 7,000 and are described as *mawālī* from the *muqātila* of Khurāsān.[6] This allows us to infer that this figure was the number of the Iranian converts who were enlisted in the *dīwān* and received the regular '*aṭā*' of the *muqātila*. Though al-Mufaḍḍal had started this experiment in Merv, Qutayba seems to have applied it to all of Khurāsān. It seems that he went further and made it a requirement that each district in Khurāsān should supply him with a certain number of men, who would join his expeditions in the spring and go home for the winter, not necessarily being enlisted in the *dīwān*. He apparently did not require them to be converted to Islam, which was a good enough reason not to enlist them in the *dīwān*. As we shall see, he soon applied this measure to Bukhārā and Samarqand. Thus we learn from

[1] Ṭabarī, vol. II, pp. 1202, 1245; al-'Ali, *Tanẓīmāt*, pp. 34–42, 287–95.

[2] Ṭabarī, vol. II, pp. 1184–5, 1195, 1204; Balādhurī, *Futūḥ*, p. 420; Ya'qūbī, *Tārīkh*, vol. II, p. 342.

[3] Ṭabarī, vol. II, pp. 1188–9; Balādhurī, *Futūḥ*, p. 420; Ibn A'tham, *Futūḥ*, vol. II, p. 135B.

[4] Ṭabarī, vol. II, p. 1204.

[5] Ṭabarī, vol. II, p. 1204; Ya'qūbī, *Tārīkh*, vol. II, p. 342; Balādhurī, *Futūḥ*, p. 337.

[6] Ṭabarī, vol. II, pp. 1291–2.

Madā'inī that when Qutayba returned to Merv after the conquest of Bukhārā in 90/709, leaving there an Arab garrison, his army disbanded for the winter and, when he needed them, he had to write to Abrshahr, Bīvard, Sarakhs and Harāt and to wait until the following spring for these men to assemble in Merv in preparation for the campaign.[1] Yet in the same winter he was able to spare 12,000 men from Merv alone to be stationed in Balkh.[2] All these indications lead us to believe that the number of men conscripted in Khurāsān to join Qutayba's expeditions was far more than the 7,000 *mawālī* mentioned in our sources.[3]

The emergency which compelled Qutayba to send 12,000 men to Balkh in the winter of 90/709 was a concerted uprising of the Hephthalite principalities of the region of Gūzgān, including Ṭālqān and Fāryāb, led and organized by Nēzak and supported by Balkh and Bādām, the *dihqān* of Merv ar-Rūd.[4] Summing up the reasons given in our Arabic sources, Gibb concluded that "Nēzak, finally realizing that all hope of recovering independence must be extinguished if Arab rule was strengthened in Khurāsān, and perhaps putting down to weakness Qutayba's willingness to gain his ends if possible by diplomacy, determined on a last effort to overthrow Muslim sovereignty in Lower Ṭukhāristān, at the moment it was least to be expected".[5] It is also possible that these Hephthalites were encouraged to revolt, at this particular time, by the success against the Arabs of their cousins in the south led by Zunbīl. Nēzak, Madā'inī indicates, made an effort to ask them for help when he decided to revolt against Qutayba,[6] which explains why Qutayba's following campaign was directed against Zunbīl. Nēzak also forced the weak Jābghū of Ṭukhāristān to join his cause, in an attempt to persuade all the princes of the Principalities of Ṭukhāristān to rise in defence of their nominal suzerain.[7] However, Nēzak's plan to stage the revolt in the spring of 91/710 was frustrated by the swift strategy of Qutayba in dispatching the 12,000 men to Balkh, and when Qutayba marched against the rebels there was hardly any fighting.

Qutayba first advanced to Merv ar-Rūd, the *dihqān* Bādām

1 *Ibid.*, pp. 1206–7.
2 *Ibid.*, p. 1207.
3 Ibn A'tham, *Futūḥ*, vol. II, p. 141 B.
4 Ṭabarī, vol. II, p. 1206; Ibn A'tham, *Futūḥ*, vol. II, pp. 138 A–9 B; Ya'qūbī, *Tārīkh*, vol. II, p. 342.
5 Gibb, *Arab Conquests*, p. 36.
6 Ṭabarī, vol. II, p. 1206.
7 Gibb, *Arab Conquests*, p. 37; Ṭabarī, vol. II, p. 1206.

fleeing to Ṭālqān.[1] From there he advanced to Ṭālqān, "concerning which the traditions are hopelessly confused".[2] However, he met with no resistance in either Ṭālqān, Fāryāb or Balkh. From the last place, where he was reinforced by the garrison, he pursued Nēzak until finally by the help of some of the lesser princes he was able to capture him. Sulaym an-Nāṣiḥ (the counsellor), a *mawlā* from Khurāsān, helped to make Nēzak submit to Qutayba, who had promised to pardon the helpless rebel. Nevertheless Qutayba had to execute him on direct orders from al-Ḥajjāj. With Nēzak were also executed at least 700 of his followers.[3] The Jābghū of Ṭukhāristān was sent to Damascus as a valuable hostage, or rather as a symbol of victory.[4]

One must agree with Gibb's statement that "The results of this expedition were of the greatest importance: not only was Nēzak's scheme crushed and Lower Ṭukhāristān henceforth incorporated in the Arab empire, but also for the first time Arab authority was extended over the Jābghū and his immediate vassals in the Oxus basin".[5] There is no indication, however, that there were any changes in the administration of this region other than the appointment of Arab representatives along with the native princes who were left to continue their administration.[6] It is worth mentioning that Qutayba's resident and garrison in Balkh were not stationed in the city itself, but in the village of al-Barūqān in the vicinity of Balkh.[7]

In the same year (91/710) Qutayba had to deal with another revolt in Shūmān which he crushed, and then he advanced through the Iron Gate into Soghdiana. After reducing Kish and Nasaf he went to Bukhārā where he took the decisive step of establishing a military colony. Here, also, as happened before in Merv, the Arabs were quartered in the houses of the inhabitants of Bukhārā.[8]

The campaign of 92/711 was directed against Zunbīl in Sīstān according to al-Ḥajjāj's instructions.[9] Sīstān, which was also included in al-Ḥajjāj's governorship, certainly posed a difficult problem for him. First in 78/697 he sent an expedition under

[1] Ya'qūbī, *Tārīkh*, vol. II, p. 342; Ṭabarī, vol. II, p. 1218.

[2] Gibb, *Arab Conquests*, p. 37.

[3] Ṭabarī, vol. II, pp. 1220–4.

[4] *Ibid.*, p. 1225.

[5] Gibb, *Arab Conquests*, p. 81.

[6] Ṭabarī, vol. II, pp. 1218–19.

[7] *Ibid.*, pp. 1206–7.

[8] Gibb, *Arab Conquests*, pp. 38–9; Barthold, *Turkestan*, p. 185; Narshakhī, *The History of Bukhārā*, tr. R. N. Frye, Cambridge, Mass., 1954, p. 53; Ṭabarī, vol. II, pp. 1228–9, 1230.

[9] Ya'qūbī, *Tārīkh*, vol. II, p. 343.

ʿUbaydullah ibn Abī-Bakra to Sīstān with the specific purpose of wiping out Zunbīl. Instead, Zunbīl was able to wipe out this expedition, whose leader died of grief at the destruction of his army.[1] This major disaster for the Arabs in Sīstān called for strong and immediate action if al-Ḥajjāj's plans for the East were to have any success. Al-Ḥajjāj, determined as he was, prepared another bigger expedition in 80/699, reportedly of 40,000 men from Kūfa and Baṣra, known as the "Army of Peacocks" and under the leadership of Abdurraḥman ibn Muḥammad ibn al-Ashʿath.

Al-Ḥajjāj did not spare any expense in equipping this army with the best available horses and arms. This in itself is enough justification for calling it the "Army of Peacocks", but the name also suggests that it included many proud men. Al-Ḥajjāj, who had by then completed the demilitarization of Kūfa and Baṣra, decided that it was best for the stability of Iraq to dispatch the veteran tribesmen of Kūfa and Baṣra to Sīstān and gradually persuade them to settle there. Many of them were proud descendants of the founders of Kūfa and Baṣra, who would vehemently object to the centralizing policies of al-Ḥajjāj and to the permanent stationing of Syrian troops in Iraq. Ibn al-Ashʿath himself was the grandson of al-Ashʿath ibn Qays al-Kindī, undoubtedly one of the most powerful and strong-minded tribal leaders of Kūfa. The elimination of such proud and powerful elements from Iraq would serve the double purpose of securing the stability of this troublesome region and advancing the Arab conquests further in the east.

Arriving in Sīstān in the spring of 79/699, the Peacock army advanced eastwards into Zābulistān and achieved some military success against Zunbīl. Nevertheless, Ibn al-Ashʿath and his followers, realizing the difficulties involved in campaigning in such inhospitable lands, began to have second thoughts about their situation. At this point al-Ḥajjāj showed his true intentions, that they should settle permanently in this remote region. The Arab tribesmen of the Peacock army had probably assumed that they had joined this expedition for the duration of the campaign in the spring and the summer, after which they would return to their homes in Kūfa and Baṣra according to the usual practice. Instead, al-Ḥajjāj repeatedly instructed Ibn al-Ashʿath to continue his attacks and advance into the heart of Zunbīl's kingdom. Ibn

[1] Ṭabarī, vol. II, pp. 1036–9, 1056; Balādhurī, *Futūḥ*, p. 399.

al-Ash'ath and his men clearly understood these instructions as condemning them to stay in Sīstān permanently.[1] They mutinied against al-Ḥajjāj and marched back into Iraq, only to be crushed by the Syrian troops. The remnants of the Peacock army fled back east where they were dispersed; Ibn al-Ash'ath himself sought refuge with Zunbīl in Zābulistān where he met his death in 85/704.[2] After this episode a truce was declared between al-Ḥajjāj and Zunbīl on condition that the latter would pay a tribute in kind, and in return al-Ḥajjāj promised not to attack him.[3] From al-Aghānī we learn that only 700 Arab tribesmen from Tamīm decided to stay in Sīstān at that time.[4]

According to Balādhurī, when Qutayba became governor of Khurāsān and Sīstān, he appointed his brother 'Amr to Sīstān. 'Amr asked Zunbīl to pay the tribute in cash, and, when the latter refused, Qutayba marched against him.[5] Qutayba's move against Zunbīl at this particular time was also motivated by his desire to eliminate any possibility of support from the southern Hephthalites, the Zābulites, for their brethren of the north which might encourage them to rise again against Arab domination. Zunbīl, surprised by this unexpected move and scared by Qutayba's reputation, hastened to offer his submission. Qutayba, who had realized the real strength of Zunbīl, accepted it and returned to Merv, leaving only an Arab representative in Sīstān.[6] During the rest of the Umayyad period no other expeditions were sent against Zunbīl, in spite of the fact that he ceased to pay tribute to the Arabs.[7]

In the years until the end of his governorship in 96/715, Qutayba's attention was again focused on Transoxiana, where he penetrated as far as Farghāna. First, in 93/712 he conquered Khwārizm on the pretext of helping its king against his rebellious brother and settled an Arab colony there.[8] On his way back he

1 Balādhurī, *Anonyme Arabische Chronik*, ed. W. Ahlwardt, Griefswald, 1883, pp. 324–6; Ṭabarī, vol. II, p. 1054.

2 Ṭabarī, vol. II, pp. 1042–77; Balādhurī, *Anonyme*, pp. 315–46; Ibn A'tham, *Futūḥ*, vol. II, pp. 98A–113A. See also Wellhausen, pp. 234–49; Bosworth, pp. 52–63.

3 Balādhurī, *Futūḥ*, p. 400.

4 *Aghānī*, vol. XIX, p. 156.

5 Balādhurī, *Futūḥ*, p. 400.

6 Ibn A'tham, *Futūḥ*, vol. II, p. 140B; Ya'qūbī, *Tārīkh*, vol. II, p. 343; Balādhurī, *Futūḥ*, p. 400; Ṭabarī, vol. II, p. 1235.

7 Balādhurī, *Futūḥ*, p. 401.

8 Gibb, *Arab Conquests*, pp. 42–3; Ṭabarī, vol. II, pp. 1236–41; Balādhurī, *Futūḥ*, pp. 420–1; Ibn A'tham, *Futūḥ*, vol. II, p. 141A; Ya'qūbī, *Tārīkh*, vol. II, p. 343.

found an opportunity to take Samarqand by surprise, although he had concluded a peace treaty with its prince after the conquest of Bukhārā. However, he attacked the city, entered it and imposed a new peace treaty.[1] When he established a strong garrison in the citadel of the city, the prince Ghūrak and the merchants of the city left it and built a new city, Farankath, to the north of Samarqand.[2] Gibb points out that there was

> a radical difference between the conquest of Bukhārā and that of Samarqand. The former was a result of a series of campaigns in which the resources of the country had been exhausted and the province annexed piecemeal. The whole population had become subjects of the Arabs and were under constant surveillance: Tughshāda (the prince of Bukhārā) himself held his rank on sufferance and was compelled to maintain at least an outward show of loyalty. But Samarqand had been captured in one swift thrust; Soghd as a whole was still unsubdued and only from policy acknowledged the suzerainty of the Arabs for the time being.[3]

In the campaigns of 94–5/713–14 and 96/715, Qutayba carried the Arab arms far into the Jaxartes province, sometimes as far as Isfījāb and deep into Farghāna.[4] However, Arab authority was not destined to be established in these provinces and the death of *Amīr al-Mu'minīn* Walīd I brought the conquests to a standstill.

After the conquest of Khwārizm and specifically in the conquest of Samarqand in 93/712 we find a new element in Qutayba's army. These were the levies from Bukhārā and Khwārizm whom we find again in the campaigns of 94/713 and 95/714 in addition to other levies from Soghdiana.[5] Yet in the campaign of 96/715 there is no mention at all of any levies in Qutayba's army. Their absence from this last campaign of Qutayba could be accounted for by the fact that in 95/714 he received fresh Arab troops from al-Ḥajjāj, represented by a Kūfan army from the Arab troops in India, and another army sent from Iraq itself. Thus there was no need to raise any levies from Transoxiana. The question now is,

[1] The text of this treaty with Samarqand is preserved in full in Ibn A'tham, *Futūḥ*, vol. II, pp. 143B–144A.

[2] Gibb, *Arab Conquests*, pp. 45–7; Balādhurī, *Futūḥ*, p. 421; Ṭabarī, vol. II, pp. 1241–52; Ibn A'tham, *Futūḥ*, vol. II, pp. 142A–4B; Ya'qūbī, *Tārīkh*, vol. II, pp. 343–4.

[3] Gibb, *Arab Conquests*, pp. 45–6.

[4] Gibb, *Arab Conquests*, pp. 48–53; H. A. R. Gibb, "The Arab invasion of Kāshgar in A.D. 715", *Bulletin of the School of Oriental Studies* II (1923), pp. 467–74.

[5] Ṭabarī, vol. II, pp. 1244–56.

why did Qutayba resort to raising levies from the newly conquered lands in Transoxiana? We have a clue in the narratives of the conquest of Khwārizm. We are told that at this particular time a demand arose in Qutayba's army to return home, which he quickly crushed, advancing towards Merv.[1] On the way he changed his mind and attacked Samarqand. We are also told that soon after this Ḥayyān an-Nabaṭī was punished by Qutayba, but for no obvious reason.[2] In the siege of Samarqand the levies of Bukhārā and Khwārizm, who were called then *'abīd* (slaves) by Qutayba, were an indispensable factor.[3] When the prince of Samarqand allegedly protested that Qutayba was really fighting him with his brethren from Bukhārā and Khwārizm, Qutayba had to prove to him that he also had some Arabs in this army.[4] It would seem that a situation was created in which the Persian levies from Khurāsān were weary of the successive campaigns. While in Khwārizm they asked to return to their homes, putting pressure on Ḥayyān, their spokesman, to voice their demand to Qutayba, who later ordered Ḥayyān to be punished for failing to handle his people. Moreover, these men gained little from these campaigns, except absence from their homes and no possibility of engaging in productive work for a good part of the year.

We have a valuable hint in a tradition by Madā'inī that one of the first actions of Qutayba's successor, Wakī' ibn Abī Sūd, who accused Qutayba of causing the prices to rise, was to reduce prices, particularly of grains.[5] The wars of Qutayba which brought to Khurāsān a considerable amount of booty, particularly from the first few campaigns, had also deprived the countryside of its needed manpower. This situation, to use a modern term, had created a war economy and resulted in inflation, which caused prices to rise. Naturally, these circumstances would discourage the people of Khurāsān from joining Qutayba's army and thus he had to turn to another source for raising levies. At the same time he asked al-Ḥajjāj to supply him with fresh troops for his ever-extending campaigns.

Another feature in Qutayba's army which also appeared as early as the conquest of Samarqand but was more developed towards the end of his governorship was the Archers, whose

[1] Ya'qūbī, *Tārīkh*, vol. II, p. 343; Ṭabarī, vol. II, pp. 1240–1.
[2] Ṭabarī, vol. II, p. 1253.
[3] *Ibid.*, p. 1245.
[4] *Ibid.*, p. 1244.
[5] *Ibid.*, p. 1298.

skill is particularly mentioned in our sources.[1] Ibn A'tham tells us that they were called *rumāt al-ḥuduq* (the archers who can pierce the pupils of the eyes) and they numbered more than 10,000 from the nobility of the Soghdians, the Hephthalites and all the princes of Ṭukhāristān and Khurāsān.[2] Naturally the number given by our authority is highly exaggerated. These noble Archers remained faithful to Qutayba even when everyone else turned against him,[3] a fact which makes them appear to have been meant rather as a bodyguard than as a contingent in the army.

5 *Downfall of Qutayba*

Now we shall turn to the downfall of Qutayba and try to find the reason for his sudden revolt, or rather the revolt of his army against him. Scholars have attributed this serious turn in Qutayba's career to personal animosity between him and the new *Amīr al-Mu'minīn* Sulaymān,[4] but the issue went much deeper than that. As we know, al-Ḥajjāj remained for twenty years the first man in the empire, second only to *Amīr al-Mu'minīn*. When his patron, 'Abdulmalik, died, his son al-Walīd I left al-Ḥajjāj with all the power given to him by 'Abdulmalik. It was to be expected that al-Ḥajjāj's powers would grow even greater under al-Walīd. Having the power to appoint governors in more than half of the empire, al-Ḥajjāj started a certain school of governors, which outlived him by many years, and which is rightly called in our sources the school of al-Ḥajjāj.[5] Qutayba was one of the best graduates of this school. One of the striking examples related in our sources of the power of al-Ḥajjāj, which extended all over the empire, is that he was able to persuade al-Walīd I to dismiss his cousin 'Umar ibn 'Abdil'azīz in 93/712 from his governorship in Madīna and appoint instead one of al-Ḥajjāj's own disciples.[6]

Al-Ḥajjāj was probably the greatest empire-builder in the history of the Arabs, and as such his main preoccupation was to strengthen the authority of the central government over the territories already acquired and expand the boundaries of the empire to include new lands. His problem in Khurāsān was a

[1] *Ibid.*, p. 1244.
[2] Ibn A'tham, *Futūḥ*, vol. II, p. 151 A.
[3] Balādhurī, *Futūḥ*, p. 424.
[4] Wellhausen, p. 439; Barthold, *Turkestan*, p. 186; Gibb, *Arab Conquests*, p. 52; Bosworth, p. 68.
[5] Ṭabarī, vol. II, p. 1354.
[6] *Ibid.*, p. 1254.

difficult one. There he was faced with a disobedient Arab community in a land which promised more expansion than any other. First, he had to bring these tribesmen into line with the rest of the community and then use them to further the conquests. He probably thought he could bring about the assimilation of these tribesmen by involving them in war. When he first brought Khurāsān under his close surveillance he sent there a new group of Arab tribesmen to balance the unruly elements. His new governor was al-Muhallab, a distinguished military leader. When this policy failed he had to find an alternative. In this he was inspired by the emergence of the *mawālī* during the governorship of Umayya and particularly under al-Mufaḍḍal. He thought that if he could use them in full force they would supply the governor in Khurāsān with the power he lacked to control the Arab tribesmen, while at the same time serving as a reliable force in the Arab conquests. Thus when Qutayba went to Khurāsān he was not accompanied by any fresh Arab troops. This policy would have succeeded, in the long run, if it had been helped by an effort to consider the interests of the Iranian population of Khurāsān and assimilate them with the Arab community there. But neither al-Ḥajjāj nor Qutayba made any effort to do this. Qutayba in fact followed just the opposite policy, making use of these people and altogether neglecting their interests, a fact which reportedly was stated by Ḥayyān, when Qutayba sought the support of his followers against the rebellious Arab tribesmen in Farghāna in 96/715.[1] Qutayba went even further to prevent any assimilation and segregated the *mawālī* in a special division of his army, instead of leaving them to join the tribes, or the clans, whose clients they were supposed to be. It is clear, therefore, why the policy of al-Ḥajjāj and Qutayba had alienated the Iranian population in Khurāsān so that they turned against Qutayba when he most needed their support.

As for the Arab tribesmen, they also had their reasons for turning against Qutayba. On the one hand, the ever-increasing power of the central government and its representative became clear in the prosecution of Banū al-Ahtam of Tamīm, who were opposed to al-Ḥajjāj's policy.[2] The interference of Qutayba, who dismissed certain powerful tribal chiefs from their positions and

[1] Balādhurī, *Futūḥ*, p. 424.

[2] *Ibid.*, pp. 423, 425–6; Ibn A'tham, *Futūḥ*, vol. II, p. 133B.

appointed instead other chiefs who were more agreeable to the government, as happened in the case of Wakī‘ ibn Abī-Sūd, had gravely alarmed the tribesmen.[1] On the other hand, these same tribesmen had been long enough in Khurāsān to get used to another kind of life which did not fully agree with Qutayba's policy of constant campaigns. At the same time, and in spite of their probable objection to Qutayba's dependence on the non-Arab subjects, these tribesmen were getting closer to these very subjects, as is clearly manifested in the agreement between the two sides against Qutayba.[2]

Al-Ḥajjāj's policy, like any other, could not have passed unchallenged, and was bound to arouse some opposition in the empire. The first leader openly to oppose it was probably Yazīd ibn al-Muhallab. It seems that his close relationship to Sulaymān, the heir apparent, enabled Yazīd to convince him of his point of view. We are told that Yazīd sought the protection of Sulaymān when al-Ḥajjāj tried to prosecute him.[3] Al-Ḥajjāj was also opposed by another distinguished figure, ‘Umar ibn ‘Abdil‘azīz,[4] an opposition which cost the latter his position as governor of Madīna. In other words, we have three prominent figures who were in close alliance in opposition to al-Ḥajjāj's policy. Al-Ḥajjāj was able to get rid of two of them, but did not have enough time to get rid of the third, Sulaymān, who probably was too strong for him. He tried to persuade al-Walīd I to change the succession and appoint his own son instead of Sulaymān, thereby securing the continuation of his policy, but al-Walīd I died before taking this step.[5] It is reported that when al-Ḥajjāj received a false report of the death of al-Walīd I, he became very frightened, and was overwhelmed with panic.[6] Fortunately for him, he died in 95/714 almost a year before al-Walīd I's death. Qutayba, the faithful disciple of al-Ḥajjāj, learned about his death while he was on an expedition to Shāsh. He ordered the army back, probably in anticipation of a change of policy.[7] But al-Walīd I left everything as it was under al-Ḥajjāj without any change and confirmed the appointment of all his governors.[8]

[1] Balādhurī, *Futūḥ*, p. 426; Ṭabarī, vol. II, pp. 1290–304; Ibn Qutayba, *Ma‘ārif*, p. 212; Ibn ‘Abd Rabbih, vol. I, p. 80.
[2] Balādhurī, *Futūḥ*, p. 426; Ṭabarī, vol. II, p. 1291.
[3] Ibn A‘tham, *Futūḥ*, vol. II, p. 132B; Ṭabarī, vol. II, pp. 1211–17.
[4] Ṭabarī, vol. II, p. 1254.
[5] *Ibid.*, p. 1274.
[6] *Ibid.*, p. 1272.
[7] *Ibid.*, p. 1267.
[8] *Ibid.*, p. 1269.

In the year 96/715 Qutayba prepared for his campaign and went to the Jaxartes provinces. It is reported that he ordered his men to take their families with them and he himself sent his family to Samarqand in fear of Sulaymān. He also stationed a guard to watch the crossing of the Oxus and to prevent anybody from returning to Merv.[1] It seems that he was planning to settle some tribesmen in a military colony in Farghāna, and, sensing that his men were not very enthusiastic about this move, he stationed the guard on the Oxus to stop any attempt to thwart his plan. In Farghāna he received the news of the death of al-Walīd I and the succession of Sulaymān. Though he was confirmed by Sulaymān, he realized that this was only a temporary measure and that a change was imminent.[2] In a desperate attempt to change the course of events he revolted, hoping that his army would support him. All his army turned against him except his bodyguard (the Archers), who apparently were a relatively small force, and Qutayba met his death at the hands of his fellow tribesmen and their new allies, the *mawālī* of Ḥayyān an-Nabaṭī.[3] The Arab tribesmen agreed to render allegiance to the Tamīmite chief, Wakī' ibn Abī Sūd, on condition that he would accept whatever the new *Amīr al-Mu'minīn* Sulaymān should decide for them.[4] The first order of Sulaymān was for the army to return to Merv, where it was disbanded.[5] In the following five years, until the death of 'Umar II, the opposition party was in power and the policy followed in Khurāsān was completely different from that of al-Ḥajjāj.

[1] *Ibid.*, pp. 1275–6.

[2] Balādhurī, *Futūḥ*, p. 423; Ṭabarī, vol. II, p. 1286.

[3] Ṭabarī, vol. II, pp. 1286–96; Qutayba's speeches when he decided to revolt are quoted at length in: Ibn A'tham, *Futūḥ*, vol. II, pp. 149B–151A; Ibn 'Abd Rabbih, vol. XV, pp. 140–1; al-Jāhiẓ, *al-Bayān wa al-Tabyīn*, Cairo, 1948–50, vol. II, pp. 132–4.

[4] Ibn A'tham, *Futūḥ*, vol. II, p. 152A; also see Ṭabarī, vol. II, p. 1289.

[5] Balādhurī, *Futūḥ*, p. 423; Ibn A'tham, *Futūḥ*, vol. II, p. 150A

5

SULAYMĀN AND 'UMAR II, THE OPPOSITION IN POWER

1 *Sulaymān, precursor of 'Umar II*

The importance of Sulaymān's reign does not seem to have been realized, because in all our sources it is overshadowed by the overwhelming emphasis on that of 'Umar ibn 'Abdil'azīz. In fact the latter should be considered as a continuation of the former, or rather a period in which the trend starting under Sulaymān reached a climax and was vigorously systematized. It is because these two rulers were in power for such a short time that their policy did not take deep root. Yazīd ibn 'Abdilmalik, 'Umar's successor, as was expected and feared, revived the old imperial policy, and tried to do away with any effects which the change under Sulaymān and 'Umar might have produced.

We know that the succession of Sulaymān to the office of *Amīr al-Mu'minīn* was feared most by al-Ḥajjāj and his disciples, as they expected him to change the policy which they had advocated for almost twenty years. Nevertheless they could not prevent his eventual attainment of power. Sulaymān succeeded precisely where his opponents failed. He had to challenge his father's will that Yazīd should succeed his brothers, Walīd and Sulaymān.[1] He overruled the strong objection of members of his family, and appointed as his successor 'Umar ibn 'Abdil'azīz.[2] The latter's opposition to al-Ḥajjāj's policy was certainly known to Sulaymān, and he must also have expected 'Umar to continue on the same lines that he had started. Although 'Umar was not appointed to any position in Sulaymān's reign, it is reported that he acted like a *wazīr* for Sulaymān.[3]

There was a man behind these two rulers, about whom we would like to know more, and who may have served to ensure continuity between their reigns. This was Rajā' ibn Ḥaywa, who

[1] Ṭabarī, vol. II, p. 1317. [2] *Ibid.*, pp. 1341–5.
[3] Al-Dhahabī, vol. IV, p. 168; *al-'Uyūn wa al-Ḥadā'iq fī Akhbār al-Ḥaqā'iq*, anon., ed. M. J. de Goeje, Leiden, 1869, p. 29.

was quite influential under Sulaymān, then played the role of the "king maker" with regard to ʿUmar II and finally served as his secretary and close associate. Rajā' ibn Ḥaywa was well acquainted with affairs of state as he is reported to have been in charge of all the treasury under ʿAbdulmalik.[1] It is possible that he was the source of inspiration for ʿUmar II's fiscal reforms.

In our sources we find some traditions according to which Sulaymān was a man only concerned with food and women, but these traditions should be taken only as an attempt by his opponents to blacken his name, probably taking advantage of the fact that he was renowned for his enormous appetite.[2] The true Sulaymān is to be found in other traditions where he is highly praised for his good deeds throughout his reign, such as undoing the oppressive acts of al-Ḥajjāj, releasing the prisoners in the jails of Baṣra, bringing back those who had been long on campaign, and finally the appointment of ʿUmar ibn ʿAbdilʿazīz as his successor.[3]

2 *Yazīd ibn al-Muhallab, governor of the East and Iraq*

When Sulaymān became *Amīr al-Mu'minīn*, his first action was to change the governors appointed by his predecessor on the advice of al-Ḥajjāj. Makka and Madīna were given new governors. To Iraq he appointed Yazīd ibn al-Muhallab, accompanied by Ṣāliḥ ibn ʿAbdirraḥman, a client of Tamīm, who was especially capable in *al-kharāj* (fiscal administration). There are some contradictory traditions concerning the reason for Sulaymān's appointment of Ṣāliḥ for *al-kharāj*. Some traditions claim that it was the advice of Yazīd who wished to be relieved from this heavy responsibility, particularly in Iraq.[4] Other traditions insinuate that it was because of Yazīd's extravagance that this arrangement was made, and, that when he was pressed by his associate Ṣāliḥ, he had to beg Sulaymān for the governorship of Khurāsān where he would be able to exercise more freedom with regard to the province's income.[5] Subsequent developments make these explanations seem far-fetched. Yazīd was not demoted to Khurāsān, but this province was included in his governorship, which

[1] Ṭabarī, vol. II, pp. 1341–5; Ibn ʿAbd Rabbih, vol. XVI, p. 24, vol. XVIII, p. 74.
[2] Ṭabarī, vol. II, pp. 1273, 1309.
[3] *Ibid.*, p. 1337.
[4] *Ibid.*, pp. 1306–7.
[5] *Ibid.*, pp. 1304–10.

means that he was given more power in the empire.[1] Sulaymān had seen in Yazīd his own "al-Ḥajjāj", and from the beginning was planning to give him these powers in the empire. Since the situation in Khurāsān was not yet clear, and probably to give Yazīd enough time to prepare himself and formulate a policy for the province, Yazīd was first appointed to Iraq with the understanding that he would soon have to take care of Khurāsān. Sulyamān must have realized that what was needed most in Iraq was a new fiscal policy which would eliminate the complaints of his subjects there. It is no wonder then that he should send a financial expert like Ṣāliḥ ibn ʿAbdirraḥman to make a close study of the financial policy of al-Ḥajjāj, in the light of which any reforms would be introduced in Iraq.

As for Khurāsān, after the death of Qutayba, there was naturally uncertainty about the course of action to be taken there. Since all the tribesmen and the Iranian population were in favour of the new *Amīr al-Mu'minīn* Sulaymān, he had no option but to confirm what had been done by them, at least for the time being, until he could form a clearer opinion about the situation. Therefore he immediately, in 96/715, confirmed Wakīʿ ibn Abī Sūd as his governor of Khurāsān, but only for *al-ḥarb*, i.e. military affairs.[2] Sulaymān also confirmed Wakīʿ's own appointment of Abū-Mijlaz Lāḥiq ibn Ḥumayd al-Sadūsī for *al-kharāj*, i.e. fiscal affairs. This step, according to Balādhurī, had been taken by Wakīʿ and accepted by the people as an appointment of Abū-Mijlaz for Merv.[3] The latter was a man well known for his honesty and vast experience in the affairs of Khurāsān.[4] The statement that his appointment was subject to the approval of the people is a clear indication that in spite of the general acceptance of Wakīʿ as a provisional governor, the tribesmen in Khurāsān were still trying to take matters into their own hands and were determined to deal with Wakīʿ as a tribal chief, not as a governor with full authority. Wakīʿ, in his nine months in office, tried forcibly and with great zeal to maintain law and order in Khurāsān.[5] Nevertheless, Sulaymān was alarmed at the possibility of an awakening of tribal tendencies in Khurāsān and was advised against leaving it in the hands of a tribal chief who might himself lead a revolt

[1] *Ibid.*, p. 1310; Balādhurī, *Futūḥ*, p. 425.
[2] Ṭabarī, vol. II, p. 1305.
[3] Balādhurī, *Futūḥ*, p. 424.
[4] Ṭabarī, vol. II, pp. 1354, 1356.
[5] *Ibid.*, p. 1301; Balādhurī, *Futūḥ*, p. 424.

against the central authority.[1] Having resolved to put an end, once and for all, to the power of the tribesmen in Khurāsān, Sulaymān in 97/716 dismissed Wakīʿ and the province was fully incorporated into the governorship of Iraq under Yazīd ibn al-Muhallab. The importance of Khurāsān was emphasized by the fact that the new governor was to move to Khurāsān, leaving only representatives in the three important cities of Iraq, Kūfa, Baṣra and Wāsiṭ.[2]

Most important of all, Yazīd was not going to depend on the loyalty of the Arab tribesmen or the *mawālī* of Khurāsān, both of whom had proved to be unreliable. Instead he brought with him to Khurāsān a great number of the Syrian imperial troops. The number quoted in our sources, 60,000 men, is of course a gross exaggeration.[3] Nevertheless, it indicates that the Syrian troops were numerous enough to impose the will of the central government over both the Arab and the Iranian communities, and to establish its authority firmly in the entire region. Yazīd was also accompanied to Khurāsān by some of the tribesmen of Kūfa and Baṣra, but they do not seem to have been very numerous.[4] In Yazīd's expeditions, in addition to the *muqātila* of Kūfa, Baṣra, Khurāsān and the Syrian troops, we find mention of the slaves, the *mawālī* and the volunteers (*al-mamālīk wa al-mawālī wa al-mutaṭawwiʿīn*).[5] We have no definite figures in our sources for these three groups, though by comparing two different narratives in Ṭabarī it can be determined that they numbered in all about 20,000 men.[6] From the presence of Ḥayyān an-Nabaṭī in the expeditions, we can conclude that the *mawālī* mentioned there were his followers, the Iranian converts registered in the *dīwān*.[7] The volunteers were also probably from the Iranian population of Khurāsān, either non-Muslims or converts, but not registered in the *dīwān*, who went along with the Arab expeditions in the hope of sharing the booty. The last group, the *mamālīk*, poses a problem, because this is the first time we find this term used for the slaves in our sources. In Qutayba's army the term *ʿabīd* was used for slaves, but only in reference to the levies from Transoxiana. We also know of Qutayba's bodyguard which was formed

[1] Ṭabarī, vol. II, pp. 1309–10; Balādhurī, *Futūḥ*, pp. 424–5.
[2] Ṭabarī, vol. II, pp. 1310, 1314; *ʿUyūn*, p. 29.
[3] Ṭabarī, vol. II, p. 1327.
[4] *Ibid.*, pp. 1318, 1328; Balādhurī, *Futūḥ*, p. 335; Ibn Aʿtham, *Futūḥ*, vol. II, p. 158 A.
[5] Ṭabarī, vol. II, p. 1318.
[6] *Ibid.*, pp. 1318, 1327.
[7] *Ibid.*, p. 1329.

from the nobility of the whole region, and who remained faithful to their master until he was killed.[1] The *mamalīk* in Yazīd's army were probably the remnants of Qutayba's bodyguard, now reduced to a comparatively insignificant group joining the Arab army.

Another significant feature of the new policy in Khurāsān is the direction in which Yazīd led his expeditions. He is reported to have objected to Qutayba's policy of furthering the Arab conquests in central Asia while leaving behind him, in Gurgān and Ṭabaristān, hostile territory which might threaten his line of communication with Iraq.[2] Yazīd spent most of his stay in Khurāsān leading expeditions into Gurgān. There he had some success, reducing it to tributary status. Leaving there a garrison of 4,000 men, he advanced against Ṭabaristān. Here, in spite of his big army and probably because of the difficult terrain, he met strong resistance, which encouraged the people of Gurgān to rise against the Arab garrison and slaughter all its members. Yazīd then made peace with the prince of Ṭabaristān, through the mediation of Ḥayyān an-Nabaṭī, and returned to Gurgān where he won a decisive victory and avenged the slaughter of his garrison. The amount of booty Yazīd won in this campaign is described in detail in our sources, and it is considerable.[3]

At the end of the campaign, he left only a representative in Gurgān and returned to Khurāsān.[4] But, instead of going back to Merv, he went to Nīshāpūr,[5] where apparently he was planning to settle the Syrian troops. We have no information on how and where exactly this settlement was planned, but it is possible that Yazīd had in mind the establishment of another "Wāsiṭ" in Khurāsān. This was probably a calculated move to make it clear to the Arab tribesmen of Khurāsān that they were no longer the centre of power in the province and henceforth the government's

1 See above, p. 75.
2 Ṭabarī, vol. II, p. 1327.
3 Ṭabarī, vol. II, pp. 1318–35; Yaʿqūbī, *Tārīkh*, vol. II, p. 355; Balādhurī, *Futūḥ*, pp. 335–8. The reports about the amount of this booty as given in Ṭabarī (vol. II, pp. 1320, 1321, 1325, 1329) and Balādhurī (*Futūḥ*, pp. 337–8) on the authority of Abū Mikhnaf and Madāʾinī are rather confusing, because Ṭabarī and Balādhurī do not agree even when they quote the same authority. However, the great size of the booty is clearly indicated. Furthermore, it is implied in the fact that Yazīd, after the distribution of the stipends and the shares of his men, was left with twenty-five or twenty-six million dirhams according to Madāʾinī, twenty million according to Ibn Aʿtham (vol. II, p. 161 B), or four million according to an anonymous report in Ṭabarī (vol. II, p. 1334).
4 Ṭabarī, vol. II, p. 1353; Balādhurī, *Futūḥ*, p. 338.
5 Yaʿqūbī, *Tārīkh*, vol. II, p. 355; Ibn Aʿtham, *Futūḥ*, vol. II, p. 165 A.

representative, supported by the imperial troops, would have the upper hand.

As for Transoxiana, Yazīd appointed his son Mukhallad as his representative in Samarqand and probably made him responsible for the whole of Soghdiana.[1] Mukhallad is reported to have made only a minor raid in the Buttām mountains.[2] Yazīd's refraining from any conquests in this region is an indication of the policy soon to be openly stated by ʿUmar II of the complete withdrawal of the Arabs from Transoxiana. On the other hand, Yazīd's military activities in Gurgān and Ṭabaristān could also indicate a policy of consolidating the conquests already achieved by the Arabs, before making any more in new directions. However, the very sudden death of Sulaymān, early in 99/717, did not allow him to implement and make clear his policy himself as was to be done by his very carefully selected successor, ʿUmar II.

3 *The distribution of the revenues from Khurāsān*

The news of the death of Sulaymān reached Yazīd while he was in Nīshāpūr, and there he waited for instructions from ʿUmar II.[3] The latter dismissed Yazīd from the governorship of Iraq and presumably from its dependency Khurāsān, and proceeded with a new organization of this extensive governorship. He divided it into three separate governorships—Kūfa, Baṣra and Khurāsān—appointing an independent governor to each.[4] This does not mean at all that ʿUmar II was proposing a decentralization of the empire. On the contrary, he followed a policy of more centralization with all the authority concentrated in his own hands, and of keeping a close watch on his governors in the various parts of the empire.

Yazīd, dismissed from his position, returned to Iraq, where he was arrested, according to ʿUmar II's orders, by ʿAdiyy ibn Arṭā, the new governor of Baṣra.[5] Although we do not have any reports about what happened to the Syrian troops which accompanied Yazīd to Khurāsān, in all probability they returned to Iraq, since we have no reports of their being in Khurāsān in

[1] Yaʿqūbī, *Tārīkh*, vol. II, p. 356; Ibn Aʿtham, *Futūḥ*, vol. II, p. 156B; Ṭabarī, vol. II, p. 1324.
[2] Gibb, *Arab Conquests*, p. 54; Balādhurī, *Futūḥ*, p. 425.
[3] Ibn Aʿtham, *Futūḥ*, vol. II, p. 165A. [4] Ṭabarī, vol. II, p. 1346.
[5] *Ibid.*, p. 1350; Ibn Aʿtham, *Futūḥ*, vol. II, p. 167A.

the reign of ʿUmar II and there is reason to believe that he ordered them to be withdrawn from this province. This also could be related to the dismissal of Yazīd ibn al-Muhallab. From Ibn Aʿtham we learn that even Sulaymān had thought of recalling Yazīd from Khurāsān.[1] It is stated in our sources that Yazīd, who depended on the Syrian troops to enforce his authority in Khurāsān, had neglected the Arab tribesmen there, including his own kinsmen from al-Azd. He also showed some favouritism towards his Syrian troops, probably in the distribution of the booty.[2] Naturally, this would give rise to complaint from the Arab tribesmen, who were against the increasing authority of the governor, particularly when it was imposed with the help of the Syrian troops, whom they considered strangers. After Yazīd had been dismissed, a delegation was sent from the tribesmen of Khurāsān to voice these complaints to the authorities in Baṣra, in the presence of Yazīd who was still there under the custody of the new governor. This delegation asserted, in no uncertain terms, their objection to the policy of bringing the Syrian troops to Khurāsān and emphatically denied Yazīd's right to misappropriate what they considered their own money.[3]

ʿUmar II had his own grievances with regard to Yazīd's misappropriation of the income from that province. Yazīd was arrested on the pretext that he had not delivered to the treasury the share promised to Sulaymān.[4] Yazīd, in a letter to Sulaymān, after informing the latter about his conquests in Gurgān and Ṭabaristān, continued: "and I have acquired from the fifth of what God caused to return to the Muslims, after delivering to each one whatever belongs to him, from the *fay'* and the *ghanīma*, six million [dirhams], and I shall carry [send] that to *Amīr al-Mu'minīn*".[5] This statement is related by Madā'inī as well as Ibn Aʿtham, but the latter gives us more information about Yazīd's handling of the *fay'* and *ghanīma*, from which it is clear that Yazīd had combined the hitherto separate income from what he called *fay'* with the income that he called *ghanīma*, and he proposed to send the fifth of the total to Sulaymān.[6] In doing this Yazīd

1 Ibn Aʿtham, *Futūḥ*, vol. II, p. 162A.
2 *Ibid.*, pp. 127A–127B; Ṭabarī, vol. II, p. 1313; Yaʿqūbī, *Tārīkh*, vol. II, p. 355.
3 Ibn Aʿtham, *Futūḥ*, vol. II, pp. 167A–8B.
4 Ṭabarī, vol. II, p. 1350; Ibn Aʿtham, *Futūḥ*, p. 167A.
5 Ṭabarī, vol. II, pp. 1334–5; Ibn Aʿtham, *Futūḥ*, vol. II, p. 161B, he gives the amount as twenty million.
6 Ibn Aʿtham, *Futūḥ*, vol. II, pp. 158B, 161A, 161B.

had infringed on what the Arab tribesmen of Khurāsān considered their own. It is also clear that ʿUmar II had accepted this arrangement and that he only ordered Yazīd to be brought to account when he did not deliver it to the treasury.

This whole situation suggests that there was a misunderstanding, or rather a conflict, involving the Arab tribesmen of Khurāsān, the governor of the province and *Amīr al-Mu'minīn* himself. This conflict centred around what belonged to whom or, at least, who claimed what, in respect of the income (*amwāl*) accruing from the *fay'* and *ghanīma* from Khurāsān. If we try to seek the answer to this problem in the principles laid down by the *Qur'ān* as applied by the Prophet, we find that Løkkegaard was right in saying that, "according to the *Qur'ān*, Muḥammad had free scope in his dealing with the booty".[1] But what was accorded to the Prophet in his lifetime was not accorded to his successors, particularly when the conquests yielded more and more returns to the Muslims. The system developed by *Amīr al-Mu'minīn* ʿUmar ibn al Khaṭṭāb was primarily concerned with Iraq, and it did not take into account the sort of situation that arose in Khurāsān, where the Arab tribesmen were settled in a land far from home, in an almost constant state of war, and were in a position to demand what they believed to be their right. On the other hand, the central government under the Umayyads was gradually trying to assert its rights to a greater share of the income from this rich province. The struggle between these two sides is an outstanding example of the circumstances in which the system of the distribution of the income from the conquered lands was developed until it reached the stage explained to us by the Muslim jurists. Fortunately, we have enough material, thanks to Ibn Aʿtham, to enable us to follow the different phases of this struggle until it reached this significant stage during the governorship of Yazīd ibn al-Muhallab and the reign of ʿUmar II.

The income from Khurāsān was derived mainly from two sources: one was the booty won on the battlefield, and the other was the tribute paid by the different districts of the region according to the peace treaties concluded with the conquerors. We shall not try to identify any of these items by any specific term lest the issue be confused, because it seems that the terms applied to them differed according to the claims of the parties involved. We

[1] F. Løkkegaard, *Islamic Taxation in the Classic Period*, Copenhagen, 1950, p. 42.

recall that at the very beginning of the Arab arrival at Khurāsān, Qays ibn al-Haytham, the leader of the garrison in Merv in 32/653, was responsible for collecting the *kharāj* and sending it to the governor, ʿAbdullah ibn ʿĀmir, in Baṣra.[1] The *kharāj* then could not have been other than the tribute. We do not hear of any problems arising from the distribution of this tribute, or the booty won in the campaigns undertaken by the governor of Baṣra in Khurāsān at that time.

The first problem we hear about occurred in the governorship of al-Ḥakam ibn ʿAmr al-Ghifārī, probably in 47/667, who was sent to Khurāsān at the head of an army. Muʿāwiya, apparently trying to make use of the principle of *sawāfī* applied by the Prophet, ordered al-Ḥakam to choose and set aside for him all the cash he had acquired in Khurāsān and not to divide it among his men.[2] Al-Ḥakam, who did not share Muʿāwiya's point of view and who considered the tribute was collected by virtue of the army's presence, and that this as well as the booty won in his campaign was *ghanīma* for his men, rejected Muʿāwiya's instructions and sent him only one-fifth of it, dividing the rest among the Arab tribesmen.[3] This action of al-Ḥakam was naturally supported by the tribesmen, and it established a precedent asserting the right of the tribesmen in Khurāsān to four-fifths of the tribute collected there as well as of four-fifths of the booty won on the battlefield. The rest, i.e. a fifth of each, was sent to the *Amir al-Muʾminīn* as his legitimate right, in a strict application of the principle laid down in the *Qurʾān*, "Know that a fifth of what ye have won belongs to Allah, to his apostle, his family, to the orphan, the needy and the traveller, if ye believe in Allah",[4] and also in keeping with the ancient Arab tradition of giving a certain portion of the booty to their chiefs.[5] In this case, the Arab tribesmen held Muʿāwiya to be the chief as well as the recognized authority to deal with the fifth as allocated by the *Qurʾān*.

Although Muʿāwiya tried successfully in the governorship of ʿUbaydullah ibn Ziyād 54/674 to extract more of the tribute from

[1] Ṭabarī, vol. II, p. 65; see also above, p. 25.

[2] Løkkegaard, p. 43; Ibn Sallam, pp. 7, 11–12; al-Jāḥiẓ, *al-Ḥayawān*, Cairo, 1938–45, vol. I, p. 330.

[3] Ṭabarī, vol. II, p. 110; Ibn Aʿtham, *Futūḥ*, vol. I, p. 170 A; Ibn al-Athīr, *Kāmil*, vol. III, p. 391.

[4] Sūra, VIII, 41.

[5] Al-Jāḥiẓ, *Ḥayawān*, vol. I, p. 330.

Khurāsān, the tribesmen scored another victory against the central government under the leadership of Alsam ibn Zurʿa, and had him appointed to watch over the finances of the province so that the central government would not infringe their rights.[1] Under Yazīd I, in the governorship of Salm ibn Ziyād, 61–4/681–4, the tribesmen gained a further victory and definitely established their right to all the tribute collected in Khurāsān. From that time on, it is reported that only the fifth of the booty won on the battlefield was sent to the central treasury. But the victory of the tribesmen was not complete. They had to concede that any tribute paid on the conclusion of a peace treaty, after any military action had been undertaken against a certain place, *ṣulḥ ʿājil*, should be considered as part of the booty won on the battlefield. Thus the central treasury would be entitled to one-fifth of it in the year of the specific campaign but not in the following years.

This principle was still in application in Qutayba's governorship. When he concluded a peace treaty with Samarqand in the year 93/712, of which the full text is preserved by Ibn Aʿtham, he accepted a tribute of two million dirhams for that same year (*ʿājila*), and 200,000 dirhams for each of the following years; then he sent one-fifth of the two million dirhams to the central treasury after the campaign. Ibn Aʿtham, who is very consistent in reporting the share sent to the central treasury, does not report any other portion of the yearly tribute sent there from Khurāsān, starting from the governorship of Salm Ibn Ziyād until the governorship of Yazīd ibn al-Muhallab. The term *ghanā'im*, which had been used by al-Ḥakam ibn ʿAmr to indicate all the income from the province, both the tribute and the booty won in the battlefield, was now applied to this same booty in addition to any tribute paid as a *ṣulḥ ʿājil*, thus excluding the yearly tribute collected in Khurāsān, which was now kept there.[2] Of course, the *ʿaṭā'* of the *muqātila* in this province, and also the expenditure involved in preparing the various expeditions, were taken out of the income from the tribute. We have no information about the way any remaining income, should there be any, was disposed of, though the fact that al-Mufaḍḍal had no treasury while he was

[1] See above, pp. 37–8.

[2] Ibn Aʿtham, *Futūḥ*, vol. I, p. 232A, and vol. II, pp. 90A, 135A, 138B, 141A, 143A, 144A, 144B, 145B, 158A, 161A; Balādhurī, *Futūḥ*, p. 421.

governor of Khurāsān[1] may indicate that it was divided among the Arab tribesmen or possibly their tribal chiefs.

Yazīd ibn al-Muhallab's new system was an attempt to establish more rights for the central government to the income from Khurāsān, and was a challenge to the long-established rights of the Arab tribesmen there. Besides depriving them of a great part of their income through the participation of the Syrian troops, Yazīd was proposing to cut down that income by giving a new share to the central government. This share was the fifth of what he called *fay'*, i.e. the yearly tribute collected peacefully in Khurāsān. It is no wonder then that the Arab tribesmen of Khurāsān protested vigorously against Yazīd's, or rather the central authority's, encroachments on their rights so that ʿUmar II had to interfere to put an end to their grievances.

4 *ʿUmar II, a Muslim statesman*

In spite of the great amount of material we have in our sources about the short rule of ʿUmar II, we find very little concerned directly with Khurāsān. ʿUmar II first, in 99/717, appointed al-Jarrāḥ ibn ʿAbdillah al-Ḥakamī as governor for the separate governorship of Khurāsān.[2] Though al-Jarrāḥ was trained in al-Ḥajjāj's school, he also served under Yazīd ibn al-Muhallab as his representative in Wāsiṭ.[3] According to al-Balādhurī, al-Jarrāḥ sent a minor expedition, under ʿAbdullah ibn Maʿmar al-Yashkurī, to the Jaxartes provinces, which met with ignominious failure.[4] However, as the same source states that the leader of this expedition was killed during the campaign of Yazīd ibn al-Muhallab in Gurgān at an earlier date, there is some doubt about the report's authenticity.[5] From Madā'inī we learn that it was only a very minor raid in Khuttal, which was undertaken on the initiative of a certain tribal chief, not on that of al-Jarrāḥ.[6]

In any case, it is certain that there were no major expeditions in the governorship of al-Jarrāḥ, and indeed in the reign of ʿUmar II. Instead, we are told that the latter had written to the princes of Transoxiana, inviting them to accept Islam, and that

[1] See above, p. 62.
[2] Ṭabarī, vol. II, p. 1350; Yaʿqūbī, *Tārīkh*, vol. II, p. 362; Ibn Aʿtham, *Futūḥ*, vol. II, p. 169B.
[3] Ṭabarī, vol. II, pp. 1310, 1354.
[4] Balādhurī, *Futūḥ*, p. 426; Gibb, *Arab Conquests*, p. 54.
[5] Balādhurī, *Futūḥ*, pp. 336–7.
[6] Ṭabarī, vol. II, p. 1353.

some of them actually became converted.[1] ʿUmar II instructed al-Jarrāḥ to invite the local population in Khurāsān to accept Islam, saying that whoever did so should be exempted from the *jizya* (in Balādhurī, *kharāj*), enlisted in the *dīwān* and treated like the rest of the Muslims, having the same duties and sharing the same rights.[2] According to Madāʾinī, ʿUmar II took this action when a complaint reached him that 20,000 men of the *mawālī* were taking part in the campaigns without receiving the *ʿaṭā*ʾ, and a like number of the converts were still paying the *kharāj*. In the same complaint al-Jarrāḥ was also accused of being prejudiced in favour of his people, the Arabs, against the others in Khurāsān, and as a disciple of al-Ḥajjāj his rule was oppressive.[3] Allowing for some exaggeration in these complaints, they would still indicate some elements of unrest among the Iranian population of Khurāsān. However, the number reported to have been converted at that time is only 4,000 persons,[4] which shows that as late as 100/718, and in spite of the promise of exempting the converts from the tribute, Islam was not yet widespread in Khurāsān.

Al-Jarrāḥ's qualities as a military leader, as proved later in his career,[5] were much better than his qualities as an administrator. He himself wrote to the ruler complaining that he could not handle the situation in Khurāsān except by using extreme measures, which ʿUmar forbade him to do.[6] Al-Jarrāḥ, feeling his weakness vis-à-vis the tribal chiefs, had tried to form a party of his own by using gifts, naturally mostly from the income of the province, to attract supporters.[7] All these factors made his stay in Khurāsān impossible, and after seventeen months in office he was recalled by ʿUmar II.[8]

On the advice of the man long acquainted with Khurāsan, Abū Mijlaz Lāḥiq al-Sadūsī, ʿUmar II appointed ʿAbdurraḥman ibn Nuʿaym al-Ghāmidī as governor of Khurāsān, but only for *al-ḥārb wa al-ṣalah*, i.e. all administration excluding fiscal affairs, and with him for *al-kharāj*, fiscal affairs, was ʿAbdurraḥman ibn

[1] Balādhurī, *Futūḥ*, p. 426.
[2] Ṭabarī, vol. II, p. 1354; Balādhurī, *Futūḥ*, p. 426; Ibn Saʿd, vol. V, p. 285.
[3] Ṭabarī, vol. II, p. 1354.
[4] Ibn Saʿd, vol. V, p. 285.
[5] Ṭabarī, vol. II, p. 1453; Balādhurī, *Futūḥ*, p. 206.
[6] Ṭabarī, vol. II, p. 1355; Balādhurī, *Futūḥ*, p. 426.
[7] Balādhurī, *Futūḥ*, p. 427.
[8] Ṭabarī, vol. II, p. 1352.

ʿAbdillah al-Qushayrī,[1] who was replaced later by ʿUqba ibn Zurʿa al-Ṭāʾī.[2] In contrast with the rough al-Jarrāḥ al-Ḥakamī, ʿAbdurraḥman ibn Nuʿaym, the new governor, was mild and lenient, and this was precisely the reason he was chosen by ʿUmar II. On the other hand, ʿAbdurraḥman al-Qushayrī, who was appointed for *al-kharāj*, was a strong, capable man.[3] ʿUmar II instructed his new governor to withdraw all the Arabs from Transoxiana, and not to undertake any expedition in any direction.[4] The Arab tribesmen refused to obey the order for withdrawal from Transoxiana on the pretext that there was no room for them in Merv.[5] Shortly after, the Soghdians withdrew their allegiance, though Bukhārā seems to have continued to be under Arab rule.[6]

ʿUmar II also issued instructions to ʿUqba ibn Zurʿa al-Ṭāʾī to collect the tribute (*kharāj*) without oppression and, should there be a surplus after distributing the stipends, to divide it among the needy in Khurāsān. In case the *kharāj* should not cover the stipends, ʿUmar offered to send money to Khurāsān to offset the shortage.[7] This was obviously intended to eliminate one of the grievances of the Arab tribesmen of Khurāsān. It took ʿUmar II almost two years to concede this point—that all the tribute in Khurāsān should be distributed to the tribesmen—but their continual pressure during the governorship of al-Jarrāḥ finally forced him to do so. As for the other point which the tribesmen in Khurāsān bitterly resented, namely the introduction of the Syrian troops, it was fortunately ʿUmar's policy for the whole empire to eliminate them. ʿUmar II realized that Sulaymān's sending of the Syrian troops to Khurāsān was in fact an extension of ʿAbdulmalik and Ḥajjāj's policy in this part of the empire. In the light of the opposition of Sulaymān to this particular policy, it is hard to believe that he intended to continue his rule on the same lines. However, ʿUmar II definitely established the principle that the empire should be ruled without the help of the Syrian troops. In Khurāsān we do not find any traces of them during his time, and even in Iraq their numbers seem to have been greatly reduced.

1 Ṭabarī, vol. II, pp. 1354–6; Balādhurī, *Futūḥ*, p. 427; Yaʿqūbī, *Tārīkh*, vol. II, pp. 362–3.
2 Ṭabarī, vol. II, p. 1366.
3 *Ibid.*, p. 1356.
4 *Ibid.*, p. 1365; Yaʿqūbī, *Tārīkh*, vol. II, pp. 362–3.
5 Ṭabarī, vol. II, p. 1365.
6 *Ibid.*, p. 1418; Gibb, *Arab Conquests*, pp. 55–6.
7 Ṭabarī, vol. II, p. 1366.

ʿUmar II was an Umayyad and an Arab, but he considered himself first and foremost as a Muslim statesman. He was not trying to destroy the Arab empire nor was he planning to sabotage Umayyad rule. He was trying to change the whole structure to a Muslim empire. He realized that the Arab rule established by Muʿāwiya had resulted, after much strife, in the Syrian domination under ʿAbdulmalik. This was bitterly resented in Iraq and then in Khurāsān, and was ultimately leading to the breakdown of the empire. To ʿUmar II it seemed that the way to prevent this imminent breakdown was not by using the force of Syrian arms but by substituting for it an ideology around which all his subjects would rally. The ideology was there, and all that was needed was to apply its principles to all the members of society without discrimination, giving everybody the same rights in return for the same duties.

Naturally, the first step was to persuade the non-Muslim subjects to become Muslims, and this was precisely what he proposed to do in Transoxiana and Khurāsān as well as in the rest of the empire. In his rescript circulated to all his governors, which Gibb believes "carries every indication of genuineness",[1] ʿUmar II wrote:

Wherefore, whosoever accepts al-Islam, whether Christian or Jew or Magian, of those who are now subject to the *jizya* and who joins himself to the body of the Muslims in their abode, *dar*, and who forsakes his abode wherein he was before, he shall enjoy all the privileges of the Muslims and shall be subject to all the duties laid upon them, and it is their duty to associate with him and to treat him as one of themselves.[2]

As noticed by Gibb, the rescript avoids the term *mawālī*,[3] a fact which suggests that ʿUmar II was trying to underline that citizenship in the new society was going to be based on being a Muslim and not on being a member or a client of a certain tribe. He realized that the maintenance of the empire required not only the assimilation of the Arab tribesmen to the structure of the Arab empire, but also the assimilation of the different subjects to a united

[1] H. A. R. Gibb, "The Fiscal Rescript of ʿUmar II", *Arabica*, Tome II, Fascicule I, janvier 1955, Leiden, 1955, pp. 1–16, at p. 2.

[2] Ibn ʿAbdilḥakam, *Sīratu-ʿUmar ibn ʿAbdilʿazīz*, Cairo, 1927, pp. 94–5, translated by Gibb, "Rescript of ʿUmar II", p. 3.

[3] Gibb, "Rescript of ʿUmar II", p. 8.

Muslim community. In keeping with his policy, ʿUmar II emphasized that the *ʿaṭā'* was not to be given to the *muqātila* by virtue of their Arab race, but by their acceptance of enrolment in the army. While he denied the *ʿaṭā'* to the Arab tribesmen who did not enrol as *muqātila*, he decreed it for the non-Arab Muslims who accepted this obligation.[1] He also "reasserted the principle that converts become liable only to the taxes imposed on Muslims in the like occupations".[2] In other words, all Muslim citizens, Arabs or non-Arabs, should have the same rights, the same obligations and in principle be treated equally in matters of taxation.

ʿUmar II laid down the general principles of a long-term policy for the whole empire, while at the same time instructing his governors how to implement this policy according to the specific circumstances in each province. Again, because of his short reign, the efficacy of his policy could not be sufficiently tested, though its impact outlived its duration. Khurāsān provided the ideal circumstances for its implementation. There, in Merv and in the surrounding villages, was a relatively large Arab community which had been living in close proximity to the local Iranian population for almost half a century. This local Iranian community had never had real grievances against Arab rule. Furthermore, they had co-operated with the Arabs, and Islam had already struck some roots amongst them. With some encouragement a complete assimilation could be brought about, and it could serve as a good example for the whole province if not the whole empire. At first ʿUmar II thought he could undertake the same experiment in Soghdiana, probably making use of the Arab colony in Bukhārā and the established garrison in Samarqand. When this met with little, if any, success, he decided to concentrate on Khurāsān, at least for the time being, and ordered a complete withdrawal from Transoxiana. However, he did not make any effort to enforce his will when the Arab tribesmen stationed there defied it, probably hoping that his policy would be served just as well by their staying there.

Turning to Khurāsān, he definitely eliminated all the grievances of the Arabs and even went so far as to appease them by appointing a governor like ʿAbdurraḥman ibn Nuʿaym. As for the Iranian population, he instructed his governor, al-Jarrāḥ, to

[1] Ibn ʿAbdilḥakam, p. 95; Gibb, "Rescript of ʿUmar II", pp. 3, 9.

[2] Gibb, "Rescript of ʿUmar II", p. 16.

invite them to accept Islam, promising them remission from the *jizya* and complete equality with the Arab settlers. Those who accepted Islam and joined the *muqātila* were naturally exempted from their *jizya* in any form, and became entitled to the *ʿaṭā'*, and the ruler offered to send money to Khurāsān if the income from the province was not sufficient to pay all the stipends. As for those who accepted Islam but preferred not to join the *muqātila,* their situation demands some explanation. The principle laid down by ʿUmar II was that their *jizya* should be remitted and they should be treated like the Arabs. As we know that each province had a different system of taxation, particularly of land, it is assumed that the Arabs ʿUmar II meant were the Arabs settled in Khurāsān. Thus, if we can elucidate the system of taxation regarding the Arabs and non-Arabs in Khurāsān, previous to ʿUmar's reform, we can find out exactly how these converts were treated under the new rules. As we know, at the time of the conquest the chiefs or *dahāqīn* of the different cities and districts in Khurāsān had negotiated peace treaties with the Arabs, according to which the relationship between the conquerors and the conquered people was determined. As far as we know, until the time of ʿUmar II nothing had happened to change the situation created by these treaties. Each treaty stipulated a fixed sum of money to be paid yearly to the Arabs as tribute. Also, according to these treaties, the assessment and collection of the taxes was left completely to the local chiefs and *dahāqīn*. The treaty of Merv stipulated that "it was their function to apportion the quota of their taxes and not that of the Muslims [Arabs] who would merely receive them".[1] As Dennett aptly put it, "what the Arabs had done was to create a series of protectorates".[2] These protectorates were left to handle their own financial administration without any interference from the Arab rulers. They continued to carry on the old Sāsānian system according to which there was a tax imposed on the land as well as on trade and other occupations. There was also a poll tax imposed on every person, peasant or city dweller, between the ages of twenty and fifty, graded according to income. The nobility, the warriors, the priests and the civil servants were exempt from this poll tax.[3]

[1] Balādhurī, *Futūḥ*, pp. 405–6; text translated by D. C. Dennett, *Conversion and the Poll Tax in Early Islam*, Cambridge, Mass., 1950, p. 118.

[2] Dennett, *Conversion*, p. 118.

[3] Christensen, *L'Iran*, pp. 118–24, 315–16, 362; Dennett, *Conversion*, p. 116.

Under Arab rule this system was continued, and the tax-payer continued to pay his land tax or trade tax in addition to the poll tax. We have mentioned before that in the governorship of Umayya ibn 'Abdillah (78/697), some Arab tribesmen complained that he supported the *dahāqīn* in extracting the "taxes" from them. We also suggested that these taxes were the land tax which was supposed to be paid by the original owners of the land. The Arabs who were able to purchase certain lands in some villages, had to pay the tax imposed on this land to the *dahāqīn*,[1] so from the beginning the rule was established in Khurāsān that a landowner, Arab or non-Arab, Muslim or non-Muslim, was supposed to pay a land tax according to the assessment of the *dahāqīn*. If the Arabs were paying a land tax, they certainly were not paying a poll tax, and that was precisely where the new reform of 'Umar II declared equality between the Arab and non-Arab Muslims in Khurāsān. Thus, the new rule regarding the converts in Khurāsān, who preferred not to join the *muqātila* and instead stayed on their land or continued to practise their occupation, was that they should not pay the poll tax, *jizya,* but they were not exempt from their land tax or trade tax. We have no information that the tribute was reduced to meet this decrease in income resulting from the remission of the poll tax on conversion. One would assume that, since the number of the converts at that time was not too great, the *dahāqīn* continued to pay the same tribute, in spite of the fact that the Arabs had actually committed a breach of contract by their interference in the assessment of the taxes, definitely the function of the *dahāqīn*. As we shall see later, this precedent created serious problems, and twenty years later Naṣr ibn Sayyār, governor of Khurāsān, had to step in and try to put an end to the abuses of the taxation system in this province.

'Umar's reign was a turning point in the history of Khurāsān. His death in 101/720 brought the rule of the opposition party to an end, and the events in Khurāsān and indeed in the whole empire took a sharp turn which ultimately led to the 'Abbāsid Revolution. Most important was the victory of 'Abdulmalik-Ḥajjāj's policy under Yazīd ibn 'Abdilmalik.

[1] See above, p. 47.

6

VICTORY FOR THE IMPERIALISTS

1 *The revolt of Yazīd ibn al-Muhallab*

The reign of Yazīd ibn ʿAbdilmalik 101–5/720–4 was inaugurated by a serious revolt in Iraq, led by the last surviving leader of the opposition party, Yazīd ibn al-Muhallab. The latter, who had been imprisoned by ʿUmar II for not delivering to the treasury its share of the income of Khurāsān and the booty from his expeditions in Gurgān and Ṭabaristān, accepted ʿUmar II's judgement and stayed in jail. Once he learned that the reign of ʿUmar II had come to an end, he actually walked out of his prison and descended on Baṣra.[1] There he entered the city without resistance, and almost immediately many men from all tribes rallied around him. Tribesmen from Bakr, Rabīʿa, Tamīm and Qays were among Yazīd's supporters, and even some of the Syrian troops in Iraq sided with him.[2] He was also joined by two small dissident groups —a Khawārij group led by al-Samaydaʿ, and an activist Murji'a group led by Ru'ba.[3] The governor of Baṣra, ʿAddiyy ibn Arṭā, who was supported by a small number of the Syrian troops, was also joined by men from all the tribes of Baṣra, amongst whom are specifically mentioned some from al-Azd, Yazīd's own tribe.[4] Yazīd's movement gained more momentum when he was able to defeat ʿAddiyy, who personally fell into Yazīd's hands. Men from all the tribes of Kūfa flocked to Yazīd's camp, and it is even mentioned that tribesmen from the frontier posts (*thughūr*) came to join him.[5]

Yazīd II, realizing the danger, called on his brother Maslama, the renowned general of the Umayyad house, and sent him to Iraq at the head of a big Syrian army. Yazīd ibn al-Muhallab's slogan was "the holy war (*jihād*) against the Syrians is more rewarding religiously than the *jihād* against the Turks or the Daylamites".[6] His oath of allegiance was "to uphold the Book of

[1] Ṭabarī, vol. II, pp. 1359–61.
[2] *Ibid.*, pp. 1382–3.
[3] *Ibid.*, pp. 1386, 1389.
[4] *Ibid.*, p. 1381.
[5] *Ibid.*, p. 1397.
[6] *Ibid.*, p. 1391; Ibn Aʿtham, *Futūḥ*, vol. II, p. 172B.

God and the traditions of the Prophet, and to prevent the *jund* (Syrian troops) from stepping on our lands; further, the policy of al-Ḥajjāj must not be reimposed on us".[1] Twenty years after the mutiny of Ibn al-Ash'ath, Yazīd was raising the same objection to the presence of the Syrian troops in Iraq, but for other reasons. Ibn al-Ash'ath was not against al-Ḥajjāj's expansionist policies; he was objecting to being sent to the remote region of Sīstān while the Syrian troops were staying comfortably in Iraq. Yazīd's revolt was against the reimposition of the basic principles of the expansionist imperialist policies, including, of course, the use of Syrian troops in Iraq. Certain traditions claim that Yazīd had repudiated Umayyad rule and tried to transfer the office of *Amīr al-Mu'minīn* to any accepted member of Banū Hāshim and had even suggested that a certain Hāshmite be installed.[2] Other traditions relate that Yazīd called himself al-Qaḥṭānī, or that he raised the "black banner".[3] All of these traditions should be taken only as later romantic accounts of Yazīd's revolt. There is no evidence at all that Yazīd tried to supplant Umayyad rule by any other, and it is reported explicitly that he did not withdraw his allegiance from Yazīd II.[4]

While Sulaymān and 'Umar II were able to pursue their opposition to al-Ḥajjāj's policy by legitimate means because of their positions, Yazīd ibn al-Muhallab had no other way to stop the overwhelming tide but to resort to armed revolt. Wellhausen's attempt to find in Yazīd's revolt a tribal struggle between Azd-Rabī'a and Qays-Tamīm is certainly not borne out by our sources, and it is a strong proof of Wellhausen's misunderstanding, not only of the situation in the "Arab Kingdom", but also of these sources.[5] The most important aspect of this whole episode is that while some of the Syrian troops were reported to have joined Yazīd's revolt, the Arab tribesmen of Khurāsān, especially al-Azd, Yazīd's own kinsmen, did not support his revolt. When he tried to persuade them by sending his brother Mudrik to seek their support, the Azdites co-operated with the Tamīmites to keep him out of Khurāsān.[6] The Arab tribesmen of Khurāsān who were satisfied with the policy of 'Umar II saw no reason to

[1] Ṭabarī, vol. II, p. 1398.
[2] *'Uyūn*, pp. 22, 29, 30.
[3] al-Dhahabī, vol. IV, p. 150.
[4] *'Uyūn*, p. 16.
[5] Wellhausen, p. 314.
[6] Ṭabarī, vol. II, p. 1390; and a clearer version in Ibn al-Athīr, *Kāmil*, vol. V, p. 56.

revolt, particularly when Yazīd II had, so far, left 'Umar II's governor in charge of the province.

After a poor fight against Maslama's Syrian army, Yazīd ibn al-Muhallab was defeated, his followers dispersed and he himself killed on the battlefield.[1] Yazīd II, who wanted to erase any traces left of the opposition rule, combined the two important provinces of Iraq and Khurāsān in one governorship and entrusted it to his chief general, Maslama, in 102/720.[2] This was meant to stabilize Iraq, as well as to be a warning to the tribesmen of Khurāsān, in case they had any illusions about the new rule. Maslama sent his son-in-law, Sa'īd ibn 'Abdil'azīz, nicknamed Khudhayna, who was also an Umayyad, to Khurāsān as his governor.[3]

Sa'īd Khudhayna's governorship marks the beginning of a period lasting a quarter of a century in which the social and political situation in this region was developing rapidly to the point at which the Umayyad government and governors actually became unable to control it. Therefore it is necessary to pause and describe the situation in Khurāsān at this crucial stage.

2 *The varying interests of the Arabs and the Iranians in the east*

Although military colonies had been established in Bukhārā and Khwārizm, and Arab garrisons were stationed in Samarqand, Balkh and, temporarily, in a few other places, the bulk of the Arab tribesmen in Khurāsān were still in the oasis of Merv, and no attempt was made to settle them in any other part of the province. We have noticed that the process of assimilation of this Arab community and the local Iranian community had started as early as the time of 'Abdullah ibn Khāzim 64–72/683–91, but it was on a very small scale which did not upset the existing social pattern in that area. Qutayba's policy, though it was not directed towards the assimilation of these two groups, helped to bring the Arab tribesmen and some of the Iranian subjects closer together, if only on the battlefield, and as we have seen the result was their co-operation against Qutayba. Still, the two communities were kept separate.

[1] Ṭabarī, vol. II, pp. 1402–5.
[2] *Ibid.*, pp. 1416–17.
[3] *Ibid.*, pp. 1417–18.

The plan according to which the Arab tribesmen were brought to Khurāsān did not envisage the possibility of their settling down. They were meant to provide the necessary forces for furthering the Arab conquests, using Merv only as a winter camp and spending the rest of the year busy on the battlefield. Thus they were deliberately kept outside the structure of Iranian society, and were even organized, as we have noticed, by Qutayba along tribal lines to emphasize the division of the two communities. As for the Iranian population, the Arab conquest introduced no change in their social structure. As we know, Merv was a part of the Sāsānian empire, and thus the social structure there was the Sāsānian class system, according to which the local nobility (*dahāqīn*) enjoyed a very privileged position. They were certainly intent upon keeping their privileges and authority even if it meant defying their own sovereigns, as we have clearly seen from the episode of Māhūyeh and Yazdgird III. Under Arab rule, and in accordance with the treaties of capitulation, the *dahāqīn* managed to keep their status and their authority over the Iranian population, and the treaty of Merv particularly provided the best proof and assurance for the continuation of the old régime. When some of the Iranian subjects were converted, their social status does not seem to have changed. Though they were attached to the Arabs as *mawālī*, they were not integrated into the Arab community. They were used by the Arabs in their campaigns, and were tolerated or even encouraged by the *dahāqīn* as a sign of their co-operation with the Arab rulers. Another possibility is that these first *mawālī* were actually the remnants of the warrior class, left without work after the Arab conquest, and it was to the advantage of the *dahāqīn* to let the Arabs take this problem off their hands and pay them in the form of the '*aṭā*'. It was also advantageous to the Arabs to have such well-trained men in their ranks. In fact, it is reported in our sources that Qutayba used to assign to them some of the difficult tasks in his campaigns.[1] If the *dahāqīn* had lost their authority over a few thousand *mawālī*, the rest of the Iranian population was left under their direct control, and their privileged position continued unmolested, with the acquiescence, if not the support, of the Arabs.

It was not until the time of 'Umar II that this social structure was faced with a serious threat. 'Umar II's policy, aimed as it

[1] *Ibid.*, p. 1280.

was at the integration of the two communities into one Muslim community, would ultimately result in the demolishing of the old régime, not only in Merv but in all of Khurāsān. If complete assimilation was to be achieved, the Arab tribesmen could not be kept outside this social structure, and a suitable place would have to be found for them in it. This would not only change the basic structure of society, but would also do away with the *dahāqīn*'s authority over their subjects.

The *dahāqīn* realized that if they were to keep their privileged position the "old régime" had to be maintained, and the Arab tribesmen kept in their place outside the social structure. Naturally, the easiest way to achieve this was to encourage the policy of expansion, in the hope of keeping them as a fighting force continually engaged on the battlefield. But many of them were getting used to a new way of life and also beginning to realize the benefits of their position in Khurāsān. They were tending to settle down and make their living by peaceful means in preference to receiving the pension and taking part in the campaigns. However, they were not craftsmen and they were easily excluded from this activity; nor was it difficult for the *dahāqīn* to exclude them from farming, since they owned and controlled the land, and we have little evidence that much land was acquired by the Arabs at that time. The only occupation for which the Arabs were instinctively qualified, and in which they could use the wealth acquired from their share in the booty, was trade, particularly in such a place as Merv, located between Soghdiana and the rest of the empire. Also, as we shall see, a tendency clearly developed among the Arab tribesmen of Khurāsān not to join the expeditions, defying the governors' orders in this respect. Thus, while some of them were still attached to their nomadic background and favoured the policy of more conquests, others were becoming increasingly interested in a different way of life and tempted to settle down and take advantage of their new circumstances.

In a story told by Madā'inī we have a clear illustration of this difference in the attitude of the Arab tribesmen in Khurāsān, though the story itself should not be taken very seriously. Madā'inī relates that Yazīd ibn al-Muhallab had made a garden in his house in Khurāsān but, when Qutayba became governor there, he used this garden to shelter his camels. When the *marzbān* of Merv expressed his surprise at Qutayba's action, the latter said:

"My father was a *shuturbān* (camel driver), and Yazīd's father was a *bustāniān* (gardener)".[1] It might have seemed most natural for the *dahāqīn* to find common ground with the party favouring settlement, but, since this would have led in fact to the accelerated assimilation of the Arab tribesmen in the Iranian population and to the subsequent loss of their own power, they found it more politic to ally themselves to the party of expansion, putting more pressure on the central government to direct the tribesmen towards the battlefield instead of allowing them to turn to a more peaceful way of life.

Soghdiana had always been attractive to the Arabs of Khurāsān for its riches, and as an important step towards furthering the Arab conquests in this direction. Because of the political division of the area and because of the fact that they received no help from the Turks or the Chinese, the Soghdians were not able to resist the Arab advances.[2] Although the Arabs under the leadership of Qutayba were able to establish their rule there, the Soghdians, particularly in Samarqand, did not submit altogether. There was always a party of resistance, and at times it was successful in gaining the upper hand. Ṭarkhūn, the prince of Samarqand who had agreed to pay tribute to Qutayba, was quickly deposed and an opponent, Ghūrak, was elected in his place.[3] When 'Umar II ordered the general evacuation of the Arabs from Transoxiana, Samarqand withdrew its allegiance, but soon after it was restored without any military action from the Arab side. As there was a party for resistance, there was also a party for co-operation with the Arabs.[4] Since trade was the most important factor in Soghdian life, it is reasonable to assume that each party was motivated by its trade interests. The party for co-operation was in favour of keeping on good terms with the Arabs even at the price of paying a tribute, because they saw more profit in the flow of trade between Soghdiana and Khurāsān. The party for resistance was more interested in the trade with the east and was supported by the landowners who were for independence.[5] Ghūrak's problem was to keep a balance between the two parties, particularly when the party for resistance gained strength by the rise of the Turgesh power in the east. Under the Khan Sü-Lü (716–738), the Turgesh

[1] Ibn Qutayba, *Ma'ārif*, p. 283.
[2] Gibb, *Arab Conquests*, pp. 30–1.
[3] *Ibid.*, p. 42; Ṭabarī, vol. II, p. 1229.
[4] Gibb, *Arab Conquests*, p. 48; Ṭabarī, vol. II, p. 1365.
[5] See below, pp. 101–2.

tribes were able to assert their independence and win the hegemony of the western Turks. With the help of the Chinese they established a new kingdom in the Ili basin.[1] The Soghdians turned to the new rising power for help against the Arabs and for almost twenty years the latter had to fight the Turgesh armies to maintain Arab rule across the Oxus.

The Arabs were not all blind to the value of the east–west trade and, since Qutayba's time, there had been attempts to control the trade route across central Asia. Qutayba is reported to have sent an embassy to the Chinese court, probably for trade purposes as well as for political reasons.[2] The numerous Arab embassies to China that followed are evidence of the continued interest of the Arabs in the east–west trade.[3] The Arabs must have realized that the Soghdians were playing the major role in this trade and were consequently the natural partners of any aspirants to taking part in it. It was to be expected that those Arabs in Khurāsān who were interested in trade would favour a policy of conciliation towards the Soghdians, their would-be partners in the east–west trade.

3 *Sa'īd Khudhayna: conciliation or expansion?*

Now we shall try to find out what was the policy followed by the Umayyad government and its representatives in Khurāsān to meet these internal and external pressures until the end of the Umayyad period. At the same time we shall try to follow the reactions of the different parties to this policy in the light of their interests. Sa'īd Khudhayna does not seem to have deviated much from the policy of 'Umar II, except in a very few cases where his actions were influenced by external pressures threatening his hopes or plans. In other words, while willing to give 'Umar II's policy a good trial, he decided not to introduce any changes on his own initiative. The best example of his attitude is his campaigning policy. This was certainly not expansionist; on the contrary, he stayed on the defensive. When a small Turgesh force was sent under Köl-chur in 102/721 to help the Soghdians against the

[1] Gibb, *Arab Conquests*, pp. 59–60; H. A. R. Gibb, "Chinese Records of the Arabs in Central Asia", *Bulletin of the School of Oriental Studies* II (1922), pp. 613–22, at p. 615.

[2] Gibb, *Arab Conquests*, pp. 49–51; Gibb, "Invasion of Kashgar", p. 469; Ṭabarī, vol. II, p. 1280.

[3] Gibb, "Chinese Records", pp. 619–21.

Arabs, he satisfied himself with chasing the invaders out of Soghdiana.[1] It is reported specifically that although he crossed the Oxus twice, he did not advance beyond Samarqand.[2]

Sa'īd's attitude towards the Soghdians was one of extreme conciliation. He sent, as his representative in Samarqand, Shu'ba ibn Ẓuhayr, probably with the agreement of the *dahāqīn* there.[3] Shu'ba was probably the son of Ẓuhayr, an old acquaintance of the Soghdians through his association with Ḥurayth ibn Quṭba. He was accompanied to Samarqand by only twenty-five men, to be joined by another 200 men from Bukhārā, but he was able to handle the delicate situation there.[4] In the fight against the Turgesh, Ghūrak, prince of Samarqand, as Gibb notes, had outwardly at least supported the Arabs.[5] Khudhayna prohibited any plundering or raiding in Soghdiana, which is certainly a remarkable contrast to the attitude of the previous governors.[6] Most remarkable, and rather surprising, is that while the Arab governor was prohibiting plundering, Ḥayyān al-Nabaṭī, who was present with Khudhayna in this brief campaign in Soghdiana, is reported to have been eager to plunder the Soghdians, and vigorously tried to persuade the governor to attack them.[7] Of course as a representative of the *dahāqīn* of Merv, of whom he was a leading figure, Ḥayyān was advocating a policy of constant campaigning and trying to sabotage any chance that the Arab elements would establish trade relations with the Soghdians.[8] He must have realized that the continuation of 'Umar II's policy by the new governor, Khudhayna, was going to lead eventually to the destruction of his own class; consequently he tried to persuade the governor to change this policy. When he failed in this, he resorted to intriguing against Khudhayna, probably among the Arab tribesmen of Khurāsān. Finally the governor had him poisoned.[9] By getting rid of Ḥayyān, Sa'īd might have been able to keep the *dahāqīn* under control temporarily, but he could not apply the same method to the Arab leaders in Khurāsān who disagreed with his policy, and wanted instead a policy of expansion and more booty.

While this was happening in Khurāsān, Yazīd II recalled his

[1] Ṭabarī, vol. II, pp. 1421–8; Balādhurī, *Futūḥ*, p. 427; Gibb, *Arab Conquests*, p. 60.

[2] Ṭabarī, vol. II, p. 1430.

[3] *Ibid.*, pp. 1420–1.

[4] *Ibid.*, p. 1418.

[5] Gibb, *Arab Conquests*, p. 62.

[6] Ṭabarī, vol. II, pp. 1428, 1430.

[7] *Ibid.*, p. 1430.

[8] Balādhurī, *Futūḥ*, p. 337.

[9] Ṭabarī, vol. II, p. 1431.

brother Maslama from Iraq and appointed in his place 'Umar ibn Hubayra, from the school of al-Ḥajjāj. The new governor of Iraq and the East soon received a delegation from the dissatisfied Arab leaders of Khurāsān, led by Mujashshir ibn Muzāḥim al-Sulamī, himself a renowned military leader in Khurāsān,[1] who were complaining about Sa'īd Khudhayna.[2] It is now easy to understand why Sa'īd was nicknamed Khudhayna (little lady), probably by some of the Iranian elements in Khurāsān, while he was described by some Arabs as "a sword held over our heads".[3] His policy alienated two powerful groups in Khurāsān, and in 103/721–2 he was recalled and replaced by Yazīd's own choice, Sa'īd al-Ḥarashī.

4 *Sa'īd al-Ḥarashī and Muslim ibn Sa'īd: more assertion of the powers of the central government*

This new governor was a military leader who had just distinguished himself in the fight against Yazīd ibn al-Muhallab.[4] He was appointed by Yazīd II to Khurāsān and Transoxiana as far as Farghāna.[5] He sent ahead of him to Khurāsān Mujashshir ibn Muzāḥim, the military leader who had just been complaining to 'Umar ibn Hubayra about the policy of Khudhayna.[6] These were all strong indications of a change to a more aggressive policy.

The Soghdians appreciated this and a great number of them decided to emigrate to Farghāna. In spite of Ghūrak's pleas to them to stay and submit to Arab rule, they actually left before Ḥarashī's arrival.[7] It is strange that they did not choose to emigrate to the Turgesh lands rather than to the semi-independent kingdoms of Khujanda and Farghāna. It is also strange that they did not ask for help from the Turgesh, who did not appear at all in Transoxiana during the governorship of al-Ḥarashī, and left the Soghdians completely at his mercy. It is possible that the Turgesh were trying to consolidate their power and were not yet ready to meet a strong Arab army. It is also possible that these Soghdians had decided to move their trade centres further to the east away from Arab domination, while at the same time avoiding domination by the Turgesh. They do not seem to have

[1] *Ibid.*, p. 1544.
[2] *Ibid.*, p. 1436; Balādhurī, *Futūḥ*, p. 427.
[3] Ṭabarī, vol. II, p. 1431.
[4] *Ibid.*, p. 1438.
[5] Ibn A'tham, *Futūḥ*, vol. II, p. 178 A.
[6] Ṭabarī, vol. II, p. 1438.
[7] *Ibid.*, pp. 1439–40.

had any doubts about their acceptance by the king of Farghāna, but as it turned out he did not feel strong enough to antagonize the Arabs, and while he outwardly professed to assist the Soghdians, he secretly betrayed them and called in the Arabs against them.[1]

Al-Ḥarashī did not waste any time, and on his arrival in Khurāsān he announced his intention of leading an expedition into Transoxiana.[2] He first tried to persuade the Soghdians to return to their lands, but when they refused he proceeded to bring them back by force.[3] He advanced to Khujanda, and the Soghdians, receiving no help from the king of Farghāna, were obliged to surrender to the Arabs.[4] The nobles and the peasants, numbering between three and seven thousand, were massacred, but the merchants, of whom there were four hundred, were spared.[5] The eagerness of al-Ḥarashī to bring back the Soghdian merchants must indicate that he was not willing to let the Soghdian trade slip out of Arab control. By the end of this campaign 103–4/722 he had pacified all of Soghdiana and restored Arab rule over the whole area.[6] Along with the *mawālī* who took part in this expedition under the leadership of Sulaymān ibn Abī al-Sarī, we find mention of levies from Bukhārā, Shūmān and Khwārizm.[7]

Al-Ḥarashī sent to the central treasury the fifth of the booty won on the battlefield, but the income of the province was kept in Khurāsān and no part of it was sent either to Damascus or to the governor-general in Iraq.[8] Al-Ḥarashī was therefore maintaining the principle long established in Khurāsān and reasserted under ʻUmar II, that the income from the tribute should be disposed of in Khurāsān. ʻUmar ibn Hubayra was not satisfied with this arrangement and tried to persuade al-Ḥarashī to send part of the income to the central government.[9] When al-Ḥarashī refused to obey these instructions, he was dismissed in 104/723 and replaced by a new governor, who was particularly noted for his "honesty", i.e. readiness to carry out the central government's orders regarding the finances.[10]

The new governor was Muslim ibn Saʻīd, a grandson of Aslam

[1] Gibb, *Arab Conquests*, pp. 62–3.
[2] Ṭabarī, vol. II, p. 1438.
[3] *Ibid.*, p. 1440; Balādhurī, *Futūḥ*, p. 427.
[4] Ṭabarī, vol. II, pp. 1441–3.
[5] *Ibid.*, p. 1445.
[6] *Ibid.*, p. 1448; Balādhurī, *Futūḥ*, p. 427.
[7] Ṭabarī, vol. II, p. 1447.
[8] *Ibid.*, p. 1448; Ibn Aʻtham, *Futūḥ*, vol. II, p. 178B.
[9] Ṭabarī, vol. II, pp. 1456, 1459–60.
[10] *Ibid.*, p. 1458; Ibn Aʻtham, *Futūḥ*, vol. II, p. 179A.

ibn Zur'a whom we have known earlier as one of the leaders of the Arab tribesmen in Khurāsān. At the time of his arrival in 104/723 the situation looked promising. Transoxiana was quiet, the Turgesh had not yet posed a threat to the Arabs, the Iranian population seemed co-operative, and there were no signs of unrest after the poisoning of Ḥayyān, while the Arab tribesmen did not seem unhappy. The central government thought the time was ripe to assert more control over the province. Although Muslim advised 'Umar ibn Hubayra against appropriating any part of the income from the province, the measure rejected previously by al-Ḥarashī, Ibn Hubayra refused to take this advice, and Muslim was ordered to go ahead with the plan. This was to restrict the right of the Arab tribesmen to their stipends, and to send the rest of the yearly tribute to the central treasury. Ibn Hubayra also ordered his governor to require from the Arab leaders (*ashrāf*) whatever money they had already received over and above the amount needed to pay the stipends of their men.[1] This was contrary to the long-established principle of disposing of the tribute in Khurāsān itself, and the Arab tribesmen could not be expected to accept the central government's challenge of their hard-gained rights easily. However, since a great number of them were becoming increasingly interested in other sources of income, the challenge was accepted quietly.

The Arab tribesmen resorted to a more passive way of resisting the new measure. They simply refrained from joining the expeditions, and this tendency began to alarm the governor. He tried to persuade them to join by threats, but to no avail. Finally he had to appoint Naṣr ibn Sayyār specifically to compel the tribesmen to join the campaigns.[2] The use of force brought the dispute to a climax in Barūqān, a strategically situated village in the vicinity of Balkh. An Arab garrison was temporarily stationed there to protect the area against any surprise attacks from the Turgesh. In view of subsequent events, this measure was a military necessity dictated by the rise of Turgesh power and the threat it posed to the Arabs in the east. This Arab garrison depended completely on their income as *muqātila* and any cut in that income would affect them most of all. When Muslim, pressed for men to join his campaign of 106/724, sent Naṣr ibn Sayyār to force the garrison of Barūqān to join him, they refused and

[1] Ṭabarī, vol. II, pp. 1460–1. [2] *Ibid.*, pp. 1477–8.

fighting broke out between them and Naṣr's force. Though the incident is represented in our sources as a tribal clash between Muḍar and Yaman, it was not basically so; only chance circumstances gave it a tribal colour. The garrison of Barūqān was apparently composed mostly of Azdites and Bakrites, but there were also Tamīmites among them and they too fought against Naṣr. The leaders of the garrison were certainly not Tamīmites. Naṣr's force was, as in most cases, drawn from men from his own tribal grouping (Muḍar, i.e. Tamīm and Qays), but was also assisted by a group of levies from Chaghāniān. The incident itself, judging from the number of men reported to have been killed in the fighting, between eighteen and thirty, was not particularly serious.[1] It had no long-term effect on the relationship of the two antagonists, as is witnessed by their co-operation less than a year later against the policy of Muslim's successor.[2]

Muslim was instructed by 'Umar ibn Hubayra to appoint a chamberlain who could make peace with his Iranian subjects, and to appoint to the different districts individuals acceptable to the local population.[3] These instructions were faithfully executed by Muslim in the appointment of two persons to two important offices. He appointed Bahrām Sīs as *marzbān* of Merv.[4] There was no precedent for such an action on the part of the Arab governor of Khurāsān. It is, as far as we know, the first time an Arab governor had interfered in any appointment to any office in the local administration, particularly to such a high office. Hitherto, the administration had been left entirely in the hands of the local nobility and there is no evidence that they were not left free to choose their officials. The only measure the Arab governors are reported to have taken was to appoint representatives of their own to watch over the affairs of the different districts and, more important, to secure the delivery of the tribute. The new measure of appointing Bahrām Sīs as *marzbān* of Merv meant that he, as an appointee of the Arab governor, would rule over the Iranian population in the name of the Arab governor. This was a shrewd attempt to incorporate the local administration into the structure of the Arab government. The *dihqān* Bahrām Sīs, who was selected to start this experiment, was

1 *Ibid.*, pp. 1473–7; Ya'qūbī, vol. II, p. 374; Balādhurī, *Futūḥ*, p. 428.
2 See below, p. 108.
3 Ṭabarī, vol. II, p. 1481.
4 *Ibid.*, p. 1462.

certainly acceptable to the Iranian population, for we find echoes of his popularity among them in our sources.[1] To ensure the success of the new policy, 'Umar ibn Hubayra ordered a new office to be created. It was that of chamberlain, called by 'Umar *ḥājib* and called in Khurāsān *'alā al-khātam* (i.e. in charge of the seal). It was essential that the person selected for this office should be on good terms with the Iranian population, indicating the role he was to play regarding them. Tawba ibn Abī Usayd, himself a client of Banū al-'Anbar, well known for his strictness, honesty and efficiency, was appointed, and he handled the office so well that he was retained by Muslim's successor in Khurāsān.[2]

[1] *Ibid.*, p. 1688.

[2] *Ibid.*, pp. 1481–2.

7

THE TURGESH THREAT

I *The Day of Thirst*

Muslim ibn Sa'īd, in his governorship (104–6/723–5), led a campaign each year into Transoxiana. The first two met with little success. The third, and the last in Muslim's governorship, met disaster. In the Arabic sources it is known as the "Day of Thirst" (106/724). This was the first time the Arabs had encountered the full strength of the Turgesh armies, and the result was not promising for any future expeditions. In Gibb's words, "It was practically the last aggressive expedition of the Arabs into Transoxiana for fifteen years, but of much greater importance was the blow which it struck at Arab prestige. The roles were reversed; from now onwards the Arabs found themselves on the defensive and were gradually ousted from almost every district across the Oxus."[1] However, the remnants of the Arab army were able to retreat to Samarqand.

After Yazīd II's death in 105/724, his brother Hishām succeeded him, and he appointed Khālid al-Qasrī as his governor for Iraq and the East. In 106/724 Khālid appointed his brother Asad to replace Muslim in Khurāsān.[2] Asad arrived at Samarqand while Muslim was on his unfortunate campaign, and the only measure he was able to take was to appoint the more experienced 'Abdur-raḥman ibn Nu'aym to take command of the retreating army.[3] It is noteworthy that the *mawālī* and the levies from Samarqand were taking part in this expedition, while some of the Soghdians together with the forces of Shāsh and Farghāna fought on the side of the Turgesh.[4]

It must be kept in mind, while trying to follow developments in Khurāsān at this time, that the defeat which the Arabs suffered at the hands of the Turgesh was a severe blow not only to Arab prestige but also to the Arab position in the whole region. The Arabs must have realized the serious threat that the Turgesh

[1] Gibb, *Arab Conquests*, p. 66.
[2] Ṭabarī, vol. II, pp. 1478–80.
[3] *Ibid.*, pp. 1484–5.
[4] *Ibid.*, pp. 1478–9.

posed to Arab rule in the east, and the elimination of this threat became the cornerstone of Arab policy in Khurāsān until the downfall of the Turgesh.

In Asad's governorship (106–9/724–7), although the Turgesh penetrated deep into Soghdiana and appeared before Samarqand, the Arab front there remained quiet. Asad appointed al-Ḥasan ibn Abī al-'Amarraṭa of Kinda, who was on good terms with the Soghdians, as his representative in Samarqand, and he himself returned to Merv. Al-Ḥasan satisfied himself with being able to maintain Arab rule in Soghdiana without receiving any help from the headquarters in Khurāsān.[1] In Merv Asad continued the policy initiated by his predecessor, of incorporating the local administration into the Arab structure. Tawba was retained by Asad as *'alā al-khātam*,[2] and in all probability Bahrām Sīs was also kept as *marzbān* of Merv.

2 *Asad al-Qasrī: an unsuccessful attempt at an alliance with the Hephthalites against the Turgesh*

Asad then turned his activities to a completely unexpected area. Throughout his governorship he was busy leading expeditions into the mountainous regions of Gharchistān and Ghūr. In 108/726 he was reported to have attacked Khuttal; but when the prince called on the Turgesh for help, Asad quickly turned back to raid the Ghūr mountains.[3] These expeditions cannot have been taken for the sake of booty, and there is no evidence or suggestion in our sources that this area was a source of trouble to the Arabs, or that there were any signs of unrest. The Hephthalite principalities were firmly under Arab control, and had been since the time of Qutayba; and Asad in his expeditions certainly did not take any measures against them. The reasons behind Asad's activities in this area should be sought elsewhere.

We know that when Asad came to his governorship he was not accompanied by any fresh troops from Iraq or Syria. There is also evidence that the Arabs of Khurāsān were reluctant to join his expeditions against the Turgesh, a tendency which had become very clear in the governorship of Muslim and which continued

[1] *Ibid.*, pp. 1485–6; Balādhurī, *Futūḥ*, p. 428.

[2] Ṭabarī, vol. II, p. 1482.

[3] *Ibid.*, pp. 1488–9, 1492–3, 1496; Balādhurī, *Futūḥ*, p. 428; Gibb, *Arab Conquests*, p. 68.

under Asad.[1] The levies from Transoxiana would not be very dependable against an enemy of the Arabs, to whom these people looked for deliverance from the Arab yoke. Asad thought of a plan, which proved later to be workable; this was to strike up an alliance with the traditional enemies of the Turks, i.e. the Hephthalites. Since the Arabs were not an attractive ally against an enemy as formidable as the Turgesh, particularly under the prevailing circumstances, Asad proceeded to make a show of strength around the Hephthalite region. He subdued the nomadic elements in the mountains of Gharchistān, and those in the Ghūr mountains, who used to raid the more settled Hephthalite population around Harāt. This may explain his close friendship with Khurāsān, the *dihqān* of Harāt.[2]

Furthermore, Asad, in his attempt to appeal to the Hephthalites, started to move his headquarters from Merv to Balkh. He first moved the garrison from Barūqān to the city.[3] This may have antagonized Balkh's small population, and is probably why they nicknamed Asad *zāgh* (raven).[4] However, he went ahead with his plan and ordered the city to be rebuilt.[5] Although he did not move officially to Balkh until ten years later, his intentions at that time were very clear.

The alliance between Asad and the Hephthalites did not materialize at the time for two reasons. First, the Hephthalites were apparently reluctant to get involved against the Turgesh while the Arabs, their would-be allies, were in such a weak position. Second, the projected alliance was opposed by the Arabs of Khurāsān themselves. The tribesmen, probably persuaded by the *dahāqīn* of Merv, realized that if this plan succeeded the centre of power would shift from Merv to Balkh, and they would lose all the power and prestige they had enjoyed under the existing régime. We are told that Naṣr ibn Sayyār and his antagonists at Barūqān were united in their opposition to Asad's policy and went so far as to plot against him. Asad took the unusually harsh measure of punishing and humiliating these important Arab leaders in Khurāsān.[6] When he sent them to Iraq, his brother Khālid and Hishām realized that the price they had to pay for the alliance with the Hephthalites would practically be the loss of

[1] Ṭabarī, vol. II, p. 1482.
[2] *Ibid.*, pp. 1635–6.
[3] *Ibid.*, p. 1490.
[4] *Ibid.*, p. 1500.
[5] *Ibid.*, p. 1490.
[6] *Ibid.*, pp. 1498–9; Balādhurī, *Futūḥ*, p. 428.

Khurāsān itself. Subsequently, Asad was peremptorily recalled, and on his return he was accompanied by the "*dahāqīn* of Khurāsān",[1] who could not have been other than some of the Hephthalite princes who were in favour of an alliance with the Arabs.

3 *Ashras al-Sulamī, a good general but a poor governor*

After the failure of Asad's plan to use the Hephthalites against the Turgesh, Hishām had to find another way to meet this threat. Apparently he did not want to send any tribesmen from Iraq to add fuel to the fire, but since outside help was necessary to enable the army of Khurāsān to fight against the Turgesh, Hishām had no choice but to send some of the Syrian troops. We have no clear statement in our sources to this effect, but Ibn A'tham is the only source who states that Ashras, the new governor, came to Khurāsān in 109/727 at the head of an army.[2] Furthermore, Madā'inī, in reporting the campaign of al-Junayd in 112/730, attests the presence of Syrian troops in the Arab army, and we know that Junayd did not lead a Syrian army to Khurāsān.[3] The choice of Ashras ibn 'Abdillah al-Sulamī as the new governor is another indication that Syrian troops were sent to Khurāsān, because Ashras himself was one of the generals of the imperial army.[4] Judging from the part they played in the campaigns of Junayd,[5] these Syrian troops could not have been very numerous, but they were probably enough to help the governor to persuade the Arab tribesmen to join in the campaigns against the Turgesh. Hishām did not want to send a big Syrian army to Khurāsān for fear that he would antagonize the Arab tribesmen there, as had happened to Yazīd ibn al-Muhallab.

Another way of persuading the tribesmen was to eliminate the grievance they had had since the governorship of Muslim ibn Sa'īd (104–6/723–5), namely the appropriation of part of the revenue from the province. Hishām meant to make it clear to the Arab tribesmen of Khurāsān that this practice was going to be discontinued when he made Khurāsān a separate governorship under Ashras, while the latter continued to be under the supervision of Khālid al-Qasrī, the governor-general of Iraq.[6]

1 Ṭabarī, vol. II, p. 1501.
2 Ibn A'tham, *Futūḥ*, vol. II, p. 202B.
3 Ṭabarī, vol. II, pp. 1527, 1533, 1539.
4 Ibn A'tham, *Futūḥ*, vol. II, p. 202A.
5 Ṭabarī, vol. II, pp. 1533, 1539.
6 *Ibid.*, p. 1504.

Ashras was well received in Khurāsān, and the people were delighted by his coming, and probably still more so by the arrangements which accompanied it. He was a man of such good reputation that he was called *al-kāmil*, the perfect.[1] But very soon, after he had stayed a while in Khurāsān, he was nicknamed, by both Arabs and Iranians, *jaghr*, a Persian word meaning frog.[2] Madā'inī states that Ashras used to attend personally to every affair, whether important or not.[3] Even if we credit Ashras with being a "perfect" man, he, like any military man without much experience in political affairs, would not necessarily be expected to be a successful governor, particularly of a province such as Khurāsān with its many complicated problems. In attending to every detail he would complicate the situation ever more, creating further dissatisfaction among Arabs and Iranians alike.

Yaḥya ibn Ḥuḍayn, the old Arab leader of Bakr in Khurāsān, described Ashras as "the traitor of his own people".[4] It is very possible that Ashras, in a drive to recruit men from the Iranian population, had allied himself more with the *dahāqīn* of Khurāsān, who saw in him the man to help them keep the Arab tribesmen on the battlefield. In fact Muqātil, the son of Ḥayyān al-Nabaṭī, became one of Ashras's chief advisers.[5]

Madā'inī informs us that Ashras was the first governor of Khurāsān to form the *rābiṭa* and he placed them under the command of 'Abdulmalik ibn Dithār al-Bāhilī, one of the Arab leaders in Khurāsān.[6] The *rābiṭa* was a garrison of horsemen stationed at the frontiers. We have no information as to exactly where the *rābiṭa* were stationed or what precisely was their role. It is difficult to believe that they were on the Transoxianan frontier against the Turgesh, particularly as we do not hear about them at all in Ashras's campaign. It is possible that they were in the district of Gūzgān to protect the right flank of Khurāsān against any possible attack from the Turgesh through Khuttal, particularly while Ashras was campaigning in Soghdiana.

Ashras's main duty was to deal with the Turgesh threat. He first had to secure his position with the Soghdians, and the way he dealt with this problem is sufficient explanation for his being called "the frog". Thinking first about peaceful means to

[1] *Ibid.*, p. 1504.
[2] *Ibid.*, p. 1505.
[3] *Ibid.*, p. 1504.
[4] *Ibid.*, p. 1505.
[5] *Ibid.*, pp. 1504–5.
[6] *Ibid.*, p. 1504.

achieve his purpose, he invited the Soghdians to accept Islam and in return the *jizya* would be remitted. The people accepted, apparently in great numbers. When, on the advice of the Soghdian princes, he realized that this would mean a great decrease in the revenue, and that consequently the tribute could not be met, he went back on his promise and ordered the *kharāj* to be taken from the converts.[1] Dennett, in his attempt to explain the situation that resulted from the remission of the *jizya*, realized that the fiscal arrangement in both Khurāsān and Transoxiana was identical in so far as a fixed tribute was paid from both to the Arabs, but he did not realize that this was the only similarity between the two regions.[2] Dennett's mistake was to assume that the system of taxation in Transoxiana was the same as that of Sāsānian Khurāsān. Although we do not have enough information about the taxation system of Transoxiana, there is no reason whatever to assume that the Sāsānian system was applied there. If the social structure of the Sāsānian empire had allowed a poll tax to be imposed on a certain class, the social structure outside the Sāsānian domain, particularly in the principalities of Soghdiana, did not allow such a poll tax. Thus, in all probability, the people of these principalities had only to pay a land tax or a trade tax to their princes, and it was from this tax that they were exempt upon their conversion, according to the instructions of Ashras. The argument put forward by Dennett, to justify his thesis that Ashras had ordered the remission of the poll tax, *jizya,* from the converts, on the basis of defining the meaning of the words *kharāj* and *jizya* in Ṭabarī's narrative of this event, cannot be accepted, because even in this same tradition these two words are used to mean the same thing.[3] At that time a clear definition of either of these terms had not been developed.

Ashras had given these instructions on the misleading advice of Abū al-Ṣaydā' Ṣāliḥ ibn Ṭarīf, his special representative with the Soghdians with responsibility for this problem, who himself was a *mawlā* on very good terms with the Soghdians. Abū al-Ṣaydā' was so interested in obtaining this special treatment for the Soghdians that he actually revolted when Ashras changed his mind. The latter realized his mistake when he saw that the new system would not work in Soghdiana in the way it had worked in Merv,

[1] *Ibid.*, pp. 1507–8.
[2] Dennett, *Conversion*, p. 121. [3] *Ibid.*, pp. 122–3.

and received complaints from the *dahāqīn* of Soghdiana that the new system was a real threat to the revenue of the whole region, since nobody would be left to pay taxes. In his military manner, he ordered the taxes to be taken from everybody in Soghdiana, as had been done before, regardless of their position or religion. This naturally infuriated not only the Soghdians but also those Arabs who saw in the governor's action a breach of faith, and those who favoured a better relationship with the Soghdians.

7,000 Soghdians went out of Samarqand and supported by the indignant Arabs resorted to armed resistance. They were easily suppressed.[1] The problem was that the Soghdians asked for Turgesh help, and Ashras was confronted with the Khāqān and his troops in Soghdiana itself in 111/729.[2] The war between Ashras and the Khāqān ended in the latter's favour and the Arab position steadily deteriorated.[3] When Hishām learned about the situation, he realized that he had sent the wrong man to Khurāsān. Ashras was dismissed in favour of another general of the imperial army, al-Junayd ibn 'Abdirraḥman al-Murrī, who hurried to Khurāsān, accompanied by 500 men of his own clan.[4]

4 *Al-Junayd al-Murrī: the Battle of the Pass*

Junayd took over from Ashras the command of the campaign of 111–12/730, after having had some difficulty in reaching the battlefield because of the overwhelming strength of the Turgesh. However, he was able to change the balance in favour of the Arabs, and finally claimed a victory against the Turgesh at Zarmān, seven leagues from Samarqand.[5] Soghdiana was saved for the Arabs and he returned to Merv, leaving a garrison of about 11,000 men in Samarqand.[6]

It seems that Junayd was satisfied with this success, because the following year 112–13/731 he prepared a big expedition and marched in full force through the Hephthalite lands where he camped close to the Oxus and sent various expeditions in different directions. An army of 18,000 men was sent to the principality

[1] Ṭabarī, vol. II, pp. 1508–9; Balādhurī, *Futūḥ*, p. 428.
[2] Ṭabarī, vol. II, p. 1510.
[3] *Ibid.*, pp. 1512–25; Gibb, *Arab Conquests*, pp. 70–2.
[4] Ṭabarī, vol. II, pp. 1527–33; al-Dhahabī, vol. IV, p. 239.
[5] Ṭabarī, vol. II, pp. 1528–9; Gibb, *Arab Conquests*, pp. 72–3.
[6] Ṭabarī, vol. II, pp. 1540, 1546.

of Ṭukhāristān where a revolt was suppressed. We do not have much information about the other expeditions, though one of them numbered as many as 10,000 men. It seems they were sent to the area between Ṭālqān and Harāt, in the mountains of Ghūr and Gharchistān, where Asad had been active during his governorship.[1] Through this campaign Junayd intended to re-assert the position of the Arabs and forestall any attempts to revolt which might have been encouraged by the appearance of the Turgesh. Contrary to the expectation of Junayd the Turgesh again appeared before Samarqand. He hastily suspended all the operations south of the Oxus and hurried to the help of Samarqand, where the Arab garrison was in a critical position, particularly when Ghūrak, the prince of Samarqand, openly sided with the Turgesh. The Jābghū of Ṭukhāristān also appeared on the side of the Khāqān in this attack. Although the garrison of Samarqand was practically annihilated and the Battle of the Pass between the Arabs and the Turgesh was not wholly an Arab victory, Junayd was able to save Samarqand. After a few battles, the Turgesh withdrew, leaving Soghdiana again in the hands of the Arabs, and Junayd, satisfied with this result, marched back to Merv.[2]

The army of Junayd in this campaign was composed mostly of Arab tribesmen from Khurāsān. There is mention of some Syrian troops but they do not seem to have been very numerous. The infantry was formed from only 1,600 men from the *mawālī* of Khurāsān, under the leadership of 'Abdullah ibn Abī 'Abdillah, a client of Sulaym, whose advice was quite valuable to Junayd in this campaign.[3] There is also mention of 1,000 Muslim converts from the people of Samarqand, who formed a part of the garrison there.[4] The slaves, called *'abīd*, who accompanied the Arab army, were promised their freedom by Junayd because they fought very bravely on the side of the Arabs.[5]

On his way back to Merv after this campaign, Junayd was joined in Chaghāniān by reinforcements from Iraq, 10,000 tribesmen from Kūfa, and 10,000 from the tribesmen of Baṣra.[6]

[1] *Ibid.*, p. 1532; Balādhurī, *Futūḥ*, p. 429.
[2] Gibb, *Arab Conquests*, pp. 73–6; Ṭabarī, vol. II, pp. 1532–52.
[3] Ṭabarī, vol. II, pp. 1538–52.
[4] *Ibid.*, p. 1546.
[5] *Ibid.*, pp. 1543, 1553.
[6] *Ibid.*, p. 1552.

8

THE REORGANIZATION OF HISHĀM

1 *The Arab Settlers in Khurāsān*

It is surprising that, in spite of these new reinforcements, Junayd in his remaining two years in office did not undertake any expeditions. It is reported that in 115/733 there was a famine in Khurāsān, possibly in Merv only, but this does not seem sufficient reason for suspending military activities a year earlier.[1] There is a surprising gap in our sources about the events of these two years, although in 116/734 we hear of the serious revolt of al-Ḥārith ibn Surayj, and the presence of Arab tribesmen outside Merv, not only in Balkh but also in the district of Gūzgān and in Merv ar-Rūd. The stationing of the Arab tribesmen in these last two places took place, almost certainly, in the last two years of Junayd's governorship.

It seems that during this period a certain reorganization had taken place in Khurāsān to deal with the current situation, particularly with regard to the Arab tribesmen. The important new factors in the situation in Khurāsān were the arrival of these 20,000 men from Kūfa and Baṣra, and Hishām's order to Junayd, which was issued at the same time as these men were sent to Khurāsān, to enlist 15,000 men. It is very important to notice that the text of Hishām's order, as related to us, is "*Fa'friḍ falā ghāyata laka fī al-farīḍa li khamsata 'ashra alfan*".[2] As for the new men from Kūfa and Baṣra, Gibb believes that they were sent to Samarqand, and the text of the tradition of Madā'inī seems, to some extent, to support this belief.[3] Yet, if we take another part of the same tradition, together with the part cited above, it becomes clear that they were sent to Merv and not to Samarqand.[4] Moreover, the fact that we find the men from Kūfa in Merv in 117/735 as a major part of Asad's army against al-Ḥārith ibn Surayj,[5] and that there is no mention that they were withdrawn

[1] Ṭabarī, vol. II, p. 1563. [2] *Ibid.*, p. 1545.
[3] Gibb, *Arab Conquests*, p. 75; Ṭabarī, vol. II, pp. 1552–3.
[4] *Ibid.*, p. 1554. [5] *Ibid.*, p. 1582.

from Samarqand, confirms our belief that they were not sent to Samarqand at all but to Merv. Furthermore, the ease with which Samarqand regained its independence during this period would indicate that the garrison there was very small and certainly did not number 20,000 men.[1] If the 10,000 men from Kūfa remained in a separate group, the 10,000 men from Baṣra had probably joined their *akhmās* in Khurāsān, and this is the reason we do not hear about them as a separate group after their arrival.

The second factor in the situation in Khurāsān, Hishām's order to enlist 15,000 men, needs some explanation. According to Ibn A'tham, all the Muslims in Khurāsān at the beginning of Junayd's campaign of 112–13/731, before the sudden Turgesh attack on Samarqand, numbered 43,000.[2] Naturally, one would expect this to reflect the number of men enlisted in the *dīwān*, and there is no reason to doubt this figure since it seems to be reasonable. From Madā'inī we know that the *mawālī* in Junayd's army of that year were only 1,600 in addition to 1,000 men from Samarqand who could have been included in Ibn A'tham's figure.[3] If we take into consideration that 10,000 men, at least, had perished among the garrison of Samarqand during the Turgesh attack, this would mean that the Arab tribesmen enlisted in the *dīwān* when Hishām issued his order were 30,000 men.[4] In spite of the probability that there were a number of the Arab tribesmen who were not enlisted in the *dīwān*, the figure 30,000 would represent the great majority of the Arab tribesmen in Khurāsān. Hishām knew that these men had been so reluctant to join the expeditions against the Turgesh that sometimes they had to be forced to go out. We also know that Hishām was very strict about the duty of the men enlisted in the *dīwān* to join the campaigns.[5] Under these circumstances it is hardly conceivable that Hishām meant to enlist 15,000 more men from the Arab tribesmen of Khurāsān. It is also difficult to conceive that Hishām meant to enlist this number of men from the *mawālī*, since the number of the converts in Khurāsān was not big enough to allow the conscription of 15,000 men, particularly if we notice that all the *mawālī* Junayd had in his army were 1,600 men. If we take a close look at the text of Hishām's order, we will find that Hishām was not ordering

[1] Gibb, *Arab Conquests*, p. 79.
[2] Ibn A'tham, *Futūḥ*, vol. II, p. 204A.
[3] See above, p. 113.
[4] Ṭabarī, vol. II, p. 1541.
[5] *Ibid.*, pp. 1731–2.

the enlistment of new men; on the contrary, he was limiting the number of enlisted men to only 15,000. The text of the order should be translated as, "Enlist [only] 15,000 men because enlistment is purposeless to you". In other words Hishām, who had realized that a great number of the Arab tribesmen in Khurāsān did not want to join the campaigns, was instructing his governor to drop them from the *dīwān*, while at the same time he was sending there fresh troops from Kūfa and Baṣra who were more willing to go to the battlefield. Thus, Hishām was in fact introducing a radical change in the situation of the Arab tribesmen of Khurāsān. He realized the futility of resisting the process of assimilation which had struck deep roots among these Arab tribesmen, and had made them unreliable in the pursuit of a policy of expansion or even in defending the conquered lands against outside attacks. He decided, therefore, to yield to the assimilation movement, and to enlist only 15,000 Arab tribesmen in the *dīwān*, thus allowing the same number, or more, to settle down. But to fill the vacuum created by these "Arab Settlers" he transferred 20,000 fresh, unassimilated tribesmen from Kūfa and Baṣra to Khurāsān.

The problems of the assimilation of the Arab tribesmen of Khurāsān into the Arab imperial structure of the Umayyad empire had eased sufficiently to allow the problems resulting from the assimilation of these tribesmen into the local Iranian population to come to the fore. Before the reorganization of Hishām the Arab tribesmen were kept outside the social structure of Merv, where they were settled, and derived their income mostly from their stipends. According to the new reorganization, they were divided into two distinctive classes: the *muqātila* and the Settlers. While the *muqātila* continued to live outside the social structure of Merv, the Settlers had to find a place within this structure. The *dahāqīn* might be expected to resent any special status being accorded to these Settlers which might threaten their own privileged position within the prevailing social structure.

That this reorganization took place quietly and without any signs of unrest from any party involved indicates that it was administered in a manner satisfactory to all. The precedent established in Merv at the time of Umayya ibn 'Abdillah (78/697), which subjected some Arab tribesmen to the authority of the *dahāqīn* in matters of taxation, was stretched to cover the new situation.[1] Thus, the Settlers were merged into the social structure with practically the same status as the converts from the Iranian population, all subject to the authority of the *dahāqīn* of Merv. It was against the abuse of this authority by the *dahāqīn* that Naṣr ibn Sayyār had to interfere in 121/739 during his governorship of Khurāsān.

Following Hishām's reorganization, the Arab army *muqātila* of Khurāsān was composed of 15,000 men from the Arab tribesmen and the *mawālī* of Khurāsān and 20,000 new tribesmen from Kūfa and Baṣra. There was also a small contingent of Syrian troops. At the time of the death of Junayd in 116/734 the greater part of these troops were stationed outside Merv. In Balkh there was an army of 10,000 men led by Naṣr ibn Sayyār. Since a cousin of Junayd held a prominent position in Balkh, it seems likely that part of this army of Balkh consisted of Syrian troops, possibly 2,500 men. The rest of that army was composed of Arab tribesmen of Khurāsān led by the old warrior of Khurāsān, Naṣr ibn Sayyār.[2]

At the three crossings of the Oxus we find three Arab garrisons, one at Tirmidh led by Sinān al-A'rābī al-Sulamī, the second at Zamm led by al-Haytham al-Shaybānī, and the third at Āmul led by Khālid ibn 'Ubaydillah al-Hajrī.[3] Among the garrison at Tirmidh there were some of the Syrian troops.[4] In An-Nakhūd (Andkhūy), in the district of Gūzgān, there was an army of at least 4,000 men, led by Al-Ḥārith ibn Surayj of Tamīm. This army consisted mostly of tribesmen of Azd and Tamīm from the Arab tribesmen of Khurāsān.[5] Finally there was apparently a small garrison in Merv ar-Rūd led by 'Abdullah ibn 'Amr of Māzin.[6]

Therefore, it seems that, although Hishām allowed some of the Arab tribesmen of Khurāsān to settle down in Merv, he planned to prevent any further loss of tribesmen from the army of Khurāsān, and at the same time to break up the hegemony that these tribesmen had over Merv. The newcomers from Kūfa and Baṣra were stationed in Merv, close to the governor, to serve as a standing army or rather to play the role of the Syrian imperial troops. The rest of the tribesmen of Khurāsān enlisted in the *dīwān* were moved out of Merv, to new locations where they

[1] See above, p. 47.

[2] Ṭabarī, vol. II, pp. 1566–7.

[3] *Ibid.*, pp. 1582, 1583, 1585.

[4] *Ibid.*, p. 1583.

[5] *Ibid.*, pp. 1569–70.

[6] *Ibid.*, p. 1580.

could defend Khurāsān itself against outside attacks, particularly from the Turgesh. The report that these tribesmen were accompanied by their families indicates that this move was designed to be a permanent rather than a temporary settlement.[1] The presence of some Syrian troops among the tribesmen in these new locations was probably to ensure that in these important posts there was an element whose faithfulness to the government was beyond doubt, and who would support the representatives of the governor in these areas.

2 *The revolt of al-Ḥārith ibn Surayj*

The reaction of the Arab tribesmen of Khurāsān to the new plan varied from full support in only one case to outright revolt in many others. They felt that it was an unfair reward for their obedience to the government to be sent from Merv, which they considered their home, to new locations which virtually amounted to exile. Not only were they deprived of the benefits resulting from their long establishment in Merv but these benefits were forfeited either to newcomers who had not engaged in the long struggle to gain these advantages, or to the Settlers who were not enlisted. The change from the half-settled life in Merv to the more military life in the new locations was certainly disadvantageous to these tribesmen.

The first outbreak against this situation occurred on the death of Junayd in 116/734. The 4,000 tribesmen stationed at Andkhūy in Gūzgān, the most isolated location, revolted under the leadership of al-Ḥārith ibn Surayj. They immediately marched on to Balkh where they were met by very little resistance from Naṣr ibn Sayyār and his army of 10,000 men.[2] Although the army of Balkh did not join the forces of Ḥārith, they did not side with the forces of Merv when the later attacked them. Furthermore, the new governor of Khurāsān, ʻĀṣim ibn ʻAbdillah al-Hilālī, did not call on this army of Balkh to support him against al-Ḥārith, in spite of the fact that their support would have been of great strategic importance, putting Ḥārith's forces between two fires. When the Hephthalite princes of Gūzgān, Fāryāb and Ṭālqān saw the revolt in the Arab ranks, and particularly after they realized the neutral stand of the army of Balkh, they joined Ḥārith's forces with their armies. They probably saw it as a

[1] *Ibid.*, p. 1589. [2] *Ibid.*, pp. 1566–7.

chance to regain their independence and possibly establish an Arab principality in Merv under their domination. The garrison of Merv ar-Rūd also joined, and Ḥārith, now with an army of 60,000, marched against Merv.[1]

From the beginning, the new governor of Khurāsān, ʻĀṣim, realized the difficulty and the danger of trying to use the army of Merv against their fellow Arabs, the followers of Ḥārith. Thus, upon learning of the revolt in Andkhūy, he sent a delegation from the Arab leaders in Merv, accompanied by Muqātil ibn Ḥayyān an-Nabaṭī, to negotiate a peaceful settlement with Ḥārith.[2] The latter was not ready for negotiations, probably because he knew that the governor could not do much to change the situation without Hishām's orders. When Ḥārith advanced towards Merv, the governor found out that part of the population there, probably some of the fellow tribesmen of Ḥārith's followers, were in league with Ḥārith and not prepared to fight.[3] ʻĀṣim then thought of withdrawing to Nīshāpūr where he would ask Hishām to send him a Syrian army of 10,000 men to deal with Ḥārith.

At this point the presence of the Hephthalites with Ḥārith worked against him. The Arab tribesmen in Merv finally realized that they were called upon not to fight fellow Arabs, but to repel what was essentially a foreign invasion. Their leaders rallied around ʻĀṣim and promised him full support against Ḥārith.[4] One would expect the local Iranian population also to be aroused by a Hephthalite invasion, and from the active role of Muqātil ibn Ḥayyān at this time it would seem that the *dahāqīn* rendered their support to the governor. The latter helped rouse the enthusiasm of his growing army by distributing money.[5] To the surprise of the Hephthalites, in the first encounter a great number of the followers of Ḥārith from Azd and Tamīm (from Azd alone 2,000 men) deserted their leader and joined their fellow tribesmen in the army of Merv. The Hephthalites, realizing then that they probably would soon have to fight all the Arabs, withdrew from the battle, gave up their hopes and returned to their lands.[6] Ḥārith, whose army then shrank to 3,000 men, was defeated and had to accept the peace terms offered by ʻĀṣim, who also realized

[1] *Ibid.*, p. 1569.
[2] *Ibid.*, p. 1566.
[3] *Ibid.*, p. 1568.
[4] *Ibid.*, p. 1569.
[5] *Ibid.*, pp. 1566, 1571.
[6] *Ibid.*, p. 1570.

that after the withdrawal of the Hephthalites his army would not fight with the same enthusiasm against Ḥārith's followers alone. 'Āṣim turned again to peaceful means and was able to persuade Ḥārith to return to Andkhūy.[1]

This peace did not last for long, because the following year (117/735) Ḥārith, encouraged by the spread of revolt to Āmul and Zamm, returned to attack 'Āṣim in Merv.[2] Apparently the governor was not able to persuade the population of Merv to fight Ḥārith again, and he himself was reduced to taking refuge in a village outside Merv with 1,000 Syrians, presumably the only troops he could muster.[3] Here again, the followers of Ḥārith could not have been very numerous and, in fact, at this point the garrison of Merv ar-Rūd is mentioned as the only followers of Ḥārith.[4] In the ensuing battle, 'Āṣim was able to defeat Ḥārith, who fled to Merv ar-Rūd.

Meanwhile, 'Āṣim had written to Hishām advising him that the only way to deal with the situation in Khurāsān was to include it in the governorship of Iraq.[5] 'Āṣim, who was a general of the Syrian army,[6] had found great difficulty in getting the co-operation of the tribesmen of Merv, whether newcomers or from Khurāsān, against their fellow tribesmen supporting Ḥārith. Hishām must have understood his governor's difficulty, and he included Khurāsān in the governorship of Khālid al-Qasrī, instructing him to send his brother Asad once more as governor of the troubled province.[7]

The tradition related by Madā'inī, and leading to this last battle between 'Āṣim and Ḥārith and the appointment of Asad al-Qasrī to Khurāsān, describes an agreement struck between 'Āṣim and Ḥārith when they learned about the appointment of Asad. This agreement was opposed by Yaḥya ibn Ḥuḍayn, the chief of Bakr in Khurāsān, because, in his words, "it amounted to revolt against *Amīr al-Mu'minīn* himself".[8] Since the origin of this tradition is not clear, it is hard to tell whether it was meant to glorify this particular tribal chief. However, taking this tradition at its face value, and in the light of the continued fight between Ḥārith and 'Āṣim, it is unlikely that they had reached any agree-

[1] *Ibid.*, p. 1572.
[2] *Ibid.*, p. 1576.
[3] *Ibid.*, p. 1579.
[4] *Ibid.*, p. 1580.
[5] *Ibid.*, pp. 1573–4.
[6] Ya'qūbī, *Tārīkh*, vol. II, pp. 394–5, 404–5.
[7] Ṭabarī, vol. II, p. 1573.
[8] *Ibid.*, pp. 1576–7.

ment. The report that Yaḥya ibn Ḥuḍayn had played a certain role, after which we find the fight between Ḥārith and 'Āṣim reduced to a skirmish outside Merv not involving the population, suggests that Yaḥya was able to reconcile the greater part of Ḥārith's remaining followers. These were probably mostly Bakrites.[1] The Azdites and Tamīmites had left Ḥārith's army in the previous campaign and had joined their fellow tribesmen. Therefore, Yaḥya's action reduced Ḥārith's army to the Tamīmites of Merv ar-Rūd. 'Āṣim's advice to Hishām, which amounted to resignation and his voluntary withdrawal to a small village accompanied only by the Syrian troops, indicates that he was trying to avoid any further division in the ranks of the tribesmen in Merv. When Asad arrived at Merv in 117/735 Ḥārith had withdrawn to Merv ar-Rūd, and Asad was faced with no problems in Merv itself.

3 *Asad al-Qasrī moves to Balkh*

Although Asad was not accompanied by any fresh troops, he was able, immediately after his arrival at Merv, to take up the fight against the rebels. The only troops he had were those of Merv, and these were mostly drawn from the newcomers from Kūfa and Baṣra in addition to a small number of the Syrian troops, probably a thousand men. It is to Asad's credit, and probably due to his personal relationship with the leaders of the tribesmen from Kūfa and Baṣra, that he was able to persuade them to resume battle. He divided his troops into two divisions. The tribesmen from Kūfa, supported by the Syrian troops, made up one division led by 'Abdurraḥman ibn Nu'aym, the man who had led these Kūfan troops from Kūfa to Khurāsān. This division was sent to Merv ar-Rūd to deal with Ḥārith himself and his weakening followers.[2] We have no report of any fight between them and Ḥārith. Apparently the latter, knowing that he could not support a fight, did not wait for it and fled to Transoxiana. It is important to point out that this was the last time we have any reference to these men in our sources as the Kūfans, *ahl al-Kūfa*. However, we soon find al-Miqdām ibn 'Abdirraḥman ibn Nu'aym and "his men" (*muqātila-tihi*) as a garrison in Gūzgān.[3] Apparently these tribesmen from Kūfa advanced into the district of Gūzgān where they met no resistance. There in Gūzgān they remained as a

[1] *Ibid.*, p. 1572. [2] *Ibid.*, p. 1582. [3] *Ibid.*, p. 1609.

garrison, the main body of which was in the capital of the district under Miqdām, who was appointed as Asad's representative there. The rest of the men were stationed in military posts, called *masāliḥ*, in Jazza and Shuburqān.[1]

The second division of the troops of Merv, which was made up mostly of tribesmen from Baṣra, from the newcomers, probably supported by some of the tribesmen from Khurāsān, marched on Āmul under the leadership of Asad himself.[2] There the rebels did not offer much resistance and surrendered to Asad. Accepting their allegiance, he left them in Āmul and appointed a representative there.[3] He then started to march with his division towards Balkh, but on his way received news that the army of Balkh had returned to its allegiance. Nevertheless he continued to Balkh, where he made preparations to cross to Tirmidh.[4] Ḥārith, who had fled from Merv ar-Rūd, appeared before the stronghold at Tirmidh supported by the kings of Khuttal, Nasaf and the Jābghū of Ṭukhāristān. Though Ḥārith was able to prevent Asad and his troops from crossing the Oxus, the garrison of Tirmidh was able to defeat him, particularly after he had quarrelled with the king of Khuttal.[5] Asad returned to Balkh while Ḥārith retired into Ṭukhāristān. From Balkh Asad marched again, this time against the last rebel group at Zamm. There the rebels quickly surrendered and Asad, giving them double pay, united them with his troops.[6] Gibb has shown that Asad's main objective on this expedition was to reconquer Samarqand, which had taken advantage of the dissensions in Khurāsān to regain its independence. From Zamm Asad marched on to Samarqand, but he was not successful in recapturing the city and returned to Balkh after damming the canal sluices at Varaghsar, which controlled the water distribution system of Samarqand.[7]

The following year (118/736) Asad finalized the plan he had begun to implement in his first governorship of Khurāsān, to move his capital from Merv to Balkh.[8] Balkh, rebuilt on his orders, provided a better garrison town than Merv with all its parties and their different interests. It was not affected by the assimilation movement as was Merv, and the small local popula-

[1] *Ibid.*, pp. 1604, 1613.
[2] *Ibid.*, p. 1582.
[3] *Ibid.*, pp. 1582–3.
[4] *Ibid.*, p. 1583.
[5] *Ibid.*, pp. 1583–5.
[6] *Ibid.*, p. 1583.
[7] *Ibid.*, pp. 1585–6; Gibb, *Arab Conquests*, pp. 78–80.
[8] Ṭabarī, vol. II, p. 1591.

tion would not have the same influence as that of Merv. Furthermore, Balkh was closer both to the expected field of military activities and to the Hephthalites, whom Asad wanted to use against the Turgesh. The *dahāqīn* of Merv might have disliked seeing the centre of Arab rule moving away from their influence, but they would be expected to accept any move which might help keep the Arab tribesmen on the battlefield, particularly if it would allow them a freer hand with their subjects, Arab and non-Arab, without the close supervision of the Arab governor in Merv.

The move to Balkh was not in the least difficult, and it was actually effected before it was announced. As we have seen, when Asad marched from Merv against the rebels there were hardly any troops left in Merv itself. There is no indication in our sources that any troops were returned to Merv in the governorship of Asad. On the contrary, there is every indication that all the troops Asad could muster in Khurāsān were kept in close proximity to Balkh. The garrisons at Tirmidh and Āmul were left there. A new garrison was established at Khulm, two days' march to the east of Balkh.[1] The tribesmen of Kūfa were divided into three garrisons in the district of Gūzgān. There were already 10,000 men, mostly from the tribesmen of Khurāsān, in the newly rebuilt town of Balkh. When Asad settled at Balkh, he was accompanied by the division he had brought with him from Merv, which was mostly from the newcomers from Baṣra, and also the garrison of Zamm. He ordered new villages to be built around Balkh where he settled most of these troops,[2] while sending a large section to Khulm.[3]

It is important to notice the distinction maintained by Asad between the army of Balkh and the rest of the army of Khurāsān. The tribesmen of the army of Balkh, who were led by Naṣr ibn Sayyār, were the larger part of the tribesmen of Khurāsān who had joined the *dīwān* under Hishām's reorganization. They symbolized the "old guard" of the Arab expansionist party in that province. Asad kept them isolated inside the town of Balkh, and was reluctant to use them when he was pressed for men for his

[1] *Ibid.*, p. 1604.

[2] *Ibid.*, p. 1591, *maṣāni'* meaning villages. See Ibn Manẓūr, *Lisān al-'Arab*, Būlāq, 1891, vol. v, p. 80; see also Ṭabarī, vol. II, p. 1602.

[3] This garrison was able to repel an attack by the whole army of the Turgesh. See Ṭabarī, vol. II, p. 1604.

campaigns.[1] We remember that Naṣr ibn Sayyār was opposed to Asad's policy in his first governorship of Khurāsān, and was arrested and humiliated by Asad for this reason. In his second governorship, Asad continued to have his suspicions about Naṣr's intentions, particularly after the stand taken by Naṣr and his followers in Balkh regarding Ḥārith's revolt.[2]

In contrast to Naṣr ibn Sayyār, there emerged from among the newcomers from Baṣra a strong man who appeared to have been Asad's first lieutenant and who played an important role later on the eve of the 'Abbāsid Revolution. That was Juday' ibn 'Alī al-Kirmānī, a tribal chief from Azd. The first time we hear about Juday' was as a leader of an expedition which Asad sent in 118/736 against some remnants of Ḥārith's followers who had occupied the fortress of Tabushkān in Badakhshān. This expedition was of 6,000 men, the biggest group of whom were 2,500 Syrians who had been part of the army of Balkh. The fortress succumbed to Juday''s army and he took extreme measures against the inhabitants.[3]

4 *Asad al-Qasrī and the Hephthalites end the Turgesh threat*

Having finished with all the rebels in Khurāsān, it would have seemed natural for Asad to advance against Samarqand to subdue the rebellious city, but in fact, after the failure of his wavering attempt in 117/735, he made no attempt on this front for the rest of his governorship. Instead he turned against Khuttal, as he had done in his first governorship, and in 119/737 penetrated into this area with his army.[4] The prince of Khuttal appealed for aid to the Khāqān of the Turgesh, who quickly marched to meet Asad in Khuttal. When Asad was advised by the prince of Khuttal about the Khāqān's move, he started a hurried retreat and ordered the "heavy loads" (*athqāl*) and the "old men" to be dispatched in advance under an Arab guard supported by the troops of Chaghāniān.[5] While Asad and the rest of his army were following, they were attacked twice by the Turgesh and suffered severe losses. However, the Khāqān hastened after the *athqāl*, which he was able to seize. Though Asad rushed to rescue the guard, the Chaghān Khudā and most of his men were killed in the battle. The Khāqān

[1] Ṭabarī, vol. II, p. 1605.
[2] *Ibid.*, pp. 1584–5.
[3] *Ibid.*, pp. 1589–91; Ibn al-Kalbī, *Nasab Ma'dd wa al-Yaman al-Kabīr*, British Museum Manuscript, no. ADD 22376, p. 67A.
[4] Ṭabarī, vol. II, p. 1593.
[5] *Ibid.*, pp. 1594–5.

then retired to the principality of Ṭukhāristān where he was joined by the desperate al-Ḥārith ibn Surayj. Asad returned to Balkh where he camped outside the town, but when the winter closed in he himself entered the town while his army dispersed in the villages around it.[1]

Taking advantage of the winter and on the advice of al-Ḥārith ibn Surayj, the Khāqān decided to launch a surprise attack against Asad.

The Khāqān summoned forces to join him from Sughd and the territories of Ṭukhāristān. The enumeration which Ṭabarī gives of the troops accompanying the Khāqān on this expedition shows very clearly how completely Arab rule in Transoxiana and the Oxus basin had been supplanted by that of the Turks. We are told that besides the Khāqān's own Turkish troops and Ḥārith with his followers, there were present the Jābghū, the King of Sughd, the prince of Usrūshana and the rulers of Shāsh and Khuttal. It is fairly certain, of course, that the list is exaggerated insofar as the actual presence of the princes is concerned (it is in fact partially contradicted in other parts of the narrative), but it can scarcely be doubted that forces from some, if not all, of these principalities were engaged.[2]

The Khāqān's army of 30,000 men first attacked Khulm, but the Arab garrison there repulsed the attack. Nevertheless, the attackers continued their march into Gūzgān and occupied its capital, apparently defeating the Arab garrison there and the Hephthalite army of Gūzgān itself. Here in Gūzgān, the Khāqān made his camp and sent out raiding parties in all directions.

Asad, learning about the Turgesh attack, immediately started his preparations. A fire was lit over the city of Balkh as a sign to the tribesmen lodged in the villages around the city to assemble.[3] These tribesmen, in addition to the Syrian troops of the army of Balkh, formed an army of 7,000 men. Since the tribesmen of the army of Balkh numbered more than 7,000 men, it appears they were not mobilized. This is confirmed by the report that Asad put Juday' al-Kirmānī in charge of Balkh, ordering him not to let anybody outside the city even if the Turgesh knocked at its gates. Amongst those kept in the city were many prominent tribal leaders from all tribes, the most prominent of whom was Naṣr ibn

[1] *Ibid.*, pp. 1594–1603; Gibb, *Arab Conquests*, pp. 81–3.
[2] Gibb, *Arab Conquests*, p. 83.
[3] Ṭabarī, vol. II, p. 1603.

Sayyār.[1] However, either pressed for men or because he accepted their pledge of loyalty and obedience, Asad allowed them to join his expedition, and this probably doubled the size of his army. While he was advancing into Gūzgān to meet the enemy, Asad's army was further strengthened by the arrival of the Arab garrison of Gūzgān under Miqdām ibn ʿAbdirraḥman and the Hephthalite army of Gūzgān.[2] With this large army Asad surprised the Khāqān near Kharistān (San) with only 4,000 of his men. The Khāqān suffered a disastrous defeat and, under close pursuit by Asad, he and Ḥārith retreated to the land of the Jābghū. Asad returned to Balkh and sent out al-Kirmānī to chase out any remnants of the Turgesh army.[3] Gibb asserts that the battle of

> Kharistān was not only the turning point in the fortunes of the Arabs in Central Asia, but gave the signal for the downfall of the Turgesh power, which was bound up with the personal prestige of Su-Lu. The princes of Ṭukhāristān and Transoxiana found it expedient to treat him with respect as he was returning to Nawākath, but in his own country the dissensions long fomented in secret by the Chinese broke out. Su-Lu was assassinated by the Bagā Ṭarkhān (Kursul); the kingdom fell to pieces. The Turks split up and began to raid one another.[4]

It seems that while Asad was busy fighting against the Turgesh, Badr Ṭarkhān, who was perhaps a prince of Bāmyān, established himself as king of Khuttal. Having defeated the Turgesh, Asad sent an expedition which defeated this usurper and re-established Arab authority in Khuttal.[5] Shortly after, early in 120/738, Asad died in Balkh.[6] It certainly would have given us more understanding of his policy had he lived a little longer after the disappearance of the Turgesh threat. However, it is clear that Khuttal was the field he had chosen for his military activities. It is possible that he was trying to lure the Turgesh to a new front, where he could best make use of his friendship with the Hephthalites. It is also possible that he was trying to control another east–west trade route through Khuttal and across the Pamirs. The presence of the *athqāl* in his campaign in Khuttal of 119/737 sounds strange with an Arab army. The booty, which was mostly sheep, was in fact left with the main army,[7] while these valuable *athqāl* were

[1] *Ibid.*, p. 1605.
[2] *Ibid.*, p. 1609.
[3] *Ibid.*, pp. 1609–12.
[4] Gibb, *Arab Conquests*, pp. 83–4.
[5] Ṭabarī, vol. II, pp. 1629–30.
[6] *Ibid.*, pp. 1635, 1638.
[7] *Ibid.*, pp. 1593, 1596–7.

rushed ahead well guarded. They were referred to as *amwāl* and were of great concern to Asad and his men, and most certainly to the Chaghān Khudā, as well as to the Khāqān himself.[1] It is not possible that this was ordinary booty or simply just "baggage" of the army as suggested by Gibb. These valuable "heavy loads" were, we believe, actually consignments of goods being sent eastwards through Khuttal.[2] This suggestion, combined with the interest of the Soghdian refugees, who were among the supporters of the Khāqān, as well as the interest of the king of Soghd and the princes of Transoxiana in the east–west trade, explains the anxiety of the Khāqān and his followers to destroy Asad's scheme and to get hold of these *athqāl* which, if they allowed them to go through, might have threatened their monopoly over that trade.

5 *Naṣr ibn Sayyār and the return to Merv*

Four months after the death of Asad, Naṣr ibn Sayyār was appointed governor of Khurāsān by Hishām and was put under the supervision of the governor of Iraq.[3] In other words, Khurāsān was made a separate governorship. In Iraq itself a great change had taken place shortly after the death of Asad. Khālid al-Qasrī, after almost fifteen years as governor of Iraq, was dismissed. Hishām, alarmed by the signs of unrest in Iraq which were clearly represented in the various Khawārij revolts which occurred there in 119/737, decided to appoint Yūsuf ibn 'Umar as governor to remedy the situation in this restless province.[4]

In Khurāsān the four months (Rabī' I–Rajab 120/March–July 739) between the governorships of Asad and Naṣr present some difficulty. According to Madā'inī, Asad appointed Ja'far ibn Ḥanẓala al-Bahrānī, a leader of the Syrian troops,[5] as his successor, which position he kept until the appointment of Naṣr.[6] Another tradition related by Ṭabarī asserts that the new governor of Iraq, Yūsuf ibn 'Umar, on his taking office, almost two months after the death of Asad, appointed Juday' al-Kirmānī in place of Ja'far ibn Ḥanẓala.[7] Madā'inī himself concedes that Kirmānī was,

[1] *Ibid.*, p. 1599.

[2] According to Ibn Manẓūr (*Lisān*, vol. XIII, pp. 90–2), the word *athqāl* has two meanings. One, which is apparently followed by Gibb, is as plural of *thaqal*—"the baggage of the traveller"; the other, which we follow, is as the plural of *thiql*—the "heavy load"—implying the meaning of valuable heavy loads, *kunūz*.

[3] Ṭabarī, vol. II, pp. 1638, 1663.

[4] *Ibid.*, pp. 1619–29, 1633–4.

[5] *Ibid.*, p. 1609.

[6] *Ibid.*, pp. 1660–1.

[7] *Ibid.*, pp. 1658–9.

for some time during these four months, a governor of Merv.[1] Though we have little information about events in Khurāsān at this time, we understand from a remark by Ya'qūbī that there were certain signs of unrest there. Hishām, alarmed by these signs and consulting an expert on the affairs of Khurāsān, decided to appoint Naṣr ibn Sayyār to the province.[2] According to the different traditions related by Ṭabarī, he was selected from a long list of suggested names.[3] All these names, except that of Juday' al-Kirmānī, were of men closely associated with Naṣr and of course holding the same views. The tradition that Naṣr was not a chief of a big *'ashīra* in Khurāsān should not be taken seriously: first, because we know that Naṣr was leader of a considerable following in Khurāsān, and second, because in the same tradition he is represented as the chief of Muḍar in Khurāsān, a fact which was clearly observed by Hishām himself.[4]

Another important change which had taken place in Khurāsān either during these four months or at the outset of Naṣr's governorship was the return to Merv. If the move to Balkh had political significance, the return to Merv must also have had political implications. Naṣr, as we know, did not belong to the same school as Asad, and his support came from different quarters, more specifically from the *muqātila* of the Arab tribesmen of Khurāsān. It seems that in the four months after the death of Asad there was an internal struggle for power in Khurāsān between the old tribesmen of Khurāsān, led by Naṣr ibn Sayyār, and the newcomers, led by Juday' al-Kirmānī, chief lieutenant of Asad. At the time this struggle did not develop into open fighting as it was to do six years later between the same two parties. Hishām, by appointing Naṣr, was actually siding with one party against the other, perhaps because he thought that this party held the real power in Khurāsān and that through it the Umayyad policy could be best carried out. Perhaps he was afraid of another revolt like that of Ḥarith, only led this time by Naṣr ibn Sayyār. It is significant that Ja'far ibn Ḥanẓala, during his short governorship, had offered Naṣr the governorship of Bukhārā. But Naṣr refused it, possibly expecting the bigger prize, the governorship of Khurāsān itself.[5]

1 *Ibid.*, p. 1661.
2 Ya'qūbī, *Tārīkh*, vol. II, p. 392.
3 Ṭabarī, vol. II, pp. 1659–63.
4 *Ibid.*, pp. 1661, 1663.
5 *Ibid.*, p. 1661.

Apparently one of the first actions of Naṣr after his appointment was to move the capital definitely back to Merv, an action taken for granted by our sources. If Asad was seeking the support for his rule outside Merv, Naṣr knew that his support lay there. He embarked on the restoration of the régime under which he and his *muqātila* had enjoyed their privileged position as the rulers of Khurāsān. He appointed his supporters to key positions in the province. Men whose names had been long associated with Naṣr's were appointed as sub-governors to the different districts. Thus we see Muslim ibn 'Abdirraḥman al-Bāhilī over Balkh, Ziyād ibn 'Abdirraḥman al-Qushayrī over Abrshahr (Nīshāpūr) and Qaṭan ibn Qutayba over Soghd (the garrisons in Bukhārā and probably Kish).[1] Naṣr developed a new policy with regard to these various district appointments. He created new offices for sub-governors all over the province, and in his governorship we hear for the first time about local governors of such towns as Sarakhs, Nisā and Abīvard.[2] These different sub-governors were accompanied to their localities by a few members of the *muqātila* from their own clans.[3] This was not an attempt to settle these tribesmen in the different parts of the province; it was an attempt to establish Arab rule in these districts through the Arabs themselves. At the same time it was a reward for his supporters, whose appointment to these offices would entail not only power and prestige but also a considerable income. On the other hand, Naṣr's opponents were not appointed to any office and we do not find mention of men like al-Kirmānī holding any office in his governorship. Moreover, he tried to lessen their power among their own supporters. Al-Kirmānī was dismissed from his position as chief of Azd, and was only returned to this position when his successor failed to handle his job.[4]

6 *The fiscal reform of Naṣr ibn Sayyār*

Naṣr took another step which was an appeal to a certain part of the Arab community in Merv itself. This was the famous fiscal reform of 121/739, which was in fact intended to remove the grievances of the Arab Settlers in Merv over the abuses of the taxation system imposed on them by the *dahāqīn* of Merv. It is

[1] *Ibid.*, p. 1664; Gibb, *Arab Conquests*, p. 89.
[2] Ṭabarī, vol. II, p. 1950. [3] *Ibid.*, p. 1929. [4] *Ibid.*, p. 1859.

significant that Naṣr referred to these people, whose situation he proposed to reform, as Muslims, a term which would cover the Arab Settlers and the Iranian converts. It is also interesting to note that these Muslims, numbered at 30,000 in this tradition, would roughly represent the probable number of these two groups in Merv. Naṣr noticed that the *dahāqīn* were using their authority in the assessment and collection of taxes in favour of their own people, who maintained their religion, against the Muslims whose burdens of taxation were unjustly increased. Manṣūr ibn ʻUmar was appointed as a commissioner with full power to watch over the assessment of taxes and to see that no Muslim was burdened with additional taxes. "He reclassified the *kharāj* and put it in order. Then he assessed the tribute stipulated in the treaty of capitulation."[1]

Although Dennett did not fully understand the situation in Merv, he was certainly right in saying that, in this respect, "Naṣr was a reformer, but no innovator. He did not create a new system, nor set up new distinctions, nor revolutionize the fiscal administration of the Arab empire. All he did was to correct the abuses existing in the old system."[2] It is now clear that, although Naṣr took exception to the *dahāqīn's* behaviour towards the Arab Settlers, he simply appointed a commissioner to supervise them without amending their position of authority within the social structure.

In contrast to the previous governors, Naṣr did not have to worry about a Turgesh threat, and naturally this made the task of restoring Arab authority over Transoxiana much easier. Between 120/738 and probably 123/741, he led expeditions across the Oxus and was met by no resistance from the princes and people of Transoxiana, who had no hope of outside support. Upon instructions from Yūsuf ibn ʻUmar, Naṣr advanced as far as Shāsh, where al-Ḥārith ibn Surayj was taking refuge. Although Naṣr had 20,000 men from the levies from Soghdiana in addition to his own army, he was not able to win a decisive victory against Shāsh.[3] All he was able to achieve was an agreement with the prince of Shāsh to expel Ḥārith to Fāryāb. Before returning to Merv, Naṣr raided Farghāna, and this was probably the last of his military activities.[4] The Turgesh's fall from power also led to the

[1] *Ibid.*, p. 1688–9. [2] Dennett, *Conversion*, p. 121. [3] Ṭabarī, vol. II, p. 1690.
[4] Gibb, *Arab Conquests*, pp. 89–92; Ṭabarī, vol. II, pp. 1688–95.

return of the Soghdian refugees, who were now left without support. They were granted generous conditions by Naṣr, more for trade reasons than because Naṣr respected their military abilities, as our sources imply.[1]

7 *The death of Hishām, and the ensuing struggle in Khurāsān*

Though Naṣr seems to have enjoyed the full confidence of Hishām, Yūsuf ibn 'Umar, the governor of Iraq, does not seem to have shared his master's opinion. Yūsuf was probably more aware of the struggle for power which continued in Khurāsān between the party of Naṣr and the newcomers. This struggle was aggravated by the siding of the Syrian troops in Khurāsān with the opponents of Naṣr, and they used their influence with Hishām to topple the governor.[2] Yūsuf also tried to persuade Hishām to dismiss Naṣr for his own reasons, but Hishām, who was apparently supporting Naṣr's policy in Khurāsān, continued to keep him in his governorship.[3]

Naṣr's troubles began after the death of Hishām in 125/743. Though the new *Amīr al-Mu'minīn*, Walīd II, confirmed him in Khurāsān and even gave him complete freedom there, Yūsuf was soon able to convince Walīd II of his point of view and Khurāsān was included in his own governorship.[4] Yūsuf, afraid that Naṣr might revolt if he were dismissed, only called him to Iraq. Naṣr hesitated to obey Yūsuf's order and prolonged his preparations until he was saved only by the arrival of the news of Walīd II's murder in 126/744.[5] It was a good excuse for Naṣr to retain his office and to stay in Khurāsān, but it was also a serious warning of the disintegration of the Umayyads and the imminent end of their rule. This murder was no isolated incident to be dismissed as of no consequence. Indeed it was a natural sequel to the events of the last troubled years of Hishām's rule. Undoubtedly Hishām was a very capable ruler and Khālid al-Qasrī, his governor for Iraq and the East for fifteen years, successfully administered these regions with remarkable statesmanship. Yet in 120/738 Khālid was dismissed for no obvious

[1] Ṭabarī, vol. II, pp. 1717–18.
[2] *Ibid.*, pp. 1719–23.
[3] *Ibid.*, pp. 1718–21.
[4] *Ibid.*, p. 1764.
[5] *Ibid.*, pp. 1765–8.

reason. While it is true that in 119/737 there were minor Khawārij uprisings in Iraq, these do not offer enough justification for Khālid's downfall. Hishām must have been under extremely powerful pressure, which could not have been, as subsequent events will show, other than pressure from the mainstay of the Umayyads, the Syrian army.

Throughout Hishām's reign the external threats were of a very serious nature. The Turgesh penetration in the east, the aggressive offensive attacks of the Khazar in Armenia and the widespread revolt of the Berber in north Africa, were real dangers to Arab rule in their respective regions. The Syrian army could not be expected to control the empire and at the same time contain these serious threats. In the east, Asad, Khālid's brother, was able to effect an alliance with the Hephthalites against the Turgesh. In Armenia, Syrian troops under the formidable Maslama were first deployed against the Khazar but, beginning in 114/732, they were gradually withdrawn, only to be replaced by a newly formed army. This army was recruited by Marwān ibn Muḥammad from the Arab tribesmen of Jazīra (Mesopotamia), Armenia and Aḍharbayjān.[1] All the available Syrian troops were sent to north Africa to subdue the rebellious Berber. The demands on the Syrian army became too great and the Syrians themselves were the first to recognize the need for the reconstruction of military power in the empire. Of course, Syrian troops were still stationed in Iraq and the Iraqi tribesmen were still demilitarized.

Khālid al-Qasrī, the governor of Iraq, was renowned for his land reclamation and agricultural projects there,[2] and for these he needed all possible manpower. He could be expected to oppose any plans for the reactivation of the Arab *muqātila* of Iraq, which would defeat his policies for pacifying the region. Hishām, who had already given Marwān ibn Muḥammad permission to reactivate the *muqātila* of Jazīra and adjacent provinces, was also under pressure to do the same in Iraq. To this Khālid objected and he had to go (120/738). The new governor of Iraq, Yūsuf ibn 'Umar, was faced in 122/740 with the serious Shī'ite revolt of Zayd ibn 'Ali in Iraq itself. Although this revolt was subdued, unrest continued in Iraq and spread north into Jazīra. About a

[1] Ibn al-Athīr, *Kāmil*, vol. v, p. 132.

[2] Al-Balādhurī, *Ansāb al-Ashrāf*, Istanbul manuscript, Suleymanniye Kütüphanesi, Reisulkuttap, no. 597–8, vol. II, pp. 294–7.

year before his death, Hishām sent an army of 12,000 Syrians to north Africa against the still rampaging Berber revolt.[1]

Walīd II (125–6/743–4), Hishām's successor, is represented in our sources as a self-indulgent man who was not fit to rule. These accusations are not to be taken seriously, since contradictory reports appear in the same sources.[2] Such reports should be understood as the traditionists' way of emphasizing other failings of a particular statesman. Walīd II's major failing was that he did not comprehend the effects of the heavy burdens imposed upon the limited powers of the Syrian army. He thought he could buy their wavering allegiance by increasing their stipends,[3] which other Arab rulers had found to be an effective way of commanding the loyalty of their troops. However, to the surprise of Walīd II, the Syrian generals engineered a successful coup d'état against him.[4] Scarcely a year had passed before his rule was brought to an end. He himself was murdered by the most loyal subjects of the Umayyad house, the Syrian *jund*. For all practical purposes this was the end of Umayyad rule. The very basis of its authority was destroyed when it lost the support of the Syrian army.

Yazīd III, the choice of the Syrian generals to succeed Walīd II, abolished the increase of the stipends of the Syrian troops granted to them under his predecessor.[5] Significantly, he appointed Manṣūr ibn Jumhūr al-Kalbī, the chief conspirator against Walīd II, as his governor for Iraq and the East. Manṣūr's task seems to have been to reactivate the Iraqi *muqātila* and to integrate them in the Syrian army stationed in Iraq. In no more than three months it became apparent that this approach was not acceptable to the Iraqis. He was dismissed in favour of a new governor who was not a Syrian general, but who had a more glamorous name, 'Abdullah ibn 'Umar ibn 'Abdil'azīz.[6] To the Iraqis the appeal of the name was that it represented to them a revival of his father's policy, i.e. to put an end to the Syrian domination of Iraq. The new governor proceeded to a reconstruction of the Iraqi army, in which he proposed to integrate the Syrian troops of

1 Ibn Iḍhārī, *al-Bayān al-Mughrib*, ed. G. S. Colin and E. Levi—Provencal, Leiden, 1948, vol. I, p. 54; Ṭabarī, vol. II, p. 1716.

2 Balādhurī, *Ansāb*, vol. II, pp. 310, 311, 318; Ṭabarī, vol. II, pp. 1741, 1754.

3 Ṭabarī, vol. II, p. 1825.

4 *Ibid.*, p. 1778; Balādhurī, *Ansāb*, vol. II, p. 327.

5 Ṭabarī, vol. II, p. 1825.

6 *Ibid.*, pp. 1836, 1854; Balādhurī, *Ansāb*, vol. II, pp. 170, 171, 364.

Iraq. Manṣūr ibn Jumhūr al-Kalbī was to be one of the generals of this newly constructed army.[1]

Unfortunately Yazīd III died suddenly at the end of 126/744, after ruling for no more than six months. His brother, Ibrāhīm, who succeeded him for four months, was not acknowledged by all factions as *Amīr al-Mu'minīn*. The factionalism spread among the Syrian army in Syria itself and the general situation deteriorated to complete chaos. Marwān ibn Muḥammad was the only general who had enough organized strength to re-establish some semblance of order in the empire. At the head of his army of Jazīra, he marched on Damascus, deposed Ibrāhīm and proclaimed himself the new *Amīr al-Mu'minīn*.[2]

In his short governorship of Iraq and the East, Manṣūr ibn Jumhūr appointed his brother Manẓūr as his governor of the East. Although Manẓūr himself never arrived at Khurāsān, the news of his appointment caused great excitement there, particularly among Naṣr ibn Sayyār's opponents. Naṣr himself, apparently feeling that he had enough support in Khurāsān, refused to recognize it.[3] Nevertheless, he proceeded to take certain measures to secure his position. Most important, he ordered Juday' al-Kirmānī, who by that time had been dismissed from his position as chief of Azd, to be arrested.[4] Naṣr also moved his residence from the city of Merv to his palace in the village of Mājān outside, probably because some of his supporters were scattered through the different districts of the province.[5] He tried to win over to his side other Arab chiefs from Azd and Rabī'a, from the tribesmen of Khurāsān, appointing men like Ya'qūb ibn Yaḥya ibn Ḥuḍayn of Rabī'a to sub-governorships.[6] Taking more precautions, Naṣr ordered the money in the treasury to be saved, and he gave the *muqātila* only a part of their stipends and this was paid in kind. When he was asked about the rest, he called a complete halt to all distribution. This last measure was probably directed mainly against his opponents, whom one would expect to be alienated by such a step.[7]

In less than a month, al-Kirmānī was able to escape from his prison in the citadel of Merv to a village called Nawsh, where he

1 Ṭabarī, vol. II, pp. 1883, 1898, 1902.

2 *Ibid.*, pp. 1870–9; Balādhurī, *Ansāb*, vol. II, p. 348.

3 Ṭabarī, vol. II, 1836, 1845–7.

4 *Ibid.*, pp. 1859–60.

5 *Ibid.*, pp. 1767, 1846, 1919.

6 *Ibid.*, p. 1847.

7 *Ibid.*, pp. 1855–6.

was joined by 3,000 men from the Azd, mainly from his own clan Ma'n.[1] They were also joined by an unspecified number of the Arab Settlers in Merv (*ahl al-taqādum*, people of long residence).[2] Naṣr immediately made preparations to fight al-Kirmānī, but it seems that the latter realized that his followers were not strong enough to fight Naṣr's army and, without any fighting, peace was arranged between the two parties on condition that Naṣr would pay the men some of their stipends.[3] This truce did not last for more than a month because the situation changed rapidly in favour of Naṣr.

Yazīd III, realizing that the appointment of Manṣūr ibn Jumhūr to Iraq and the East was causing great unrest, not only in Iraq but also in Khurāsān, dismissed him in favour of 'Abdullah ibn 'Umar ibn 'Abdil'azīz, who immediately confirmed Naṣr ibn Sayyār in Khurāsān.[4] Certainly this was a victory for Naṣr's party, to which al-Kirmānī and his followers reacted by resuming their revolt. After some unsuccessful negotiations between Naṣr and al-Kirmānī, the latter, with his followers, withdrew from the city and made his camp in the village of Māsarjasān.[5] There he was joined by other tribesmen from among the newcomers, of whom particular mention is made of a large faction of Rabī'a led by Yaḥya ibn Nu'aym,[6] others from Kinda,[7] some from Muḍar,[8] and probably the greater part of the Syrian troops.[9] In spite of the presence of tribesmen from Muḍar among the followers of al-Kirmānī, they were all called *yamāniyya,* or Yaman, in contrast to the followers of Naṣr who were called Muḍar.[10] When Ṭabarī found tribesmen from Rabī'a among the followers of Naṣr, he called them all *nizāriyya,* a convenient name which covers Rabī'a and Muḍar.[11] Madā'inī, realizing that there was no clear-cut tribal division to define the two camps of Naṣr and al-Kirmānī, refers to them, in most cases, as the "followers" of Naṣr versus the "followers" of al-Kirmānī. However, Naṣr apparently could not muster enough men to fight al-Kirmānī, whose support was

[1] *Ibid.*, pp. 1861–2.

[2] *Ibid.*, p. 1862. These people are referred to as *ahl al-saqādum* but, according to another reading (*ibid.*, p. 1954) and according to Ibn al-Athīr (*Kāmil*, vol. v, p. 273), this word is to be read *taqādum*, and we understand it to mean the Settlers of Merv.

[3] Ṭabarī, vol. II, pp. 1863–4.

[4] *Ibid.*, pp. 1854, 1855.

[5] *Ibid.*, pp. 1864–6, 1925.

[6] *Ibid.*, pp. 1925–32, 1992.

[7] *Ibid.*, p. 1932.

[8] *Ibid.*, p. 1933.

[9] *Ibid.*, pp. 1590, 1926.

[10] *Ibid.*, p. 1927; Ya'qūbī, *Tārīkh*, vol. II, p. 399.

[11] Ṭabarī, vol. II, pp. 1855, 1921.

gradually increasing. Moreover, his position became very precarious after the death of Yazīd III, with no recognized authority to confirm him in his governorship. In other words, he was no longer the legitimate governor of Khurāsān, and this naturally weakened his position with many of his followers. This fact, together with the re-emergence of al-Ḥārith ibn Surayj, had a deep impact on Naṣr's followers, and indeed on the course of events in Khurāsān.

Al-Ḥārith was granted an amnesty by Yazīd III upon the mediation of Naṣr ibn Sayyār, who thought that al-Ḥārith might help strengthen his position with the tribesmen of Khurāsān vis-à-vis al-Kirmānī and his followers.[1] Al-Ḥārith arrived in Merv in Jumādā II 127/March 745 while a civil war was raging in the heart of the empire and revolts were spreading to every corner of the Arab domain.[2] Though Naṣr was still in power, he was by no means in control of the situation in Khurāsān. Shortly afterwards, when Yazīd ibn 'Umar ibn Hubayra, the governor of Iraq and the East for Marwān II, confirmed or rather reappointed Naṣr to Khurāsān, the latter naturally recognized Marwān II.[3] This, apparently, was not the general opinion of Naṣr's followers and indeed Marwān II's rule continued to be disputed in most of the empire. Ḥārith was not the man to miss such an opportunity to reassert his leadership among the Arab tribesmen of Khurāsān, and he quickly denounced the rule of Marwān II.[4] In no time more then 3,000 of Naṣr's followers rallied around Ḥārith,[5] and through his chief propagandist, Jahm ibn Ṣafwān, he was able to gain more support for his movement.[6]

This time, Ḥārith posed not as a rebel but as a leader whose main concern was the unity of his community. At the same time, he was vehemently against oppression, i.e. he was going to defend all that these tribesmen believed to be their rights.[7] In fact, Ḥārith was more of a threat to Naṣr than al-Kirmānī. Naṣr realized that he would have to get rid of Ḥārith first in order to be able to deal with al-Kirmānī.[8] After exhausting all peaceful means to reach an agreement with him, Naṣr had to resort to fighting. First Naṣr was able to inflict a defeat upon Ḥārith in Jumādā II

[1] *Ibid.*, pp. 1867–8.
[2] Wellhausen, pp. 370–96.
[3] Ṭabarī, vol. II, p. 1917.
[4] *Ibid.*, pp. 1917–18.
[5] *Ibid.*, pp. 1890, 1920.
[6] *Ibid.*, p. 1918.
[7] *Ibid.*, pp. 1889–90, 1919.
[8] *Ibid.*, pp. 1919, 1928–9.

128/March 746, but al-Kirmānī took advantage of the situation and interfered in the fight on the side of Ḥārith.[1] Naṣr had no option but to withdraw, not only from the fight but from Merv itself.[2] While Naṣr retired to Nīshāpūr, al-Kirmānī, accompanied by Ḥārith, entered Merv. The alliance between Ḥārith and al-Kirmānī did not last more than a few days. Under pressure from his followers, Ḥārith had to resume the fight against al-Kirmānī. The latter won a decisive victory in a battle where Ḥārith himself was killed, and finally al-Kirmānī became the sole master of Merv.[3]

But Naṣr did not leave al-Kirmānī to enjoy his victory, and in 129/747 he sent from Nīshāpūr one expedition after another against Merv. When all these expeditions were defeated by al-Kirmānī's followers, Naṣr himself, with all his men, marched to Merv. There the two antagonists, camping opposite one another, vigorously continued their fight.[4] But, to the surprise of both parties, at this point there appeared unexpectedly a third party. This was Abū Muslim and his followers.

[1] *Ibid.*, pp. 1922–8.
[2] *Ibid.*, p. 1929.
[3] *Ibid.*, pp. 1930–4.
[4] *Ibid.*, pp. 1970–2.

9

THE REVOLUTION

1 *The nature of the movement*

Muslim heresiographers present us with a misleading picture of the various Islamic sects. These are depicted as major sects, divided into numerous sub-sects, each sub-sect having clear religious or philosophical ideas. In this elaborate network of sects and sub-sects, attempts have been made to relate sub-sects to each other and to the major sects. For the sake of completeness some sub-sects are only mentioned by name without any more information. On the other hand other sub-sects are overemphasized, although modern research questions their very existence. W. M. Watt has recently concluded that, "despite the elaborate notices of the Jahmiyyah in the heresiographers, there was never such a sect...Definite information about particular men of whose history something is known is more reliable and more valuable than general descriptions of sects."[1] Indeed, later polemics severely distorted the heresiographers' descriptions of the early history of the sects in much the same way as contemporary practices distorted the jurists' exposition of legal practices in the early history of Islam. Following the heresiographers, modern scholars classified the Hāshimiyya as a sub-sect of the extremist *ghulāt*. Bernard Lewis says:

The 'Abbāsid party that won power from the Umayyads was known as Hāshimiyya. According to the later chronicles, this name referred to Hāshim, the common ancestor of al-'Abbās, 'Alī and the Prophet, and it has been taken as asserting a claim to the succession based on kinship with the Prophet. In fact the name was of a quite different significance, and reveals very clearly the true origins of the 'Abbāsid party. During the Umayyad period the large number of Shī'ite and pro-Shī'ite sects and parties that flourished in different parts of the Empire, but especially in southern Irak, may be broadly divided into two main groups. One of them followed the pretenders of the line of

[1] W. M. Watt, "The Political Attitudes of the Mutazilah", *Journal of the Royal Asiatic Society* (1963–4), pp. 38–57, at pp. 41–2.

Fāṭima, and was, generally speaking, moderate, differing from the dominant faith chiefly by its support, on legitimist grounds, for the political claims of the house of ʿAlī. The other first appeared in the revolt of al-Mukhtār, who rose in 66/685 in the name of Muḥammad, a son of ʿAlī by a Ḥanafī woman. For the next sixty or seventy years the claims of Muḥammad b. al-Ḥanafiyya and his successors were advanced by a series of sects of a more extreme character, deriving their main support from the resentful and imperfectly Islamised *mawālī* and embodying in their teachings many ideas brought by these converts from their previous religions. After the death of Muḥammad b. al-Ḥanafiyya in 81/700–1, his followers split into three main groups, one of which followed his son Abū Hāshim ʿAbd Allah (...), and was known after him as Hāshimiyya. On the death of Abu Hāshim without issue in 98/716, his followers again split into several groups, one of which maintained that Abū Hāshim had bequeathed the Imāmate to Muḥammad b. ʿAlī b. ʿAbd Allah b. al-ʿAbbās, just before he died in the house of Muḥammad b. ʿAlī's father in Palestine. This group continued to be known as Hāshimiyya, and also as Rāwandiyya.[1]

In a recent study, C. Cahen argued for a new interpretation of the term *ghāliya*. He explains that the context of this word leaves no doubt that the *ghāliya* (extremists) are those who exaggerate with regard to a personage, conferring on him superhuman attributes.[2] This brings us to the real nature of the differences between the various Shīʿite sects. One must leave aside the elaborate theories of the heresiographers and try to reconstruct the early stages of the development of the need for such a personage with such superhuman attributes. Of course this personage is the *Imām*. The notion of an *Imām* as leader of the Muslim community is definitely a Shīʿite one. While it is common among all Shīʿite sects, there are differences regarding the extent of the *Imām*'s power. How did he come to possess such power? How is he to be installed as leader of the Muslim community to exercise his powers? To all Shīʿite sects these powers or attributes descend from the realm of knowledge (*ʿilm*). The *Imām* is supposed, through intuition, inheritance or divine guidance, to possess superhuman religious knowledge. It is by means of this knowledge that the many problems of the Muslim community are solved. Therefore, all Shīʿite sects wanted an *Imām* to occupy the office of

1 B. Lewis, "ʿAbbāsids", *Encyclopaedia of Islam*, New Edition, Leiden, 1954–.

2 C. Cahen, "Points de vue sur la 'Révolution abbaside'", *Revue Historique*, 1963, pp. 295–338, at p. 309.

Amīr al-Mu'minīn, i.e. they wanted a leader of the community who would have both secular and religious powers.

A brief description of the development and functions of the office of *Amīr al-Mu'minīn* may clarify the issues involved in the struggle over this position. Abū Bakr was not *Amīr al-Mu'minīn*; he was *Khalīfat Rasūl Allāh*. He was chosen as a rallying point around which the régime established by Muḥammad would be maintained. Obviously there was no precedent, and just as clearly he did not have the same powers as the Prophet. Commentators argued at length about the exact meaning of the word *khalīfa*, without reaching a definite conclusion. Modern scholars have continued the argument, perhaps with the same lack of success. W. M. Watt concluded that "the basic meaning is 'successor' or, as one commentator defined it, 'one who takes the place of another after him in some matter'".[1] Clearly, the application of this word to Abū Bakr was deliberately vague. Nobody in Madīna yet had any conception of the amount of authority this new office bestowed upon its holder. This vagueness would assure minimum authority while at the same time leaving the door open for any possible development.

As the experiment was a success during the two years of Abū Bakr, it was decided to continue with it. He appointed 'Umar as his successor and there was no objection. 'Umar took the title of *Amīr al-Mu'minīn*, generally translated as Commander of the Believers. This translation is wrong because it implies more powers than 'Umar had. The word *amīr* has many meanings and it is misleading to rely on this one, ignoring all the others. It means king, prince, lord, governor, leader of the blind, a husband, a neighbour, a counsellor, or adviser. The last meaning is the one which should concern us here. Thus the title of *Amīr al-Mu'minīn* was originally conceived and understood to mean the Counsellor of Believers. Indeed, the Greek historian Theophanes rendered it as *protosymboulos* (first counsellor).[2] 'Umar was chosen as a counsellor with no power to command. In the Arab tradition no power to command was granted to the chief. This was understood by 'Umar as well as by the rest of the community of believers. Although the office changed names the authority of *Amīr al-Mu'minīn* was kept to a minimum. 'Umar had a very strong

[1] W. M. Watt, *Islamic Political Thought*, Edinburgh, 1968, p. 32.
[2] Wellhausen, p. 138.

personality and he certainly took the best advantage of it, but he also scrupulously recognized the limits of the authority of his office.

The trouble started when the sudden expansion of the empire created unforeseen political and social problems. ʿUmar himself was acutely aware of these problems, but they were too complicated to be solved within the political and social framework of the existing system. The newly conquered provinces were virtually autonomous and Arab tribesmen were pouring into the newly established garrison towns. This uncontrolled mass migration was one of the most serious results of the Arab conquests, a result not yet fully appreciated by students of Islamic history. It is no wonder that at his death ʿUmar had to consider very seriously the future of the whole structure. He could have appointed a successor from among the many respected leaders around him, but he chose not to, and instead took the precaution of appointing a committee (*shūra*) to consider the question of succession. Even if their assignment was only to recommend a successor to the community, their choice must depend on the policies of the candidates and all aspects of the situation would have to be examined. This must have been the case, because after some hard bargaining two candidates were left, ʿAlī and ʿUthmān. ʿAlī was not willing to accept the nomination in the same tradition as Abū Bakr and ʿUmar, that is, ruling with limited power. He asked for freedom to act according to his own judgement to meet the new circumstances. ʿUthmān agreed unconditionally to follow the policies of the *shaykhān*, Abū Bakr and ʿUmar.[1] The result was a new *Amīr al-Muʾminīn* with limited powers in a very troublesome situation.

Subsequently the situation continued to worsen in the provinces. Successive waves of migration created social upheaval in the garrison towns, especially in Kūfa. There the distribution of the revenue from the conquered territories was originally planned for the benefit of the founders. They were all considered *ashrāf*, i.e. receiving an *atā* (stipend) of an average of 3,000 dirhams a year, compared to an average of 300 dirhams for the new arrivals. Also in the territories conquered and held by the Kūfans, there were many inequalities in the division of the spoils between those who actually conquered these territories and those who arrived at

[1] Balādhurī, *Ansāb*, vol. v, pp. 41–2; Ṭabarī, vol. 1, pp. 2793–4.

a later stage. The conquerors held to their advantages and strongly opposed any claims made by the new arrivals. The latter grew resentful and demanded a fair share of the spoils. The clan, the unit in Arab society, lost some of its social significance, since the influx of the tribesmen into the garrison towns was haphazard. Tribesmen from related, sometimes even from unrelated, clans were clustered together in various tribal groupings. This arrangement led to many unsettling rivalries for the leadership. At the same time a new Islamic leadership was trying to assert itself in competition with the old-established Arab aristocracy, like that of Ash'ath ibn Qays al-Kindī in Kūfa.

Soon 'Uthmān realized that he could not keep his promise and tried to assume more power, religious as well as secular, in order to cope with the new problems. He was not a weak ruler, on the contrary he was trying to be a strong one. He initiated new waves of conquest in North Africa as well as in Iran. He appointed new, capable and vigorous governors to lead these campaigns. Replacing 'Amr ibn al-'Ās by his foster-brother Ibn Abī Sarḥ in Egypt was not simply nepotism; an independent-minded governor was dismissed to make way for a man from his own clan over whom he would have more control. 'Uthmān was simply trying to assert his authority over the autonomous provinces through his own men. In the same way, other actions about which different sections of the Islamic community complained may all be interpreted as attempts to strengthen his position as *Amīr al-Mu'minīn*. The most vehement objections came from the tribesmen of the provinces who finally turned against him in revolt and murdered him.

The community of Madīna was shocked at the unexpected turn of events, and for five days after the murder of 'Uthmān they could not find any leader to accept the responsibility of the position of *Amīr al-Mu'minīn*.[1] Finally 'Alī, under the pressure of circumstances, had to accept the position in the most unfortunate conditions. The long expected explosion had occurred and he had the responsibility of ruling over a seriously divided community. Quaraysh never trusted 'Alī because, although he was a Qurayshite born in Makka, his early years had been spent in Muḥammad's household under circumstances unlikely to dispose him to identify himself with Meccan interests. Ṭalḥa and Zubayr, the leaders of Makkan opposition to 'Alī, failed to raise significant

[1] Ṭabarī, vol. 1, p. 3073.

support to their cause against him. 'Alī's strength was based on a coalition of various groups which hoped to influence him to favour their interests. He had become the champion of the Madīnans' (*Anṣār*) cause, particularly when they began to feel neglected in favour of the Makkans after Muḥammad's death. The Madīnans stood by 'Alī until the very end though they never became Shī'ites. Kūfa with all its factions, from the founders to the latest comers, was also behind 'Alī. The founders, with their established interests in the region, thought that 'Alī would reverse the trend that threatened their position under 'Uthmān. 'Alī's other supporters were mainly the latecomers to Kūfa, who hoped that he could help them redress their grievances by introducing important amendments in the distribution of spoils. 'Alī was well known for his views about using his own judgement to meet new developments, that is, to allow change to take place as long as he considered it justified. This approach was of the utmost importance because those with established interests were, of course, against any change. Furthermore, they had begun to formulate justifications for their claims in religious terms. A leader who promised to bring about change and who could reinterpret the elusive Qur'ānic references to the distribution of *fay'* and *ghanīma* in favour of the latecomers was what they needed to bring justice and harmony to the community.

Soon 'Alī found that it was impossible to reconcile the various interests so as to satisfy all the Kūfan factions. Their interests were so contradictory that to satisfy one was to antagonize another. The Khawārij were the first of 'Alī's supporters to fall out. Any reinterpretation by 'Alī would certainly affect their interests, and they vehemently turned against him. The Khawārij took their uncompromising stand not only, as has been suggested, because they felt insecure as a result of the great social upheaval following the stupendous Arab conquests; nor was it simply to make a public protest against the domination of an impersonal system, even if it cost them their lives.[1] What they wanted was the application of the rule (*ḥukm*) of God, i.e. Qur'ānic rules as interpreted by them and not as interpreted by anybody else. They saw their *Amīr al-Mu'minīn* as a figurehead without any power at all.

[1] W. M. Watt, "The Conception of the Charismatic Community in Islam", *Numen* VII (1960), pp. 85–98, at p. 85; also by the same author, "Kharijite thought in the Umayyad Period", *Der Islam*, vol. 36, part 3 (1961), pp. 215–31, at p. 217.

Those latecomers who hoped that 'Alī could bring about changes to redress their grievances continued to support him and became his Shī'a. To them he was the *Imām–Amīr al-Mu'minīn* who would use his interpretative religious powers to set all things right. The religious knowledge (*'ilm*) of the *Imām* became a cornerstone in Shī'ite thought and it was left to later generations of Shī'ites to argue about the nature of this particular knowledge and the means by which an *Imām* should acquire it. In 'Alī's lifetime he was perhaps credited with certain intellectual powers, but the community at large was not ready to grant *Amīr al-Mu'minīn* any religious powers in the conduct of his office. When 'Alī's coalition disintegrated his own following was in the minority. In spite of hesitant support from Baṣra and even without the inconclusive opposition from Syria, 'Alī's cause was doomed. After his assassination, his son and successor Ḥasan failed to rally any significant support and wisely abdicated.

Mu'āwiya was acclaimed as the new *Amīr al-Mu'minīn* but with no religious powers at all. His secular powers were perhaps intended to be the same as those of Abū Bakr and 'Umar. His acceptance was a compromise between all parties concerned. Although he was a leader of Quraysh, he did not identify himself with Makkan interests as much as Ṭalḥa and Zubayr. He had the power of the Syrian army, yet he prudently kept it in the background and allowed the tribal leadership to share power with him in the empire. He was *Amīr al-Mu'minīn*, yet employing his *ḥilm*, he was equal among equals. He tried to rectify some of the injustices of the system in Iraq but, because of his limited authority, he could not satisfy all factions. The very delicate balance he maintained was too dependent on his own personality, and upon his death the situation in the empire reverted to what it had been before his reign. First Ḥusayn, 'Alī's son, thought he saw a chance for power, but he was mistaken. Then the Makkans, taking advantage of the collapse of the central government, tried to regain lost ground and set up a rival régime under the leadership of 'Abdullah ibn al-Zubayr. This régime was widely recognized but not vigorously supported. The Muslim community was not willing to submit to Makkan domination. The Syrian power was still intact and still supporting the Umayyad cause. The Syrians were satisfied with their social organization and the land distribution system set up from the time of the conquest and carefully maintained by Mu'āwiya in his forty years in power in Syria. It was only a question of time before the Syrians, using their military power, were able to impose unity throughout the empire.

Nevertheless, during this period there was a great deal of confusion and instability. Baṣra, threatened by the Khawārij, was willing to accept any authority to fend off the danger. Kūfa continued to be the hotbed of revolutionary activities in its quest for change. Some Kūfans thought that after the death of Yazīd I the Umayyads were finished. In 64/684, 4,000 Arab tribesmen from Kūfa calling themselves the Penitents claimed that they repented of the betrayal of Ḥusayn and would avenge his murder. Although most of those responsible for the massacre at Karbalā were living in Kūfa, the Penitents marched against Syria where they were easily defeated. There is no doubt that these Penitents were from the original Shī'a of 'Alī, but in contrast to other Shī'ite movements they did not proclaim an *Imām*. However, they were immediately followed by a better organized Shī'ite movement, also in Kūfa, under the leadership of al-Mukhtār ibn Abī 'Ubayd al-Thaqafī.

Mukhtār's revolt is, perhaps, one of the most misunderstood and misrepresented movements in early Islamic history. Of course it was a revolt of Shī'ites in Kūfa clamouring for change, but the nature of this change cannot be fully understood unless the socio-economic factors are clearly explained. No study of Kūfa has so far appeared to allow us to understand the way it was settled or indeed any aspect of unrest in this troubled centre. Unfortunately, modern scholars have not given enough attention to this problem, concentrating rather on misleading interpretations of the aims of the various revolts there. The revolt of Mukhtār is unjustifiably ascribed to *mawālī* unrest, in spite of the overwhelming evidence to the contrary.[1] The largest *mawālī* group we can find among his followers—and the tendency of our sources to exaggerate must be taken into account—numbers 2,300.[2] His main support came from Ibrāhīm ibn al-Ashtar and his men, none of whom were *mawālī*.[3] Mukhtār himself was no more than an opportunist who saw the breakdown in the political structure of the empire. He thought that he could fill the power vacuum

[1] C. Cahen, pp. 303–5; Watt, "Shī'ism under the Umayyads", *Journal of the Royal Asiatic Society* (1960), pp. 158–72, at pp. 162–5.

[2] Balādhurī, *Ansāb*, vol. v, p. 246.

[3] *Ibid.*, p. 222.

by establishing himself in Kūfa. As a resident of long standing, he certainly understood the real reasons for its internal strife and decided to use it to his best advantage. He knew the predicament of the latecomers in their struggle against established interests. He also realized that if he was to have their support he must provide an *Imām* who could bring about the desired change. The legacy of ʿAlī still survived among his Shīʿa in Kūfa. Mukhtār decided to proclaim his revolt in the name of ʿAlī's son, Muḥammad, who was then living in Ḥijāz. The latter only ambiguously consented to lend his name to Mukhtār's revolt and no other noticeable contact between them is noted. Nevertheless, Muḥammad ibn ʿAlī (Ibn al-Ḥanafiyya) was proclaimed the *Imām* in whose name the revolt was launched. Mukhtār even went a step further and designated him as the *Mahdī*, the divinely guided *Imām*. At this point it is difficult to say whether this was meant to emphasize the religious role of the *Imām* in contrast to the role Mukhtār reserved for himself as emissary, *wazīr* and *amīn*, who would presumably hold the secular power in case of success. On the other hand, it may have been a propaganda move on the part of Mukhtār, who was apparently a master of this art, as is evident from his celebrated rhymes, predictions and his adoption of a *tābūt* (Ark of the Covenant). Our sources leave no doubt about the ambitions and opportunism of Mukhtār. However, they make it clear that for a while he captured the imagination of the dissatisfied Arab tribesmen of Kūfa and that his support rested with them. Any support from the *mawālī* was incidental and unimportant, and in any case is reported in only one incident where the *mawālī* were not effective. It is most significant that the strongest opposition to Mukhtār in Kūfa came from the *ashrāf*, the only satisfied group there, who finally had to leave Kūfa altogether and join Ibn al-Zubayr in Baṣra. They formed a powerful contingent in his army which finally put an end to Mukhtār's revolt.[1]

When Umayyad rule was re-established under ʿAbdulmalik, a new, powerful central government put forward a vigorous imperialist policy. Neither the new *Amīr al-Muʾminīn* nor any of his successors claimed any religious powers, but they certainly had more secular powers than Muʿāwiya. In spite of his much cele-

[1] *Ibid.*, pp. 214–273. Balādhurī gives the best account of Mukhtār's revolt and it is confirmed by all our sources.

brated religiosity, 'Umar II assumed as much temporal authority as any other Umayyad ruler. His short-lived opposition was primarily to the imperialist policies of his predecessors but not necessarily to the strengthening of the central government. Although the Umayyads were able to establish effective control in Iraq and the rest of the empire, their policies did not satisfy all elements, and the increasing power of the central government aroused much opposition. In most cases this opposition took the form of frequent Khārijite and Shī'ite uprisings. These various uprisings, especially among the Shī'ites, rarely took the form of a concerted effort. Each uprising had its own reasons in the circumstances of the region concerned, and its own solution in the political system it advocated. They were all complaining about one kind of injustice or another imposed on them by the established order and its supporters. The Khawārij generally agreed that they wanted an *Amīr al-Mu'minīn* with no secular or religious powers. All the Shī'ites believed that they needed an *Imām* with interpretative religious powers to occupy the office of *Amīr al-Mu'minīn*. It was in the nature of things that they should fall back on the legacy of 'Alī, which by then had been enhanced by the martyrdom of Ḥusayn. Of course, kinship to the Prophet was an added advantage. The pre-Islamic Arabs had always accepted the leadership of the people of the House (*ahl al-bayt*), a term applied to the leading family of a clan. It was almost inevitable that this term should be applied to the family of the Prophet. Consequently the Shī'a believed that the leadership of the Islamic community was their legitimate right. The knowledge with which 'Alī was accredited was also believed to be inherent in his descendants, or at least to be passed on from one *Imām* to another.

In many ways the circumstances under which the Shī'ite movements and uprisings took place in the various parts of the empire determined the basic tenets of each sect. The availability of a member of the House of the Prophet, the extent of the needed reform, or the amount of control the central government could exert in a specific region, dictated the nature of the Shī'ite sect concerned, or the method it advocated to install its *Imām* in the office of *Amīr al-Mu'minīn*. Some sects were for armed revolt while others, realizing the risks involved, were willing to wait for circumstances to allow such a move without causing a split in the Muslim community. Other minor groups were desperate enough to use any possible means, including terror, to achieve their goal.

Towards the end of the Umayyad period there was an eruption of Shīʿite activities in Kūfa which clearly illustrates the various trends among the Shīʿa. The Kūfans had vigorously demonstrated their objection to Umayyad rule in their support of al-Mukhtār, Ibn al-Ashʿath and Yazīd ibn al-Muhallab. After the failure of the latter's revolt, Syrian military presence in Iraq was strengthened under Maslama 102/720. The only recourse for any Shīʿite movement was to operate underground. Three movements of this kind were reported to have taken place in Kūfa at that time. Bayān ibn Samʿān, executed in 119/737, claimed to be an emissary of Abū Hāshim ibn Muḥammad ibn al Ḥanafiyya (d. 98/716), then changed his claim to Muḥammad al-Bāqir (d. 113/731) a descendant of al-Ḥusayn ibn ʿAlī. Al-Mughīra ibn Saʿīd al-ʿIjlī, also executed in 119/737, first preached the cause of Muḥammad al-Bāqir, but on his death turned to Muḥammad the Pure Soul, a descendant of al-Ḥasan ibn ʿAlī. The latter eventually led an unsuccessful revolt against Abū Jaʿfar al-Manṣūr and was killed in 145/762. The third claimant to be an emissary of Muḥammad al-Bāqir was Abū Manṣūr, executed in 125/742, whose supporters practised the strangulation of their opponents.[1]

Meanwhile in 122/720 Zayd ibn ʿAlī, a brother of Muḥammad al-Bāqir, led an armed revolt in Kūfa and was killed. His son Yaḥyā fled to Khurāsān where he too was killed. In 127/744 ʿAbdullāh ibn Muʿāwiya, a great-grandson of ʿAlī's brother Jaʿfar, started another armed revolt in Kūfa. Soon he too was driven out of Kūfa but was able to establish himself in western Iran, where he was again chased and defeated by Umayyad forces. When he fled to Khurāsān he was assassinated by Abū Muslim. His revolt was Shīʿite in so far as it was led by a member of the House of the Prophet. Although his supporters included many Shīʿite Kūfans, other non-Shīʿite groups joined him, especially after he had left Kūfa. Sulaymān ibn Hishām of the Umayyad house, Manṣūr ibn Jumhūr al-Kalbī, the Syrian general, and the Khārijite leader, Shaybān, were among the followers of Ibn Muʿāwiya. He was also joined by leading members of the ʿAbbāsid house including al-Manṣūr himself.[2] Obviously at this stage in the collapse of Umayyad rule and before the advent of the

[1] See Watt, "Shīʿism", p. 168.

[2] Ṭabarī, vol. II, p. 1977.

'Abbāsid Revolution, Ibn Mu'āwiya offered the best viable alternative to the disintegrating régime. Had he succeeded, we might perhaps not have heard of the 'Abbāsid Revolution. However, he made one serious mistake and that was to stage his abortive uprising in Kūfa and then in Fars, which were too close to the Syrian troops stationed in Wāsiṭ. Although his claims to the Imāmate were not any stronger than those of the 'Abbāsids, he was able to rally the opposition around him and pose a serious threat to the Umayyads. At this point, precedence was given to the practical step of bringing down the Umayyad régime. The choice of the member of the House of the Prophet to be the *Imām* was relegated to second place. Al-Manṣūr himself believed in this as is evident from his presence with Ibn Mu'āwiya as late as 129/746–7. It was not unusual among the Shī'a to change allegiance from one member of the House of the Prophet to another. In other words all members had what W. M. Watt prefers to call charismata and what would be better described as acceptance by the Shī'a.[1]

In such an atmosphere, one can understand the reason why the 'Abbāsid emissaries preached on behalf of "an acceptable member of the family of the Prophet". They were confident of their plan to bring down the Umayyads, after which the 'Abbāsids had as much of a chance as any other claimant, if not more.

2 *Machinations of the conspirators*

The rise of Abū Muslim in Merv was the culmination of a long and sustained effort. A great deal has been said about the stages of this revolutionary movement. Yet one must not forget that it was a secret movement and this secrecy was perhaps one of the important factors in its success. It is difficult enough to reconstruct some of the most celebrated episodes in Islamic history, let alone to try to unravel the shrouded mysteries of a clandestine revolutionary conspiracy. In spite of the discovery of new sources concerned with the organization of the 'Abbāsid Revolution, we are still very much in the dark about some of its important links and personages. Nevertheless, various scholars have been able to present a reasonable reconstruction of its stages, methods and propaganda. Their conclusions have been confirmed in a recent

[1] Watt, "Charismatic Community", p. 78.

study by Dr F. Omar who has made use of freshly discovered material.[1]

The ʿAbbāsids were the descendants of the Prophet's uncle al-ʿAbbās, and as such they were members of the House of the Prophet. Al-ʿAbbās himself did not particularly distinguish himself in the service of Islam. He was a relatively late convert who only accepted Islam in 8/630. His son ʿAbdullah was a man whose religious opinions were highly respected. For some time he supported his cousin ʿAlī, then, after the inconclusive battle of Ṣiffīn, he withdrew to Ḥijāz. During the second civil war he refused to lend his support to Ibn al-Zubayr, and subsequently was expelled to Ṭā'if.[2] His son, ʿAlī ibn ʿAbdillah, also enjoyed a sound reputation as a religious man, but he incurred the wrath of Walīd I, perhaps because he was suspected of political activities against the Umayyads. Twice he was ordered to be beaten, and finally he was imprisoned for a period, after which he was released to take up residence in Ḥumayma, a village in Palestine on the route from Damascus to Ḥijāz.[3] After his death in 118/736 his son, Muḥammad ibn ʿAlī, continued to live there. There is general agreement that it is with him that the history of the ʿAbbāsid movement begins. The story of the bequest of Abū Hāshim ibn Muḥammad ibn al-Ḥanafiyya to Muḥammad ibn ʿAlī is too well known to be repeated here. The fact remains that in 98/716 Muḥammad ibn ʿAlī took over the claims of Abū Hāshim and with them a small Shīʿite sect and a secret organization known as Hāshimiyya. We know very little about the political activities of Abū Hāshim or, for that matter, about his secret organization. Although neither Abū Hāshim nor his father ever lived in Kūfa, we are told that the Hāshimiyya organization was established there. It consisted of no more than thirty men, Arabs and *mawālī*.[4] From their later activities it can be inferred that many of them were involved in trade between Khurāsān, Iraq, Syria and Ḥijāz. Muḥammad ibn ʿAlī proceeded to transform this small

[1] G. van Vloten, *De opkomst der Abbasiden in Chorasan*, Leiden, 1890; also by the same author, *Recherches sur la Domination Arabe*, Amsterdam, 1894, Wellhausen, Ch. IX, pp. 492–566; S. Moscati, "Il testamento di Abu Muslim", *Rivista degli Studi Orientali* (1952), pp. 28 ff.; also Moscati, "Studi su Abū Muslim I–III", *Accademia Nazionale dei Lincei* (1949), pp. 323–35, 474–95; (1950), pp. 89–105; F. Omar, "The ʿAbbāsid Caliphate, 132–70/750–86", unpublished Ph.D. thesis, University of London, 1967.

[2] Omar, p. 76.

[3] Ṭabarī, vol. I, p. 579.

[4] *Tārīkh al-Khulafā'*, anon., ed. P. Griyaznevitch, Moscow, 1962, p. 250B.

organization into the instrument of the ʿAbbāsid party. His genius was in deciding on Khurāsān and especially Merv as the centre for the revolutionary activities of the Hāshimiyya. He must have realized the explosive situation there and that Merv was the best potential field for the recruitment of a revolutionary army. He also realized that any anti-Umayyad movement in Iraq was doomed to failure as long as the Syrian troops were stationed there. Certainly the Shīʿites of Kūfa were always ready to join any uprising, but they had never been successful. Kūfa, with its large sympathetic community, could serve best as a link between the headquarters in Ḥumayma and the field of activities in Merv. Probably some of the members of the Hāshimiyya organization in Kūfa were descendants of Shīʿites who had supported Mukhtār, but this would be the only connection between the two movements.[1] To attempt to establish continuity between Mukhtār's uprising and the Hāshimiyya–ʿAbbāsid movement is futile. While it is true that they were both Shīʿite, the conditions, the methods and the chosen fields of activity were completely different.

Muḥammad ibn ʿAlī did not waste much time in pursuing his plan to establish a revolutionary base in Khurāsān. From Kūfa emissaries (*dāʿīs*) were sent to Merv but, according to F. Omar, "the first *dāʿīs* in Khurāsān did not have much success, and in its early period the *daʿwa* was under constant surveillance on the part of the Umayyads".[2] Bernard Lewis more accurately concluded that "the accounts given by the historians of the first ʿAbbāsid missions are incomplete and in part contradictory. Broadly, they indicate that intensive propaganda began from about 100/718. From headquarters in Kūfa, and the Hāshimiyya sent emissaries to Khurāsān, one of whom, Khidāsh, won considerable success, but was executed in 118/736 after prematurely showing his hand."[3]

Soon after, the leaders of the revolution adopted a new tactic. A committee of twelve *naqībs* (leading missionaries) was chosen from the Arab Settlers in Merv: four from Khuzāʿa, four from Tamīm, one from Ṭayy, one from Shaybān, one from Bajīla and one probably a *mawlā* of Ḥanīfa. Sulaymān ibn Kathīr al-Khuzāʿī was selected to head this new organization in Merv.[4] It is also reported

[1] *Ibid.*, p. 246B.
[2] Omar, p. 88; Cahen, pp. 324–5.
[3] Lewis, "ʿAbbāsids".
[4] Ṭabarī, vol. II, pp. 1358, 1988; *Tārīkh al-Khulafāʾ*, p. 254A; Omar, pp. 88–90.

that fifty-eight *dā'īs* were nominated at that time, forty for Merv itself, and eighteen for various towns in Khurāsān. The names we have of these *dā'īs* suggest that they were from the Arab Settlers in Merv. While no specific responsibility was assigned to the forty *dā'īs* in Merv, the other eighteen are believed to have been selected to "propagate the cause in parts other than Merv, among the *muqātila* stationed in other garrison cities in Khurāsān".[1] These reports should not be taken seriously because, in the first place, we know that there were no Arab garrison towns in Khurāsān at that time. Secondly, although it is natural for revolutionaries to propagate their cause wherever possible, the number of *dā'īs* allocated to Merv is so out of proportion to the rest of Khurāsān as to suggest that the revolutionaries knew exactly where to expect support. They preferred to concentrate their efforts in Merv and the few *dā'īs* who were sent out were to investigate the situation rather than propagate the cause. It is significant that we do not hear much about these *dā'īs* in the narratives about later developments in Khurāsān. These reports about *dā'īs* outside Merv were probably meant to bring the number of all *dā'īs* up to seventy in emulation of the number of the first Madīnans who concluded the agreement with the Prophet before his flight from Makka. It is also possible that seventy was the total number of the Hāshimiyya movement in Khurāsān at that time.[2] F. Omar reports that "furthermore the central committee of twelve *naqībs* at Merv decided to choose twelve more members, called *nuẓarā' al-nuqabā'*, to substitute for any of the twelve *naqībs* should any of them withdraw or be dismissed or killed".[3] Bukayr ibn Māhān, the leader of the Kūfan organization, was in Merv as an emissary of Muḥammad ibn 'Alī to supervise the setting up of this organization in Khurāsān. Contact with Muḥammad in Ḥumayma was only maintained through Kūfa and his name was kept secret. The pilgrimage season was the only chance for some of the leaders from Merv to meet him in Ḥijāz and present him with contributions from their followers in Merv. Until Muḥammad's death in 125/743 Bukayr continued to be his usual emissary to Merv, and it was on his last visit that he brought the news of the succession of Ibrāhīm ibn Muḥammad to his father's claims.[4]

[1] Omar, pp. 91–92.
[2] Ṭabarī, vol. II, p. 1988.
[3] Omar, p. 92.
[4] *Tārīkh al-Khulafā'*, pp. 251 B, 252 A, 252 B, 254 B, 255 A, 255 B, 257 A.

Ibrāhīm's accession to the leadership of the Hāshimiyya organization coincided with the breakdown in the Umayyad government after the death of Hishām. As a result it was the beginning of a new phase of activity on the part of the revolutionaries whose hopes were heightened by these events. The partisans in Merv agitated for immediate action to take advantage of the situation in the empire.[1] In 126/744 Abū Salama al-Khallāl, the new leader of the organization in Kūfa following the death of Bukayr ibn Māhān, was hurriedly sent to Merv to control the partisans. He was accompanied by a young follower whose name was Abū Muslim. However, after four months in Merv they both returned to Kūfa, leaving Sulaymān ibn Kathīr in charge of the organization in Khurāsān.[2]

It does not seem that the situation in Merv remained under control for long. Soon the *Imām* Ibrāhīm had to send a personal representative to reside there and take charge of the Revolution in his name. Abū Muslim, who was chosen for this task, arrived at Merv in 128/746. He was not easily accepted by the local leaders, particularly Sulaymān ibn Kathīr who was, however, quickly overruled by his colleagues. Abū Muslim himself did his best to assuage Sulaymān's feelings and left him in nominal charge of the secret organization.[3] But the Revolution then moved from secrecy to open revolt, and it was Abū Muslim who was to play the vital role. The question now is, why was he chosen for this role? Or indeed, who was Abū Muslim?

3 *Abū Muslim 'Abdurraḥman ibn Muslim al-Khurāsānī*

Surprisingly we know very little before his arrival at Merv about the man to whom the 'Abbāsids owed their victory.[4] The reports about his early life do not agree on a single detail. When he was personally asked about his origin, he evaded the question and instead advised the interrogators not to attach any importance to such unimportant details.[5] In spite of the newly discovered sources, and the valiant effort of F. Omar, one must agree with R. N. Frye that "the origins of Abū Muslim cannot definitely be

[1] *Ibid.*, pp. 257A, 257B. [2] *Ibid.*, p. 258A.

[3] *Ibid.*, pp. 262B–263B; Ṭabarī, vol. II, pp. 1960–2.

[4] For discussion of the origin of Abū Muslim, see Omar, pp. 94–9; also the various articles by Moscati.

[5] Ṭabarī, vol. II, p. 1965; Ibn al-Athīr, *Kāmil*, vol. V, p. 279.

determined from Islamic sources".[1] There seems to have been a deliberate attempt to cover all traces of his past and to present him in a new image. The key to this new image is his assumed name, Abū Muslim ʻAbdurraḥman ibn Muslim al-Khurāsānī. His *kunya,* Abū Muslim, means the father of a *muslim*. His name ʻAbdurraḥman, he who worships the Compassionate, applies to every *muslim*. The name itself is reputed to have been one of the favourite names which the Prophet gave to many of his newly converted companions. Abū Muslim also assumed Muslim as his father's name. In other words the name represents a *muslim* who is a son of a *muslim* and the father of a *muslim*. His *nisba* is most significant. He related himself only to Khurāsān, and not to a tribe or a clan, either as a member or a *mawlā*, as was the practice at the time. One must not forget that he was not from Khurāsān, he only came there. There could not have been greater emphasis placed on the idea that in the new society promised by the Revolution every member would be regarded only as a *muslim*, with the same rights and the same responsibilities regardless of racial origins or tribal connections. Abū Muslim's assumed name was the best possible slogan for the Revolution he was sent to lead. Perhaps this was the real reason for sending him to Khurāsān. It was not to be one of the proven Arabs or *mawālī* of Merv who was to lead the Revolution. This could have given it a specific colour which was deliberately avoided by sending a complete outsider whose very origin was kept a secret. Of course, there were men in Merv who would have been quite capable of leading the Revolution. Qaḥṭaba ibn Shabīb, the general who led the victorious march to Kūfa, or Sulaymān ibn Kathīr, who was responsible for building up the organization in Merv, are only two examples. There was a certain risk in asking Sulaymān to subordinate himself in his own territory to a total stranger; yet the risk was taken. This arrangement must have had the approval of Abū Salama, if it was not altogether at his own suggestion. He was to remain in Kūfa in charge of the organization there and Abū Muslim was instructed to defer to him.[2] Abū Salama had just returned from Merv after a four months stay during which he was accompanied by Abū Muslim.[3] They must have formulated some opinion

[1] R. N. Frye, "The role of Abū Muslim in the ʻAbbāsid Revolution", *Muslim World* 37 (1947), pp. 28–38, at p. 28; see also Cahen, p. 326.

[2] *Tārīkh al-Khulafā'*, p. 262 B.

[3] *Ibid.*, pp. 257 B–258 A; Ṭabarī, vol. III; pp. 24–5.

about the leadership in the vital region of Merv in this crucial phase of the Revolution. At this stage there was full co-operation between these two leaders and their ideas were successfully put into effect.

Abū Muslim's spectacular success in manipulating the struggle in Merv to the advantage of the Revolution, and his undeniable political acumen, perhaps overshadow other talents employed in it. Abū Salama's talent seems to have been in the quiet preparatory work. Although one cannot credit him with the long, arduous work of the original planners, his role in the Revolution has not been given enough attention. He was in Kūfa in the heart of the empire to prepare the ground for the takeover after the expected arrival of the victorious revolutionary army or, for that matter, for any other eventuality. From 126/744 to 132/749 he was in charge of co-ordinating all efforts for the success of the Revolution. Propaganda was a major weapon long adopted by the Shī'a before Abū Salama, but it was to him that the task fell of using it to maximum effect all over the empire. Every possible sign or portent listed in the eschatological prophecies current at the time was used to herald the imminent Revolution. Black flags had been hoisted by earlier rebels and had already acquired messianic significance. Now they were adopted by the Revolution as its own emblem. Legends and prophecies were invented and widely circulated referring to the rise of the black banners in the east and pointing to the end of Umayyad rule.[1] Slogans were provided to propagate the cause. The Revolution was preached in the name of *al-riḍā min āl Muḥammad*, a member of the House of the Prophet who would be acceptable to all. This was not particularly put forward for the sake of the partisans in Merv, but more as an appeal to all the Shī'a in the empire. As has been stated, a further appeal to all members of the Muslim community was embodied in the adopted name of Abū Muslim, perhaps invented by Abū Salama as a living and expressive slogan for the Revolution.

4 *The revolutionary army*

Who were the supporters of Abū Muslim? Wellhausen's opinion is: "the majority of his [Abū Muslim's] adherents consisted of Iranian peasants and of the *mawālī* of the villages of Merv, but

[1] Van Vloten, *Recherches*, p. 46; Lewis, "'Abbāsids".

there were Arabs among them also who mostly occupied leading positions".[1] Bernard Lewis seems to agree to some extent with this opinion: "While his (Abū Muslim's) main appeal was to the Persian *mawālī*, he also found important support among the Yemenite Arabs." Then Lewis continues:

an active and war-like Persian population, imbued with the religious and military traditions of the frontier, was deeply resentful of the inequalities imposed by Umayyad rule. The Arab army and settlers, half Persianized by long residence, were sharply divided among themselves, and even during the triumphal progress of Abū Muslim diverted their own energies and those of Naṣr ibn Sayyār to Arab inter-tribal strife.[2]

Moscati prefers to avoid the problem and states: "On 1 Shawwāl 129/15 June 747 the black banners of the insurgents were publicly raised. Profiting by the internal discords of the Umayyad army, Abū Muslim gained support among the Yemenites."[3] H. A. R. Gibb notes that "the tradition of the enthusiasm of the Iranians for Abū Muslim is true only of the period after his success. In our most authentic records there is no trace of a mass movement such as has so often been portrayed."[4] The truth of the matter is that, although there were some of the *mawālī* in Khurāsān among Abū Muslim's followers, his main support came from Arab quarters in Merv, namely from the Arab Settlers. As we have shown, it was this part of the population of Merv who were opposed to the Umayyad policy, which showed no concern with their interests. They were not only deprived of the advantages of being Arabs, but were also left under the authority of the *dihqāns* and thus in a sense were treated even worse than the conquered people. It is true that there was an attempt under Naṣr ibn Sayyār to eliminate some of their grievances, but it came too late to reconcile them to Umayyad rule. After the various experiments of the successive governors, these Settlers saw no hope except in a complete change not only in Khurāsān but in the whole empire. To them no change seemed better then that to the House of the Prophet to which Abū Muslim was summoning them. It is understandable that the House of the Prophet had come to be identified in the minds of the Muslim masses, under the prevailing circumstances, with the cause of justice. Further-

[1] Wellhausen, p. 532.
[2] Lewis, "'Abbāsids".
[3] Moscati, "Abū Muslim", *Encyclopaedia of Islam*, New Edition, Leiden, 1954–.
[4] Gibb, *Arab Conquests*, p. 94.

more, the martyrdom of the Shī'ite *Imāms* at the hands of the Umayyads, particularly that of Yaḥyā ibn Zayd in Khurāsān in 125/743 at the hands of Naṣr ibn Sayyār, had further tipped the balance in favour of the House of the Prophet, and it was skilfully exploited by Abū Muslim.

Other Arab tribesmen in Khurāsān were already assimilated enough to fit into the structure of the Umayyad empire, and they all were for the Umayyads, whether they supported Naṣr or al-Kirmānī. It was the Settlers who had perhaps become too assimilated to have a place in the imperial structure. To be sure, similar situations must have existed in other parts of the empire, but there the local administration was predominantly in Arab hands, not in the hands of the local aristocracy. In short, the Arab Settlers in Merv had their reasons to revolt against the continued existence of the "old régime" which was supported by Umayyad rule. It was towards these Settlers that the Hāshimiyya propaganda campaign was directed. The Hāshimiyya missionaries to Merv must have realized that they provided the most fertile ground for recruiting supporters for the revolutionary movement.

Although Wellhausen gives a fairly good account of the propaganda campaign of the Hāshimiyya, and in fact of the different phases of the 'Abbāsid Revolution, he himself missed the implications of these accounts. He did note, however, that all the missionaries of the Hāshimiyya were sent to Merv and all their activities in Khurāsān were confined to this district. He also noticed that the Khuzā'a "owned certain villages in the oasis of Merv, and with their Iranian peasants furnished a disproportionately large contingent to the 'Abbāsid Shī'a".[1] It is highly probable that a great number of the Settlers were from this particular tribe. We shall recall that the only two names we have in our records for the first settlers in Khurāsān were of men from Aslam of Khuzā'a and they were especially connected with the village of Fanīn in the Merv oasis which still belonged to Khuzā'a in Abū Muslim's time.[2] We also remember that this tribe was deeply involved in the schemes of Ḥurayth ibn Quṭba, the Soghdian merchant of Merv, himself a client of Khuzā'a.[3] It is of some significance that most of the Hāshimiyya missionaries to Merv

[1] Wellhausen, pp. 514–15.
[2] See above, p. 33.
[3] See above, p. 60.

were merchants, or at least claimed to be merchants, who had come to Khurāsān only for reasons of trade.[1] Certainly this would provide them with a good alibi in case they were watched by the authorities, and it would also make their contacts easier, particularly if the people they were trying to contact were also involved in trade. It is interesting to note, too, that some of the financial support sent to the *Imām* from Khurāsān was in the form of merchandise,[2] which may indicate the source of this support.

When Abū Muslim finally and openly raised the black banners, probably on the 1st of Shawwāl 129/15 June 747, he did so in a Khuzā'ite village.[3] In less than two days he was joined by about 2,200 men from the two *rub 'al-taqādum* or *ahl al-taqādum* (*saqādum* according to other readings).[4] Wellhausen read the word *Suqādim* as the name of a specific place, but since there were two groups of supporters coming from two different *Suqādims* or *Taqādums*, this reading is improbable.[5] Also, although Yāqūt gives an elaborate list of the names of the villages and districts of Merv he does not mention any place so named.[6] According to another version related by Ṭabarī, these supporters came from sixty villages around Merv.[7] On this basis we prefer the reading *taqādum* and we understand it as meaning the old Settlers in Merv.

In less than a month and a half the number of Abū Muslim's army rose to 7,000, whom he ordered to be listed in a new *dīwān* according to their names, their fathers' names and their villages.[8] This was a clear indication that they were all becoming Khurāsāniyya, without any distinction as to their tribes or their Arab or non-Arab origin. In other words, complete assimilation was achieved in Khurāsān, but this was expressed first in Abū Muslim's army, and subsequently imposed upon the rest of the empire by force of arms after the success of his Revolution in Merv.

[1] Ṭabarī, vol. II, pp. 1358, 1432, 1502.
[2] *Ibid.*, p. 1962; Ibn al-Athīr, *Kāmil*, vol. v, p. 127.
[3] Ṭabarī, vol. II, pp. 1952–4.
[4] *Ibid.*, pp. 1954–5, 1957; *Tārīkh al-Khulafā'*, p. 263B: where this word occurs as *naqādum*, the editor in his notes on p. vi adds two dots to the N and reads it *thaqādum*; Ibn al-Athīr, *Kāmil*, vol. v, p. 273, where this word occurs as *taqādum*; see above, p. 135.
[5] Wellhausen, p. 523.
[6] Yāqūt, *Buldān*.
[7] Ṭabarī, vol. II, p. 1952.
[8] *Ibid.*, p. 1969.

5 *The victory of the Revolution*

From the beginning, Abū Muslim realized that Juday' al-Kirmānī and his followers would be his best allies against Naṣr ibn Sayyār. They were wavering in their support of the Umayyads and it was possible to make common cause with them against Naṣr if not to gain their support for the Revolution. In fact, some of the Settlers had already joined Juday' in his fight against Naṣr.[1] The latter must have realized also that an alliance between Abū Muslim and Juday' would certainly put an end to his power in Khurāsān. He contrived to have Juday' murdered at the hand of Hātim, son of al-Ḥārith ibn Surayj, in revenge for his father.[2] Nevertheless 'Alī al-Kirmānī, son of Juday', continued his father's struggle against Naṣr. The situation was further complicated by the arrival of a new group of Arab tribesmen at Merv. These were some of the remnants of the defeated forces of Ibn Mu'āwiya, whose anti-Umayyad revolt in Iraq and western Iran had just been crushed. They were seeking refuge in Khurāsān and were led by Shaybān ibn Salama.[3] It was to be expected that these tribesmen, originally from Iraq, would have more affinity with the tribesmen of al-Kirmānī. It was also to be expected that they would ally themselves with any forces against the Umayyad governor of Khurāsān, Naṣr ibn Sayyār. However, their role should not be exaggerated since they do not seem to have been at all numerous.

Meanwhile Naṣr's celebrated appeals to the central Umayyad government were of no avail. On the other hand, al-Kirmānī was hopeful of gaining Abū Muslim's active support against Naṣr. In the summer of 129/747, after Naṣr had managed to install himself again in one part of the city of Merv, an uneasy truce was proclaimed between the two antagonists.[4] Abū Muslim, for his part, continued to gain more recruits to his revolutionary army and now moved to Ālīn, another Khuzā'ite village in the Merv oasis in Dhū al-Ḥijja 129/August 747.[5] Taking advantage of the truce, al-Kirmānī assumed *de facto* power in Khurāsān and in Rabī' II 130/December 747 appointed his new ally Shaybān ibn

[1] See above, p. 135.
[2] Ṭabarī, vol. II, p. 1975; Ya'qūbī, *Tārīkh*, vol. II, p. 407.
[3] Ṭabarī, vol. II, p. 1992; Omar, pp. 122–3.
[4] Ṭabarī, vol. II, pp. 1964–8, 1980–4.
[5] *Ibid.*, p. 1969.

Salama as his representative in Sarakhs.[1] Abū Muslim tacitly agreed to al-Kirmānī's assumption of power and promised him his support. It was not long before fighting broke out again in Merv between Naṣr and al-Kirmānī. The latter appealed to Abū Muslim for help. On Thursday, 9 Jumādā II 130/14 February 748, Abū Muslim led his revolutionary army into Merv and brought the fighting to an end.[2] The following day Naṣr ibn Sayyār fled to Nīshāpūr, where he planned to continue the fight against the revolution in spite of his very advanced age.

It would be wrong to assume that, at this point, Abū Muslim became the master of the situation in Khurāsān or even in Merv itself. While it is true that his strength was enhanced by the defeat of Naṣr, it is important to remember that this was achieved because of the alliance with the forces of al-Kirmānī who were not members of the Hāshimiyya. After entering Merv, Abū Muslim summoned his followers to pay allegiance in public to *al-riḍā*, an acceptable member of the House of the Prophet.[3] Neither al-Kirmānī nor any of his followers were among those who took such an oath. In other words, there were two rebellious parties in Merv: Abū Muslim's, fully committed to a revolutionary cause, al-Kirmānī's which, though co-operating with the revolutionaries, stayed outside the Revolution. Their co-operation aimed at getting rid of Naṣr and was to last as long as he or any of his followers represented any danger to the allies. Naṣr himself was in Nīshāpūr trying to rally any of his followers, presumably for an attack on Merv. Abū Muslim brought them near to desperation when he ordered twenty-four of their leaders captured in Merv to be executed.[4] Other partisans of Naṣr were still strongly entrenched in Balkh and in the stronghold of Tirmidh at the crossing of the Oxus. The *dahāqīn* of Merv must not be expected to have accepted easily the destruction of the régime which supported their privileges. It was also natural that the princes of the Principalities of Ṭukhāristān would try to take advantage of the division in the Arab ranks.

Abū Muslim continued to hold on to his alliance with al-Kirmānī's followers and to use them for his purposes in Khurāsān. But he wasted no time in dispatching his own army on its major task, the march westwards towards Kūfa. Qaḥṭaba ibn Shabīb

[1] *Ibid.*, p. 1996.
[2] *Ibid.*, p. 1987.
[3] *Ibid.*, p. 1989.
[4] *Ibid.*, p. 1989.

al-Tā'ī was reportedly appointed to lead this army by the *Imām* Ibrāhīm himself.[1] The first victory was at Sarakhs, where Shaybān ibn Salama and his refugees had been installed by al-Kirmānī. Shaybān thought that he was safe and showed some defiance to Abū Muslim. He probably had too much confidence in his own alliance with al-Kirmānī, but who in fact made no effort to save him from Abū Muslim's wrath.[2] Next the revolutionary army met and defeated an army from the followers of Naṣr, led by his son Tamīm. The battle took place outside Ṭūs and the city was soon captured. Nīshāpūr also soon fell in the hands of Qaḥṭaba's army. Naṣr ibn Sayyār, who was in Nīshāpūr, had to abandon all efforts to regain his power in Khurāsān and fled westwards only to die a few months later.[3]

The Umayyad central government, which was greatly alarmed by the developments in Khurāsān, was now able to send an army to deal with the rebels. This army of 10,000 men led by Nubāta ibn Hanẓala met the advancing revolutionaries at Gurgān and was utterly defeated, Dhū al-Ḥijja 130/August 748.[4] Qaḥṭaba then advanced to Rayy where he stayed for five months preparing for the crucial stages of his march. In Rajab 131/March 749 he was confronted by a bigger Umayyad army at Jāblaq near Isfahān. This army, reputedly of 50,000 men under the leadership of 'Āmir ibn Ḍubāra, was again decisively defeated by Qaḥṭaba.[5] After a short siege Nihāvand was captured and the road into Iraq was open. In a swift move Qaḥṭaba approached Kūfa but he was first forced to do battle with Yazīd ibn Hubayra, governor of Iraq for Marwān II, who was trying to make a last stand in its defence. However, on Wednesday, 8 Murharram 132/27 August 749, Qaḥṭaba took Ibn Hubayra by surprise and forced him to withdraw from his camp, on the bank of the Euphrates in the region of upper Fallūja, to the garrison town of Wāsiṭ. Although Qaḥṭaba himself lost his life in this last battle, his son Ḥasan led the victorious revolutionary army into Kūfa, without striking a blow, on Tuesday, 14 Muḥarram 132/2 September 749.[6] On their entering the town Abū Salama was acknowledged as *Waẓīr āl-Muḥammad*, and took charge of the whole situation. At this point

[1] *Ibid.*, p. 1954.
[2] *Ibid.*, p. 1996; *Tārīkh al-Khulafā'*, p. 271 B.
[3] Ṭabarī, vol. II, p. 2004, vol. III, p. 2.
[4] *Ibid.*, vol. II, pp. 2004, 2016.
[5] *Tārīkh al-Khulafā'*, pp. 275 B–278 A; Ṭabarī, vol. II, p. 2004.
[6] Ṭabarī, vol. III, pp. 12–18.

there was definitely no mention of any *Imām* or any questioning of Abū Salama's assumption of power. He appointed some of the leaders of the Khurāsāniyya to important positions in his administration and confirmed others in the appointments they held in the army. He also increased the stipends of the men in the army from 300 dirhams a year to 80 dirhams a month, with appropriate increases also for officers and commanders.[1]

Meanwhile, Abū Muslim was busy strengthening his position in Khurāsān. From Merv he sent small expeditions to various towns and regions in Khurāsān and was easily able to establish his control there. He had difficulty only in Balkh and Tirmidh. The sub-governors of these two important places, under Naṣr ibn Sayyār, were two of his staunchest supporters: Ziyād ibn 'Abdirraḥman al-Qushayrī for Balkh and Muslim ibn 'Abdirraḥman ibn Muslim al-Bāhilī for Tirmidh. They were joined by other sub-governors of the districts of the East, particularly from the Principalities of Ṭukhāristān, in an attempt by the "old guard" to make a last stand against the Revolution. When Abū Muslim dispatched a force, led by Abū Dāwūd Khālid ibn Ibrāhīm, towards Balkh, they put together as many as possible of their supporters from the surrounding districts and quickly advanced to meet Abū Dāwūd halfway in Gūzgān. Apparently realizing that they were not fully prepared, they decided, before the encounter, to withdraw to Tirmidh, leaving Balkh to fall temporarily to Abū Dāwūd.[2] From Tirmidh they continued their efforts to combine all the forces opposed to the Revolution in the East. First they enticed Yaḥyā ibn Nu'aym, Abū Muslim's representative in Balkh, to defect and join their effort. Then they persuaded the princes of the Principalities of Ṭukhāristān to support them. Most significant is that the *dahāqīn* of Merv also joined this desperate fight against the Revolution. In fact these combined forces were put under the leadership of Muqātil, son of Ḥayyān an-Nabaṭī, an old ally of the "old guard" in Merv.[3] All these forces marched towards Balkh and camped outside the town. Again, Abū Muslim sent his trusted lieutenant Abū Dāwūd to rescue Balkh. He defeated the enemy, who once more took refuge in Tirmidh, and re-entered the town.

[1] *Ibid.*, vol. III, p. 20; *Tārīkh al-Khulafa'*, pp. 283A–284A.

[2] Ṭabarī, vol. II, p. 1997.

[3] *Ibid.*, vol. II, p. 1998; see also above, p. 100.

Abū Muslim then appointed 'Uthmān, brother of 'Alī ibn al-Kirmānī, as his representative in Balkh. Although at this point our sources are extremely brief, it appears that there was another conspiracy, this time involving 'Uthmān al-Kirmānī with the increasingly desperate leaders of the "old guard". For no apparent reason 'Uthmān left Balkh for Merv ar-Rūd, during which time the forces of Tirmidh were able to recapture Balkh. When 'Uthmān turned back for the rescue he was easily defeated. It took yet another expedition under Abū Dāwūd to expel the enemy from Balkh. Abū Muslim, realizing the futility of his alliance with al-Kirmānī, decided to take no more risks. He ordered Abū Dāwūd to get rid of 'Uthmān while he discreetly ordered 'Alī to be killed.[1] Thereafter Abū Muslim became the sole master in Merv and the East.

6 *The 'Abbāsids in power*

Abū Muslim, who was now firmly established in Khurāsān, assumed the title of *Amīr Āl Muḥammad*.[2] This title must have meant more than simply the *amīr* of a province. Abū Muslim was more than a governor of Khurāsān and the East. He expected and received wider authority, both in the revolutionary phase and later, after the establishment of 'Abbāsid rule in the empire. From Khurāsān he kept in close touch with developments in Kūfa through his agent, Abū al-Jahm ibn 'Aṭiyya. The latter was appointed by Abū Muslim as a "political commissar" for the advancing revolutionary army and then confirmed in his position by Abū Salama in Kūfa.[3]

Abū Salama was in charge in Kūfa in the newly created position of *Wazīr Āl Muḥammad*. The etymological origin of the word *wazīr* does not explain the functions of the position.[4] The responsibilities of Abū Salama amounted to those of a provisional head of state in a revolutionary phase, and his powers were duly recognized by all concerned. Nevertheless the army was not

[1] *Ibid.*, vol. II, pp. 1999–2000; see also Ibn al-Athīr, *Kāmil*, vol. V, pp. 293–5.
[2] *Tārīkh al-Khulafā'*, p. 284A; Ṭabarī, vol. III, p. 60.
[3] Ṭabarī, vol. II, p. 2001; *Tārīkh al-Khulafā'*, p. 283B.
[4] For further discussion of *wazīr* see S. D. Goitein, *Studies in Islamic History and Institutions*, Leiden, 1968, pp. 168–96; D. Sourdel, *Le Vizirat Abbaside*, Damascus, 1959–60, vol. I, pp. 65–70; H. A. R. Gibb reviewed this latter work in *The Middle East Journal*, 14 (1960), p. 344.

completely under his control. He was to provide for it and administer its affairs, but the real control stayed with Abū al-Jahm, Abū Muslim's loyal adherent.

The Revolution was proclaimed in the name of *al-riḍā min āl Muḥammad*. The time came when this member of the House of the Prophet, acceptable to all, was to be selected. Although the name of the *Imām* of the Hāshimiyya, Ibrāhīm, was by now circulating among the revolutionaries, it was perhaps only as a possible candidate for the office of *Amīr al-Mu'minīn*. Unfortunately the currency of the name led the Umayyad authorities to the discovery of the connection between Ibrāhīm and the revolutionaries. He was promptly arrested in Ḥumayma and taken to Ḥarrān where he died, or more likely was murdered, in prison in Muḥarram 132/August 749. There are endless reports, in our sources, informing us that he had appointed his brother, Abū al-'Abbās 'Abdullah ibn Muḥammad, as his successor and that he had managed to inform his followers of his choice before he met his death.[1] Abū Salama, who was supposedly informed about Ibrāhīm's will, did not take it very seriously, or at least did not think that Abū al-'Abbās was the most acceptable member of the House of the Prophet to be installed as *Amīr al-Mu'minīn*. When all the members of the 'Abbāsid house congregated in Kūfa soon after the arrival of the Khurāsāniyya, Abū Salama ordered them to remain in hiding and refused to pay them badly needed transport costs.[2]

Meanwhile, Abū Salama corresponded with the other prominent members of the House of the Prophet, Ja'far al-Ṣādiq, 'Abdullah ibn al-Ḥasan and 'Umar ibn 'Alī ibn al-Ḥasan, who were all living in Ḥijāz.[3] Presumably Abū Salama offered them the office of *Amīr al-Mu'minīn* on certain conditions. Ja'far al-Ṣādiq flatly refused. 'Abdullah ibn al-Ḥasan hesitated but wanted better terms for his son Muḥammad the Pure Soul. We have no record of the reaction of the third candidate. If it was a simple offer, it is difficult to understand why it was not immediately accepted by any of these candidates, especially by 'Abdullah ibn al-Ḥasan or his son Muḥammad who was to lead an uprising against the

1 Ṭabarī, vol. III, pp. 42–4; Ibn A'tham, *Futūḥ*, p. 220A; Ya'qūbī, *Tārīkh*, vol. II, p. 413; *Tārīkh al Khulafā'*, pp. 284B–287B.

2 Tabarī, vol. III, pp. 27–34; *Tārīkh al-Khulafā'*, p. 290A.

3 *Tārīkh al-Khulafā'*, p. 290A; Ya'qūbī, *Tārīkh*, vol. II, pp. 418–19; Omar, pp. 171–4.

'Abbāsids thirteen years later. One must raise the question as to what these conditions for holding the office of *Amīr al-Mu'minīn* were. Obviously, Abū Salama was under pressure to install an acceptable member of the House of the Prophet in the office. But at the same time one must realize that he was a responsible statesman who had a great deal of interest in the final success of the Revolution. He was undoubtedly aware of the various trends in Shī'ism and all their practical implications for the powers of the *Imām–Amīr al-Mu'minīn* especially in a place like Kūfa. He was also aware of the wishes of the Khurāsāniyya and their own conception of these powers. These revolutionaries, who were fighting to bring down a decadent régime, must have had their own ideas about the political structure that was to replace it. In the last years of Umayyad rule they had just witnessed the complete breakdown of the system. The office of *Amīr al-Mu'minīn* was too central in importance for these revolutionaries to be prepared to adopt the same institution and merely change the holder of the office. The Shī'a had long agreed that they wanted an *Imām* to occupy the office of *Amīr al-Mu'minīn*, i.e. a ruler with secular as well as religious powers. There were differences about the extent of the powers, secular or religious, with which this ruler was to be invested. The Khurāsāniyya envisaged an *Amīr al-Mu'minīn* with very limited religious and no secular powers. They accepted without any dispute the institution of Abū Salama in the new office of *wazīr* with full secular authority. On the other hand, they waited for over two months before they finally forced their choice for *Amīr al-Mu'minīn*.

During these two months Abū Salama was busy trying to find the most widely supported *al-riḍā* to accept the position of *Amīr al-Mu'minīn* on the terms of the Khurāsāniyya. He was probably hopeful of persuading one of the more respected members of the House of the Prophet who would be acceptable to the Shī'a and to the Muslim community at large.[1] The conditions imposed by the Khurāsāniyya made it difficult if not impossible for any such person to accept Abū Salama's offer. Finally, the Khurāsāniyya took matters in their own hands and forced the selection of the 'Abbāsid, Abū al-'Abbās 'Abdullah ibn Muḥammad as the new *Amīr al-Mu'minīn*. Abū Salama had no choice but to accept the *fait accompli*. Abū Muslim must have consented to

[1] Ṭabarī, vol. III, p. 66; Ya'qūbī, *Tārīkh*, vol. II, p. 424.

this action because it was accomplished through the manipulation of his agent in Kūfa, Abū al-Jahm ibn ʻAṭiyya.[1]

Abū al-ʻAbbās was more than happy to accept the office on the terms of the Khurāsāniyya. He agreed that Abū Salama should continue in the office of *wazīr* which could only mean the greatest restriction on his own secular power. His failure to assume the title *Imām* could only indicate that he was not to have any religious powers, or at least not the kind of religious power the Shīʻa advocated for their *Imām–Amīr al-Mu'minīn*. His selection for the office is a further proof of the intentions of the Khurāsāniyya. It is generally attributed to the fact that his mother was an Arab woman in contrast to his older brother Abū Jaʻfar ʻAbdullah ibn Muḥammad, whose mother was a Berber slave. In other words we are asked to believe that the Khurāsāniyya, who risked their lives to achieve complete assimilation in the Muslim community, would behave so illogically in such a celebrated and exemplary case. It is no secret that Abū Jaʻfar was the more powerful personality of the two brothers and it is just as clear that he believed in a stronger *Amīr al-Mu'minīn*. It was precisely for this reason that he was passed over for his younger and weaker brother, Abū al-ʻAbbās.

Thus from the very beginning the ʻAbbāsids set themselves apart from the rest of the Shīʻa, by deviating from the cardinal Shīʻite precept of *Imām–Amīr al-Mu'minīn*. It is no wonder that the Shīʻa continued to keep up the agitation for the fulfilment of this precept throughout ʻAbbāsid rule. Abū Salama's far-sightedness was vindicated; had his opinion been followed, it would probably have saved the Muslim community a great deal of dissension. Whatever attempts the ʻAbbāsids made to appeal to the Shīʻa were to no avail. The adoption of personal titles with increasingly messianic implications, *al-Manṣūr*, *al-Mahdī*, *al-Hādī*, was not enough to convince the Shīʻa that their demand was being met. Al-Ma'mūn certainly realized this and in his frantic attempt to reconcile the Shīʻa he assumed the title *Imām* in addition to *Amīr al-Mu'minīn al-Ma'mūn* but it was then too late to restore the confidence of the Shīʻa in the ʻAbbāsid house.[2]

Abū al-ʻAbbās, though generally known as *al-Saffāḥ*, the

[1] Ṭabarī, vol. III, pp. 27–37; Yaʻqūbī, *Tārīkh*, vol. II, p. 413; *Tārīkh al-Khulafā'*, p. 291 A.

[2] Ṭabarī, vol. III, pp. 799, 1133.

generous or the bloodthirsty, never assumed this title. "It was assigned to him by later historians, whose sense of order and propriety required that the first 'Abbāsid, like all his successors, should have a regnal title of some sort."[1] His power was meant to be kept down to a minimum and perhaps the assumption of such a title would have added an undesirable nuance to this power.

The principle of the division of power between the *Amīr al-Mu'minīn* and the *wazīr* was certainly an innovation of the Revolution, probably introduced to eliminate the abuses of the later Umayyad rule. The betrayal of this principle by Abū al-'Abbās was not very noticeable to the revolutionaries at the time. When he ordered his *wazīr*, Abū Salama, to be killed in 132/750, the latter had laid himself open by his earlier conduct to treason charges. Also Abū Muslim, *Amīr Āl Muḥammad*, whose approval of this action was secured, was still there to exercise considerable power in the empire. His agent, Abū al-Jahm ibn 'Aṭiyya, acted almost like the *wazīr* after Abū Salama's death.[2]

The rest of the reign of Abū al-'Abbās (132–7/749–54) was very much occupied with establishing 'Abbāsid rule in the western half of the empire. In Jumādā II 132/January 750, the main battle against the Umayyads was fought on the banks of the Zāb river, where Marwān II was defeated. The 'Abbāsid army, led by 'Abdullah ibn 'Alī, an uncle of Abū al-'Abbās, pursued him to Ḥarrān. He fled to Syria and then Palestine, where he could not find any support. He eventually reached Egypt where he was followed by another 'Abbāsid army led by Ṣāliḥ ibn 'Alī, also an uncle of Abū al-'Abbās. Again Marwān II was defeated, and again he fled only to be trapped in a church at Būsīr. There he was slain in Dhū al-Ḥijja 132/August 750 and Umayyad rule was ended in Syria and Egypt. The following year Wāsiṭ, the last stronghold of the Umayyads, surrendered to Abū Ja'far. Yazīd ibn Hubayra, the last Umayyad governor of Iraq, withstood an 'Abbāsid siege for almost a year. Finally he surrendered, accepting a safe conduct, but was soon treacherously murdered by the 'Abbāsids.

The reign of Abū Ja'far al-Manṣūr was inaugurated in 136/754 by the rebellion of his uncle, 'Abdullah ibn 'Alī, against him. Until that time and in spite of the insinuations to the contrary in

[1] B. Lewis, "*The Regnal Titles of the First 'Abbāsid Caliphs*", *Dr Zahir Husain Presentation Volume*, New Delhi, 1968, p. 15.

[2] Ṭabarī, vol. III, p. 88; Goitein, p. 173.

our sources, agreement and confidence between Abū Muslim and al-Manṣūr were firmly established. The latter had not shown his hand yet and the former had had no reason to suspect his intentions. It was al-Manṣūr himself who delegated to Abū Muslim the task of suppressing his own uncle's revolt. The breach between the two occurred after the successful campaign of Abū Muslim. Al-Manṣūr sent Yaqṭīn ibn Mūsā, as his representative, to watch over the booty. To this Abū Muslim objected in no uncertain terms.[1] He must have considered it outside the power of the *Amīr al-Mu'minīn* to deal with such matters. Al-Manṣūr realized that if he were to have real power in the empire, he must first get rid of Abū Muslim. That he knew the enormous risk he was taking is evident from the elaborate precautions undertaken in preparation for his execution. Nevertheless the hazardous act was carried out (137/755) and no serious objection was raised by Abū Muslim's followers.[2] The 'Abbāsids had begun to acquire an aura of legitimacy in the eyes of their subjects. For the rest of his reign, al-Manṣūr exercised secular powers in very much the same way as any Umayyad *Amīr al-Mu'minīn* without any claims to the religious powers of an *Imām*. Significantly his *wazīr*, Abū Ayyūb al-Mūriānī, was no more than a chief secretary.[3] Nevertheless the principle of the division of powers continued to survive, and under the later 'Abbāsids powerful *wazīrs* once again held all secular power while emphasis was focused on the religious aspects of the office of *Amīr al-Mu'minīn*.

The one solid achievement of the 'Abbāsid Revolution which did not suffer any diminution was the complete assimilation of all members of the Muslim community. This in itself resulted in the remarkably rapid spread of Islam among the non-Arab subjects in the empire, especially in the east. It seems that the ideas of 'Umar II had finally won through, but only at the price of a revolution which brought about the downfall of his House.

1 Ṭabarī, vol. III, pp. 103–4, 114.

2 *Ibid.*, p. 117.

3 Goitein, p. 176; Sourdel, vol. I, pp. 78–87.

BIBLIOGRAPHY

PRIMARY SOURCES

ibn 'Abd Rabbih, Aḥmad ibn Muḥammad, *al-'Iqd al-Farīd*, Beirut, 1951–4. 31 vols.

ibn 'Abdilḥakam, Abū Muḥammad 'Abdullah, *Sīratu 'Umar ibn 'Abdil-'azīz*, Cairo, 1927.

Akhbār al-'Abbās wa Waladihi, anon., manuscript in the Library of the Institute of Higher Islamic Studies, Baghdad.

ibn A'tham al-Kūfī al-Kindī, Abū Muḥammad Aḥmad, *Kitāb al-Futūḥ*, Istanbul manuscript, Library of Ahmet III, no. 2956. 2 vols. Persian translation by Muḥammad ibn Aḥmad al-Mustawfī al-Harawī, Bombay, 1300/1882.

ibn al-Athīr, 'Izz al-Dīn, *al-Kāmil fī al-Tārīkh*, ed. C. J. Tornberg, Leiden, 1866–71. 14 vols.

al-Lubāb Fī Ma'rifat al-Ansāb, Cairo, A.H. 1357–69. 3 vols.

al-Balādhurī, Aḥmad ibn Yaḥyā, *Anonyme Arabische Chronik*, ed. W. Ahlwardt, vol. IX, Griefswald, 1883.

Ansāb al-Ashrāf: vol. IV B, ed. M. Schloessinger, Jerusalem, 1938; vol. V, ed. S. D. Goitein, Jerusalem, 1936; Istanbul manuscript, Suleymanniye Kütüphanesi, Reisulkuttap, no. 597–8, 2 vols.

Futūḥ al-Buldān, ed. M. J. de Goeje, Leiden, 1866.

al-Bal'amī, Abū 'Alī Muḥammad, *Tarjama-i-Tārīkh-i-Ṭabarī*, Cawnpore, 1324/1906 (in Persian).

al-Bīrunī, Abū Rayḥān, *al-Athār al- Bāqiya*, ed. E. Sachau, Leipzig, 1923.

al-Dhahabī, Muḥammad ibn Aḥmad, *Tārīkh al-Islām*, Cairo, 1367–9. 5 vols.

al-Dīnawarī, Abū-Ḥanifa, *al-Akhbār al-Ṭiwāl*, ed. V. Guirgass, Leiden, 1888.

ibn Durayd, Muḥammad, *al-Ishtiqāq*, ed. F. Wüstenfeld, Göttingen, 1854.

ibn al-Faqīh, al-Hamadānī, *Kitāb al-Buldān*, ed. M. J. Goeje, Leiden, 1885.

Gardīzī, Abu Sa'īd 'Abdulḥayy, *Kitāb Zayn al-Akhbār*, Teherān, 1939 (in Persian).

ibn Hajar al-'Asqalānī, *Kitāb al-Iṣāba fī Ma'rifat al-Saḥāba*, Cairo, 1328. 4 vols.

Tahdhīb al-Tahdīb, Hyderabad, 1325–7. 12 vols.

Hajjī Khalīfa, *Iḍāḥ al-Maknūn fī al-dhayl 'alā Kashf al-Ẓunūn*, Istanbul, 1945. 2 vols.

Kashf al-Ẓunūn, Istanbul, 1941–3. 2 vols.

ibn Ḥawqal, Muḥammad, *Ṣūrat al-Arḍ*, ed. J. H. Kramers, Leiden, 1938–9. 2 vols.

ibn Ḥazm, ʿAlī ibn Muḥammad, *Jamharatu Ansāb al-ʿArab*, E. Levi-Provencal, Cairo, 1948.
Ḥudūd al-ʿĀlam, anon., ed. V. Minorsky, London, 1937 (in Persian).
Ibn Idhārī, al-Bayān al-Mughrib, ed. G. S. Colin and E. Levi-Provencal, Leiden, 1948.
al-Iṣfahānī, Abū al-Faraj, *al-Aghānī*: vols. I–XX, Cairo, 1285; vol. XXI, ed. R. E. Brunow, Leiden, 1888.
Maqātil al Ṭālibiyyīn, Cairo, 1949.
ibn Isfandiyār, Muḥammad ibn al-Ḥasan, *Tārīkh-i-Ṭabaristān*, ed. ʿAbbās Iqbāl, Teherān, 1942 (in Persian).
al-Iṣtakhrī, Abū Isḥāq Ibrāhīm, *Kitāb al-Masālik wa al-Mamālik*, ed. M. J. de Goeje, Leiden, 1870.
al-Jāhiz, ʿAmr ibn Baḥr, *al-Bayān wa al-Tabyīn*, Cairo, 1948–50. 4 vols.
al-Bukhalā, Cairo, 1958.
al-Ḥayawān, Cairo, 1938–45. 7 vols.
Kitāb al-Tāj, Cairo, 1914.
al-Maḥāsin wal Aḍdād, ed. Van Vloten, Leiden, 1898.
Majmūʿat Rasāʾil, Cairo, A.H. 1324.
Thalāth Rasāʾil, ed. Van Vloten, Leiden, 1903.
ibn al-Kalbī, Hishām ibn Muḥammad, *Nasab Maʿdd wa al-Yaman al-Kabīr*, British Museum manuscript, no. ADD 22376.
ibn Khallikān, Abū al ʿAbbās, *Kitāb Wafayāt al-Aʿyān*, Cairo, 1299/1881. 2 vols.
ibn Khurdādhbeh, ʿUbaydullah ibn ʿAbdillah, *Kitāb al-Masālik waʾlʾ Mamālik*, ed. M. J. de Goeje, Leiden, 1889.
Khwārizmī, Muḥammad ibn Yūsuf, *Mafātīḥ al-ʿulūm*, ed. G. van Vloten, Leiden, 1885.
ibn Manẓūr, Muḥammad ibn Makram, *Lisān al-ʿArab*, *Būlāq*, 1891. 10 vols.
al-Maqdisī, Shams al-Dīn, *Aḥsan al-Taqāsīm fī Maʿrifat al-Aqālīm*, ed. M. J. de Goeje, Leiden, 1877.
al-Māwardī, *al-Aḥkām al-Sulṭāniyya*, Cairo, Subayh.
al-Maqrīzī, Aḥmad ibn ʿAlī, *al-Khiṭaṭ*, Cairo, A.H. 1270. 2 vols.
Kitāb al Nizāʿ wa al Takhāṣum fīmā bayn banī Umayya wa banī Hāshim, ed. Von Geerhardus Vos, Leiden, 1888.
al-Masʿūdī, ʿAli ibn al-Ḥusayn, *Murūj al-Dhahab*, ed. C. Barbier de Meynard and P. de Courteille, Paris, 1861–77. 9 vols.
al-Tanbīh wa al-Ishrāf, ed. M. J. de Goeje, Leiden, 1894.
al-Mubarrad, Abu al-ʿAbbās Muḥammad, *al-Kāmil*, ed. W. Wright, Leipzig, 1874–82.
ibn al-Nadīm, Muḥammad ibn Isḥāq, *al-Fihrist*, Cairo, 1929.
Narshakhī, Abū Bakr Muḥammad, *The History of Bukhārā*, tr. R. N. Frye, Cambridge, Mass., 1954.

Tārīkh-i-Bukhārā, ed. Razavi, Teherān, 1939 (in Persian).
al-Nawbakhtī, al-Ḥasan ibn Mūsā, *Firaq al-Shī'a*, al Najaf, 'Irāq, 1936.
Qudāma ibn Ja'far, *Kitāb al-Kharāj*, ed. M. J. de Goeje, Leiden, 1889.
Qummī, Ḥasan ibn Muḥammad, *Tārīkh-i-Qumm*, Teherān, 1935 (in Persian).
ibn Qutayba, 'Abdullah ibn Muslim, *al-Ma'ārif*, ed. F. Wüstenfeld, Göttingen, 1850.
'Uyūn al-Akhbār, Cairo, 1925–30. 4 vols.
ibn Rustah, Abū 'Alī Muḥammad, *Kitāb al-A'lāq al-Nafīsa*, ed. M. J. de Goeje, Leiden, 1892.
ibn Sa'd, Muḥammad, *at-Ṭabaqāt al-Kabīr*, ed. Sachau *et al.*, Leiden, 1905–21. 8 vols.
ibn Sallām, Abū 'Ubayd al-Qāsim, *al-Amwāl*, Cairo, A.H. 1353.
al-Sam'ānī, 'Abdulkarīm ibn Muḥammad, *al-Ansāb*, ed. D. S. Margoliouth, Leiden, 1912.
al-Ṭabarī, Muḥammad ibn Jarīr, *Annales quos scripsit Abū Ja'far...aṭ-Ṭabarī*, ed. M. J. de Goeje *et al.*, Leiden, 1879–1901. 3 vols.
al-Tanūkhī, al-Ḥasan ibn 'Alī, *al-Mustajād*, ed. Kurd 'Alī, Damascus, 1946.
Tārīkah al-Khulafā', anon., ed. P. Griyaznevitch, Moscow, 1967.
Tārīkh-i-Sīstān, anon., ed. M. Bahār, Teherān, A.H. 1314 (in Persian).
al-Tha'ālibī, Abū Manṣur, *Ghurar Akhbār Mulūk al-Furs wa Siyarihim*, ed. N. Zotenberg, Paris, 1900.
al-'Uyūn wa al-Ḥadā'iq fī Akhbār al-Ḥaqā'iq, anon., ed. M. J. de Goeje, Leiden, 1869.
Yaḥya ibn Ādam, *al-Kharāj*, ed. T. W. Juynboll, Leiden, 1896.
Ya'qūbī, Aḥmad ibn abī-Ya'qūb, *Kitāb al-Buldān*, ed. M. J. de Goeje, Leiden, 1892.
Tārīkh, ed. M. T. Houtsma, Leiden, 1883. 2 vols.
Yāqūt, Shihāb al-Dīn, *Mu'jam al-Buldān*, ed. F. Wüstenfeld, Leipzig, 1924. 6 vols.
Mu'jam al-Udabā', ed. D. S. Margoliouth, Leiden–London, 1907–26. 7 vols.
Abū-Yūsuf, Ya'qūb, *al-Kharāj*, Cairo, A.H. 1302.
al-Zubayrī, Abū 'Abdillah al-Mus'ab, *Nasab Quraysh*, ed. E. Levi-Provencal, Cairo, 1953.

SECONDARY STUDIES

al-'Alī, S. A., *al-Tanẓīmāt al-Ijtimā'iyya wal Iqtiṣādiyya fī al-Baṣra*, Baghdād, 1953.

"Istīṭān al-'Arab fī Khurāsān", *Bulletin of the College of Arts and Sciences*, Baghdād, 1958, pp. 36–83.

Altheim, F.–Stiehl, R., *Geschichte der Hunnen. II Die Hephthaliten in Iran*, Berlin, 1960.

Azizi, Mohsen, *La domination Arabe et l'épanouissement du sentiment national en Iran*, Paris, 1938.

Barthold, W., *Turkestan down to the Mongol invasion*, London, 1928.

"Ṭukhāristān" and "Farqhāna", *Encyclopaedia of Islam*, Leiden, 1939.

Histoire des Turcs d'Asie Centrale, adaptation français par Mme M. Donskis, Paris, 1945.

Four studies on the history of Central Asia, tr. from the Russian by V. and T. Minorsky, Leiden, 1956. 2 vols.

Bivar, A. D. H., "Hayāṭila", *Encylopaedia of Islam*, New Edition, Leiden, 1954–.

Bosworth, C. E., *Sīstān under the Arabs*, Rome, 1968.

Brockelmann, C., "Ya'kubī", *Encyclopaedia of Islam*, New Edition, Leiden, 1954–.

Brunschvic, R., *Ibn 'Abd ul Ḥakam*, *Annales de l'Institut des Études Orientales*, vol. VII, 1942.

Cahen, C., "Points de vue sur la 'Révolution abbaside'", *Revue Historique*, 1963, pp. 295–338.

Chavannes, E., *Documents sur les Tou-Kiue (Turc) Occidentaux*, St Petersbourg, 1903.

Notes additionelles sur les Tou-Kiue, Occidentaux T'oung Pao, vol. V (1904).

Christensen, A., "L'Empire des Sassanides", *Mémoires de L'Académie des Sciences et des Lettres de Danemark*, 7th series, I (1907).

L'Iran sous les Sassanides, Copenhagen, 1936.

Czaplicka, M. A., *The Turks of Central Asia*, Oxford, 1918 (a very detailed bibliography).

Dennett, D. C., "Marwān ibn Muḥammad; The passing of the Umayyad Caliphate", unpublished Ph.D. thesis, Harvard University, 1939.

Conversion and the Poll Tax in Early Islam, Cambridge, Mass., 1950.

al-Dūrī, A., "Ḍaw jadīd 'alā al-Da'wa al-'Abbāsiyya", *Bulletin of the College of Arts and Sciences*, Baghdad, 1960, pp. 64–82.

"Niẓām al-Darā'ib fī Khurāsān", *Majallat al-Majma' al-'Ilmī al-'Iraqī*, vol. XI, 1964, pp. 75–87.

Enoki, K., "On the nationality of the Ephthalites", *Memoirs of the Research Department of the Toyo Bunko*, XVIII, Tokyo, 1959, pp. 1–58.

Fateh, Mostafa Khan, "Taxation in Persia. A synopsis from the early times to the conquest of the Mongols", *Bulletin of the School of Oriental Studies* IV (1926/28), pp. 723–43.

Fischel, W. J., "The Jews of Central Asia (Khorasan) in Medieval Hebrew and Islamic literature", *Historia Judaica* 7 (1945), pp. 29–50.

Friedlander, I., "The heterodoxies of the Shīʿā", *Journal of the American Oriental Society* XXVIII (1907), pp. 1–80; XXIX (1908), pp. 1–183.

Frye, R. N., "The role of Abū Muslim in the ʿAbbāsid Revolution", *Muslim World* 37 (1947), pp. 28–38.

"Tarxun-Turxun and central Asian history", *Harvard Journal of Asiatic Studies* 14 (1951), pp. 105–29.

"The ʿAbbāsid conspiracy and modern revolution theory", *Indo-Iranica*, S III (1952–3), pp. 9–14.

The Heritage of Persia, London, 1962.

Gabrieli, F., "al-Walīd ibn Yazīd, il califfo e il poeta", *Rivista degli Studi Orientali* XV (1934), pp. 1–64.

"Il califato di Hishām, Studi di storia omayyade", *Mémoires de la Société Archaeologique d'Alexandrie* VII/2 (1935).

"La rivolta dei Muhallabiti nel Iraq e il nuovo Balādurī", *Rendiconti della* Reale *Accademia dei Lincei*, series 6, 14 (1938), pp. 199–236.

"L'eroe Omayyade Maslamah ibn ʿAbd al-Malik", *ibid.*, series 8, 5 (1950–1), pp. 22–39.

Ghirshman, R., *Begram*, Le Caire, 1946.

Les Chionites–Hephthalites, Le Caire, 1948.

Gibb, H. A. R., "Chinese Records of the Arabs in Central Asia", *Bulletin of the School of Oriental Studies* II (1922), pp. 613–22.

The Arab Conquests in Central Asia, London, 1923.

"The Arab invasion of Kāshgar in A.D. 715", *Bulletin of the School of Oriental Studies* II (1923), pp. 467–74.

"Tārīkh", supplement of the *Encyclopaedia of Islam*, Leiden, 1939.

"The structure of religious thought in Islam", *Muslim World* 38 (1948), pp. 17–28, 113–23, 185–97, 280–91.

"Interpretation of Islamic History", *Journal of World History*, vol. I, no. I, July 1953, pp. 39–62.

"The Fiscal Rescript of ʿUmar II", *Arabica*, Tome II, Fascicule I, janvier 1955, Leiden, 1955.

"The evolution of government in Early Islam", *Studia Islamica* 4 (1955), pp. 1–17.

Goitein, S. D., *Studies in Islamic History and Institutions*, Leiden, 1968.

Grousset, R., *The Civilisations of the East*, London, 1931.

Hamidullah, M., *Muslim conduct of the state*, Calcutta, 1943.

Hodgson, Marshall G. S., "How did the early Shia become Sectarian?", *Journal of the American Oriental Society* LXXV (1955), pp. 1–13.

Housseini, A. M. El-, "The Umayyad policy in Khurasan and its effect on the formulation of Muslim thought", *Journal University of Peshawar* 4 (1955), pp. 1–21.

Irani, M. S., "Khorasan after the Arab Conquest", *All India Oriental Conference* 13 (1946), part II, pp. 530–7.

Jacobson, H., *Early History of Sogdia*, Chicago, 1935.

Jettmar, K., "Les plus anciennes civilisations d'éleveurs des steppes d'Asie Centrale", *Journal of World History* I (1954), pp. 760–78.

Kurat, Akdes N., "Kitāb al-Futūḥ", *Ankara Universitesi Dil ve Tarih Coqrafya Fakultesi Derqisi*, vol. 6, pp. 385–430; vol. 7, part 2, July 1949, pp. 255–82.

Lammens, H., "ètude sur le regne du calife Omaiyade Mo'āwia Ier", *Mélanges de la Faculté Orientale de Beyrouth* I (1906), pp. 1–108; II (1907), pp. 1–172; III (1908), pp. 145–312.

"Le califat de Yazīd Ier", *ibid.*, IV (1910), pp. 213–33; V (1911/12), pp. 79–267, 589–724; VI (1913), pp. 401–92; VII (1914/21), pp. 211–44.

"Ziād ibn Abihī, vice-roi de L'Iraq, lieutenant de Mo'āwia", *Rivista degli Studi Orientali* IV (1911/12), pp. 1–45, 199–250, 653–93.

"Mo'āwia II ou le dernier des Sofiānides", *ibid.*, VII (1916/18), pp. 1–49.

"L'avènement des Merwānides et le califat de Merwān Ier", *Mélanges de la Faculté Orientale de Beyrouth* XII (1927), pp. 41–147.

Etudes sur la Siècle des Omayyades, Beyrouth, 1930.

LeStrange, G., *The Lands of the Eastern Caliphate*, Cambridge, 1930.

Levi, S., "Le Tokharien", *Journal Asiatique*, 1933, pp. 1 ff.

Lewis, B., "An apocalyptic vision of Islamic History", *Bulletin of the School of Oriental Studies* XIII (1950), pp. 308–38.

"'Abbāsids", *Encyclopaedia of Islam*, New Edition, Leiden, 1954–.

"The Regnal Titles of the First 'Abbāsid Caliphs", *Dr Zahir Husain Presentation Volume*, New Delhi, 1968, pp. 13–22.

Løkkegaard, F., *Islamic Taxation in the Classic Period*, Copenhagen, 1950.

Margoliouth, D. S., *Lectures on Arabic Historians*, Calcutta, 1930.

Marquart, J., "Eranšahr", *Abhandlungen der Königlichen Gesellschaft der Wissenschaften zu Göttingen*, vol. III, 1901.

A Catalogue of the provincial Capitals of Eranshahr, ed. G. Messina, Rome, 1931.

McGovern, W. M., *The Early Empires of Central Asia*, Chapel Hill, 1939 (has an excellent bibliography with very useful notes).

Minorsky, V., "Ṭūs", *Encyclopaedia of Islam*, Leiden, 1939.

Iranica, Publications of the University of Teheran, vol. 775, Teheran, 1964.

Moscati, S., "Studi su Abū Muslim I–III", *Accademia Nazionale dei Lincei* (1949), pp. 323–35, 474–95; (1950), pp. 89–105.
"Il testamento di Abū Hāshim", *Rivista degli Studi Orientali* (1952), pp. 28 ff.
"Abū Muslim", *Encyclopaedia of Islam*, New Edition, Leiden, 1954–.
Mukhlis, ʻAbdullah, "Tārīkh Ibn Aʻtham al-Kūfī", *Majallat al-Majmaʻ al-ʻIlmī al-ʻArabī*, vol. VI, part 3, March 1926, pp. 142–3.
Nasr, Seyyed Taghi, *Essai sur l'histoire du droit Persan dès l'origine à l'invasion Arabe*, Paris, 1933.
Omar, F., "The ʻAbbāsid Caliphate, 132–170/750–786", unpublished Ph.D. thesis, University of London, 1967.
Pelliot, P., "Tocharien et Kotcheen", *Journal Asiatique*, 1934, pp. 23 ff.
Rabinowitz, L. I., "Notes on the Jews of Central Asia (Khorasan)", *Historia Judaica* 8 (1948), pp. 61–6 (rejoinder by W. J. Fischel, pp. 66–8).
Rosenthal, F., *A History of Muslim Historiography*, Leiden, 1952.
"Baladhuri", *Encylopaedia of Islam*, New Edition, Leiden, 1954–.
Ross, E. D., *Nomadic Movements in Asia*, London, 1929.
Schwarz, P., *Iran im Mittelalter*, Stuttgart and Berlin, 1896–1936. 9 vols.
Siddiqi, S. A., *Public Finance in Islam*, Lahore, 1948.
Shaban, M. A., "Ibn Aʻtham al-Kūfī", *Encyclopaedia of Islam*, New Edition, Leiden, 1954–.
"The Social and Political Background of the ʻAbbāsid Revolution in Khurāsān", unpublished Ph.D. thesis, Harvard University, 1960.
Sourdel, D., *Le Vizirat Abbaside*, Damascus, 1959–60. 2 vols.
Spuler, B., *Iran in Früh-Islamischer Zeit*, Wiesbaden, 1952 (has a full bibliography).
Stein, Aurel, *On ancient central Asian tracks*, London, 1933.
Storey, C. A., *Persian Literature, A bio-bibliographical survey*, section 2, fasc. 2, London, 1936.
Tavadia, J. C., "Iran in the first centuries of Islam and her unique conversion to the new religion", *Journal University of Bombay* (1954), pp. 106–17.
Tritton, A. S., *The Caliphs and their non-Muslim subjects. A critical study of the Covenant of ʻUmar*, London, 1930.
The Caliphs and their non-Muslim Subjects, Oxford, 1930.
Tyan, E., *Histoire de l'Organisation judicaire en Pays de l'Islam*, Paris, 1938–45. 2 vols.
Van Vloten, G., *De opkomst der Abbasiden in Chorasan*, Leiden, 1890.
Recherches sur la Domination Arabe, Amsterdam, 1894.
Walker, J., *A Catalogue of the Arab–Sassanian Coins*, London, 1941.
A Catalogue of the Arab–Byzantine and Post-Reform Umaiyad Coins, London, 1956.

Watt, W. M., "Shīʿism under the Umayyads", *Journal of the Royal Asiatic Society* (1960), pp. 158–72.
"The Conception of the Charismatic Community in Islam", *Numen* VII (1960), pp. 85–98.
"Khārijite thought in the Umayyad Period", *Der Islam*, vol. 36, part 3 (1961), pp. 215–31.
"The Political Attitudes of the Mutazilah", *Journal of the Royal Asiatic Society* (1963–4), pp. 38–57.
Islamic Political Thought, Edinburgh, 1968.
Watters, T., *On Yuan Chwang's travels in India*, London, 1904–5. 2 vols.
Wellhausen, J., *Das Arabische Reich und sein Sturz*, Berlin, 1902, *The Arab Kingdom and its Fall*, tr. M. G. Weir, Calcutta, 1927.
Widengren, G., *Xosrau Anosurwan, les Hephthalites et les peuples Turcs*, Orientalia Succana, i, 1952.
Wensinck, A. J., *A handbook of early Muhammadan tradition*, Leiden, 1927.
Wiet, G., "L'Empire néo-byzantin des Omayyades et l'Empire néo-sassanide des Abbasides", *Journal of World History* I (1953), pp. 63–70.
Wright, E. M., "Symbols of Iranian persistence against Islamic penetration in North Iran", *Muslim World* 38 (1948), pp. 43–59, 124–31.
Zambaur, E., *Manuel de généalogie et de chronologie pour l'histoire de l'Islam*, Hanover, 1927.

INDEX

For the purposes of the alphabetical order of this index the words Ibn, Abū and Abī are disregarded. Characters are classified according to the names following these words; for example, Ibn Abī Sarḥ will be found under "S".